D1738598

To Tom & Carol:

DILLERLAND

Bon Voyage! Buon Viaggio!
Buen Viaje!

Our years together have been a
great ride for me.
Your friend,

Jerry Tuccille

DILLERLAND

THE STORY OF MEDIA MOGUL
BARRY DILLER

JEROME TUCCILLE
BEST SELLING AUTHOR OF *TRUMP*

ALYSON*books*

©May 2009 by Jerome Tuccille. All rights reserved

Published by Alyson Books
245 West 17th Street, Suite 1200 New York, NY 10011
www.alyson.com

First Alyson Books edition: May 2009

10 9 8 7 6 5 4 3 2 1

ISBN-10: 1-59350-124-2
ISBN-13: 978-1-59350-124-2

Library of Congress Cataloging-in-Publication data are on file.

Cover design by Victor Mingovits
Book interior by Maria E. Torres, Neuwirth & Associates, Inc.

Printed in the United States of America

Distributed by Consortium Book Sales and Distribution
Distribution in the United Kingdom by Turnaround Publisher Services Ltd.

CONTENTS

DILLERLAND

CHAPTER 1

NO BRIDE FOR BARRY

SUN VALLEY WAS alive with celebrities from movieland in the winter of 1983. They all seemed to converge on this winter paradise as though on cue. It was amazing how all the "beautiful people," the ones in the "in crowd," those who thought that not being invited to the right parties was akin to death, knew instinctively where all the other beautiful folks were going to be when it mattered. The network was everything. It was the rumor mill—who was in, who was out, the right place to ski this year, the right place to summer, the precise time and place where swarms of paparazzi would be present with shutters clicking to immortalize in the glossies and tabloids everyone who was anyone. You were either plugged into it, or you were dead.

The lift lines opened early, at 8:30 A.M., so early that most of the beautiful people were still holed up in their condos, windows shuttered against the sun, sleeping off last night's excesses and waiting until a more civilized hour—the correct moment—to make an appearance. The name of the game, after all, was not so much to enjoy a day of skiing, but rather to be *seen* skiing in just the right attire. Striking the correct pose, outfit just so, hair just right, power shades reflecting the sun glare, teeth sparkling white, the very picture of health and fitness—that was far more important than *schussing* down the perfect trail in total obscurity. The only people who were out skiing at 8:30 in the morning, before the shutterbugs were present to capture them on film, were—well, skiers.

The chair lifts were virtually empty, according to sources who were present at the time, perhaps every fourth or fifth one occupied with skiers who knew that early morning was the best time to ski and that from eleven o'clock on, when all the right people were up and about being photographed, was the absolute worst time to ski. The trails fingering their way down the mountain this way and that, bellying outward from their common beginning at the apex hidden in early morning fog, were likewise devoid of skiers, save for those solitary early birds just disgorged from chairlifts. They came down singly for the most part, lonely dots against the pristine white background as yet unsullied by man-made tracks that would snake and rut and push the snow into moguls later in the day.

Suddenly, the pattern was broken. The isolated dots were joined by four black dots bunched up together on the slope, working their way down rapidly toward the base of the mountain. It was clear that these black dots were real skiers, too. After all, it *was* early, and this black quartet was actually skiing, not just posing for paparazzi. The black dots descended the mountain, growing larger and larger and evolving into human shapes as they neared the main lift at the base.

The foursome was no longer a montage of black dots. As the four figures came fully into view, breaking their momentum in tandem as they drove their edges into the snow, creating an ethereal shower of airy white powder, they resembled nothing so much as four urban *wunderkinds* all decked out in black jumpsuits as though stepping out for a night on the town. All of them were dressed in matching black ski suits, one piece from head to toe, with complementary boots and headgear. Even the goggles were *darkish*—dark gray shades with black rims and straps setting off the ski suits. One by one, they pushed the goggles back on their heads, revealing four faces that were known to everyone in Hollywood, known to every tabloid reader in America, known to everyone everywhere who followed with religious curiosity the comings and goings, the exploits and travails, the adventures and misadventures of the rich and famous. The black-clad, early-morning skiers were Barry Diller, David Geffen, Calvin Klein, and Diane von Furstenberg. The only thing not immediately apparent was who had designed their outfits, Calvin or Diane.

Barry Diller's unconventional lifestyle had been very much on the mind of Charlie Bluhdorn, who had been Barry's boss at Paramount Pictures before Bluhdorn's untimely death. Bluhdorn had been the volatile, opinionated, extremely demanding, and critical chairman of Gulf + Western, the parent company of Paramount. He was a maverick of sorts himself, a tyrannical corporate leader who ruled with an iron fist. But, as unconventional as he was in business, his private life had been a model of propriety. Culturally, he was a straight arrow, as conventional as they come.

"Barry Diller is potentially the brightest executive I've ever brought into this company," Bluhdorn was fond of saying, according to his close associates. This was high praise indeed, coming from a man who had no reservations whatsoever about publicly discussing the shortcomings of his subordinates in the minutest detail. Bluhdorn thought so highly of Diller that he wooed him away from ABC with a compensation package worthy of a sultan.

"Barry has guts," Bluhdorn maintained. "He has imagination. I can make him the greatest. But there's only one thing. He has to get married."

Those familiar with rumors of his sexual preferences figured that this was one feat beyond Bluhdorn's capabilities, notwithstanding his determination to set his protégé down the straight and narrow path toward a more conventional lifestyle.

"Barry's like a son to me," Bluhdorn said. "He's going to get married. I found just the right woman for him. I know they'll like each other. They're already friends . . . sort of."

Diller, in deference to his mentor and benefactor, went along with the old boy's paternalistic mission to the best of his ability—as painful as it was. Bluhdorn chose Diller's future "bride" well. She was attractive, gracious, wealthy, and just as confused as everyone else when Bluhdorn threw a "pre-engagement" party for her and Barry. She and Barry had indeed been friends, "sort of," for sometime now—and nothing but friends. To keep Bluhdorn happy, she and Barry even went off on an occasional weekend together, a sign according to Bluhdorn that Barry had "straightened himself out." Bluhdorn told friends that the wedding was imminent, just a "matter of time."

"So?" Bluhdorn asked Diller several months after the party.

"She's nice, Charlie. We like each other."

"So, when's the wedding?"

"We called if off. We're friends. That's all we ever want to be."

Bluhdorn was visibly shaken. Publicly, however, he refused to admit that his mission had ended in failure. Barry would come around, he told his closest friends. He'll see the light. It's just a matter of time.

Before that fateful day arrived, Bluhdorn died of a heart attack on his private jet while returning to the United States from his Casa de Campo resort in the Dominican Republic, and Barry Diller went on to achieve the success and power he craved at another company, Fox, after he had a falling-out with Bluhdorn's successor, Martin S. Davis. In short order, Diller found himself locked in a classic struggle of egos and wills with Davis. The animosity between the two men quickly assumed legendary proportions, and Diller's frustration led him to resign in disgust in 1984 and spend the better part of the next year licking the wounds he suffered on the corporate battlefield, all the while planning and plotting his next move.

Diller found a new mentor and father figure of sorts in Rupert Murdoch, the head of News Corporation of America, who hired him to run Fox Broadcasting Company. Murdoch's management style has always been basic and to-the-point, a curious blend of hands-on micromanagement and laissez faire. He believes in hiring the best people for a particular job, then leaving them alone to run things as they see fit, as long as they produce the desired results. If they fail, he steps in quickly, gets rid of them, and does the job himself.

Diller continued to keep a low profile as far as his private life, including his sex life, was concerned. It seemed the prudent thing to do, considering that his new boss, who was aggressively conservative, had his own reservations about lifestyles that varied significantly from his own. In Murdoch's case, however, he didn't insist that others change their behavior to suit him. He was an advocate of the "don't ask, don't tell" school of sexual identity, long before Bill Clinton popularized it in the 1990s.

At Fox, Barry Diller continued along the fast track to fame and power that he had been on for a couple of decades. His broad, ever-present smile, crowned by a balding pate, was displayed in newspapers, magazines, and on television with almost predictable regularity. He was a prominent fixture at the right premieres, parties, and resorts from East Hampton to Sun Valley to Palm Springs. Diller was hardly intent on hiding his flame under the proverbial bushel. He enjoyed money and power, which he sometimes wielded like a double-edged sword. He was rumored to be vindictive and merciless toward those who crossed him. In that regard, he was a more humane version of the late Roy Cohn; Cohn once told this author that "seeing people on their knees begging me for mercy gives me the greatest pleasure of all."

While there was some tension between Diller and Murdoch, Diller was clearly the right man for the job Murdoch hired him to do—take over Fox and turn it into a media powerhouse. It took a few years, but by the fall of 1988, Diller gave Murdoch the breakthrough he had been looking for with Fox; for the first time ever, a Fox program, *Married . . . with Children*, scored a perfect 10 rating. It had become one of the biggest hits on television.

Early the following year, Diller announced at the annual The Association of Independent Television Stations convention in Hollywood that Fox, which had lost almost $100 million the year before, had finished 1988 with a $400,000 profit.

Murdoch's dream for Fox was to turn it into the fourth television network, and thanks to Diller, he was well on his way to attaining that goal. Diller had a genius for coming up with the right programming at precisely the right time. He followed *Married . . . with Children* with *The Simpsons* and *In Living Color*. By the end of 1989, Fox had a lock on the youth market, the fastest-growing segment of the television-watching audience. In the movie end of the business, Fox Studios' finances had already moved into the black with *Raiders of the Lost Ark*, *Saturday Night Fever*, and *Flashdance*.

Diller enjoyed some measure of revenge against his nemesis Martin Davis by stealing Lucie Salhany away to work with him at Fox. A former Diller protégé, Lucie had risen from virtually nowhere by sheer force of her talent, and Diller elevated her to chairwoman of Fox.

As she said in January 1994, "Barry's a born risk-taker. He's truly a visionary with a great sense of where this industry is going. He's tough as iron and difficult to work with sometimes, but he rewards people who are loyal and help him achieve his goals."

Murdoch, too, had high praise for Diller, as evidenced by the $17 million salary and retirement benefits he paid him in 1991—a monumental sum at the time—as well as the $34 million termination package he bestowed on him when Diller surprisingly left Fox in February 1992.

According to Murdoch, "It was no great surprise really. l knew for a long time that Barry was dying to go out on his own, be his own man for a change instead of somebody else's player."

Diller's close friends were not altogether surprised when he decided to follow up his great success at Fox with a move to the financially strapped QVC Network in 1992.

"Barry has effectively worked for Charlie Bluhdorn at Paramount and then Rupert Murdoch at Fox for a total of almost twenty years," said ski buddy David Geffen, no small power in the industry himself. "During that time, he created billions of dollars in value for both of them. And I think now he's going to do it for himself."

Ray Stark, producer of *Steel Magnolias* and *The Way We Were* and another friend of Diller, said, "Barry loves a challenge. He's the most brilliant entertainment executive there is."

But QVC sounded like a joke to others in the industry, including James Brooks, the writer/director of *Terms of Endearment* and other films. "Home shopping? Give me a break. QVC was strictly a vehicle for Barry. It was a financial basket case. Barry's tough and smart and he knew what he had to do to turn the company around and transform it into a complete communications and entertainment company," he said.

Wall Street analysts agreed that Diller worked magic at QVC when he joined it. Media analyst Edward Hatch of UBS Securities said, "Diller's taken QVC to the next level, where he can transform it into a full-service entertainment network." The first innovation Diller made at QVC was to single-handedly change home shopping's tacky image, as a vehicle for peddling cubic zirconium rings to bored housewives, into a more glamorous marketplace for upscale retailers, such as Tiffany and Saks Fifth Avenue.

"What's Barry up to? That's what everybody wanted to know when he left his great success at Fox for a cable home shopping company that was in the toilet financially," said broadcasting analyst Herb Schlosser of Wertheim Schroder. "Is he crazy or what? Now everybody knows what his game plan is, and it makes a lot of sense. Look, he rescued Fox for Murdoch when it was virtually bankrupt, and he did it again with QVC."

"Barry knows television," said Rupert Murdoch, "and he knows the movie business. Personally, I believe he's more interested in television now. That's where all the growth is likely to be."

Before very long, Barry Diller would be the most highly compensated executive on earth, the chairman of IAC/InterActiveCorp, a media empire with a market capitalization of $18 billion at its peak, encompassing cable and television, a plethora of Web sites including Ask.com, LendingTree.com, and Ticketmaster. To understand what makes Diller tick, what motivates

him and drives him relentlessly, we have to look back a half century into
the past, back at the life of a rich kid growing up in the very heart of
La-La Land itself: Beverly Hills, California.

CHAPTER 2

GROWING UP RICH
IN BEVERLY HILLS

SOME TOWNS MAKE a sharp distinction between old money and new money, but in Beverly Hills all money is treated with equal respect. It was no different back in 1942. Some people claim that money is not important to them, but in Beverly Hills it ranks right up there with oxygen as one of the primary elixirs of life. In many communities the old moneyed families disdain the recently arrived *nouveau riche*, but in Beverly Hills they say it is better to be *nouveau* than never to have been *riche* at all.

Barry Diller personifies Beverly Hills as well as anyone else who has lived there. However, he was actually born a few hundred miles to the north, in San Francisco, on February 2, 1942, less than two months after Japanese bombs rained down with impunity on Pearl Harbor. The demonization of Japanese Americans had already begun in earnest thanks to California Attorney General Earl Warren, who ordered American citizens of Japanese ancestry to be relocated to internment camps otherwise known as detention centers.

The man who would later gain fame, ironically enough, as one of the most liberal chief justices of the Supreme Court claimed that the entire Pacific Coast was vulnerable to an invisible campaign of "organized sabotage." Warren was alarmed by the knowledge that Japanese American–owned businesses and land surrounded many of our aircraft factories. Many were also surrounded by neighborhoods filled with German and Italian Americans, though their ties to their ancestral homelands were apparently not as unbreakable as the bonds that linked Asians.

Los Angeles, the city that Barry's parents Michael and Reva (née Addison) Diller called home, endured its first wartime blackout between 2:25 and 7:21 on the morning of February 25, 1942. Anti-aircraft guns threw up heavy barrages when the army received reports of unidentified planes flying overhead. Two people died in traffic accidents, several houses were damaged by shell fragments, and thirty American citizens were arrested—twenty of them Japanese Americans. Secretary of War Henry Stimson claimed that fifteen aircraft operated by Japanese agents were involved in the attack. The Department of the Navy later corrected him when the "raid" turned out to be a false alarm.

Wartime Los Angeles was a collection of towns and villages linked by trolley car lines that were already beginning to fail. World War II delayed their final demise by a few years, but as the wartime boom came to an end, the Los Angeles Railway Company collapsed. Its property was sold to the Los Angeles Transit Lines, whose parent company was owned by General Motors, Standard Oil of California, and Firestone Tire and Rubber Company—three entities with solidly vested interests in escorting out the age of electric mass transportation and ushering in a brave new world of freeways and ubiquitous gas-guzzling, rubber-burning automobiles.

During the years following the war, electric rail service on one line after another failed in the face of mounting deficits. The powers that ran the city condemned key portions of the Pasadena line to begin construction of the San Bernardino freeway in 1950. A few electric rail lines survived through the 1950s, but their days were clearly numbered. The last Big Red Car made its final run on March 31, 1963. Painted tears streaming from painted eyes on the front of the streetcar gave it the nickname "The Crying Trolley."

Michael Diller earned his chips in one of the most mundane pursuits of all: building tract houses for GIs returning from the war. The collapse of electric rail lines and the creation of a bewildering network of freeways meant that working stiffs could live farther out in the hinterlands and still get to their downtown jobs on time. Diller seized his opportunity by becoming the West Coast version of William Levitt, who built an empire out of ugly but affordable Levittowns around New York City, and Donald Trump's father Fred, who made his fortune constructing vertical housing for the masses overlooking Coney Island and Brighton Beach. "If horizontal is good, vertical must be better," was the credo motivating old man Trump.

To say that Michael and Reva's son Barry grew up spoiled in Beverly Hills is redundant. Virtually *everyone* raised in Beverly Hills grows up spoiled. Spoiling yourself and your offspring is the whole *point* of living in Beverly Hills, since wealth means nothing unless it is visible, which means you have to flaunt it. Because of its emphasis on money without class distinctions, Beverly Hills society has more than its share of rough edges. All that matters is having the money to get in the game, and the name of the game in Beverly Hills is status as defined by worldly possessions. The most common pastime is trying to size up people's net worth the first time you meet them, judging them by the cars they drive, the clothes and jewels they wear, the homes they live in, and the value of the art they hang on their walls. Gold or silver Rolls Royces, mega-million-dollar homes, and pounds upon pounds of precious stones instantly confer social status.

Beverly Hills owes a tremendous debt to the old money that resided in Pasadena. Most of the so-called first families of Pasadena earned their money the old-fashioned way: they stole it. Prominent among them were the oil-rich Dohenys of Teapot Dome scandal fame and Burton Green, a director of the Amalgamated Oil Company, who attempted many times, without success, to find oil beneath the land that would later become

Beverly Hills. Failing to strike a mother lode of black gold, Green subdivided the land and sold it for building lots.

Beverly Hills took its name from Burton Green's hometown, Beverly Farms, located along the shore of Massachusetts north of Boston. The first known resident was the legendary Virginia Robinson, a wealthy émigré from the Midwest who allegedly drove past the undeveloped land in 1914 and shouted out the window of her limousine, "I want that property." She died at the age of 102 many decades later, after having spent most of her life on the ten-acre Beverly Hills estate her father built for her.

The Robinsons were joined in short order by a parade of early settlers, including the Gianninis who had made their fortune in banking, the Taylors and Andersons of Union Oil and Atlantic Richfield, respectively, and the Mays who founded a department store chain.

Other early arrivals were billionaire investor and movie mogul Kirk Kerkorian, who built his fiefdom at MGM; David Packard, founder of Hewlett-Packard; and David Murdock, emperor of a conglomerate spanning the real estate, meat processing, and manufacturing worlds.

Barry's father Michael had been the youngest of seven children born to Bernard Diller, an Austrian who emigrated to San Francisco in 1902. Michael (who changed his name from Meyer) grew up in an Orthodox Jewish household that strictly observed kosher dietary laws and ran a string of kosher food stores for a living. Diller Deli, a popular San Francisco breakfast nook, was a remnant of the family's mini–culinary empire.

But Michael was something of a rebel who chose a gentile, Reva Addison, for his wife in spite of his father's protests. Reva gave birth to two boys, Donald in 1938, and Barry four years later. The boys spent their early childhood in San Francisco before Michael relocated to Los Angeles in 1949 to be near his older brother Richard and his family.

By the time the Dillers arrived, Beverly Hills had already become a fashionable enclave of upwardly mobile dynamos from various walks of life. If Beverly Hills made no distinction between old money and new, the separation between two other disparate groups was extremely prominent: gentiles and Jews.

The Dillers, being Jewish, quickly learned which clubs and schools would accept them and which ones would not. (Although Reva was born a gentile, she became Jewish by osmosis so to speak and blended into the Jewish community.) In the beginning, the gentiles excluded the Jews (and other minorities), so the Jews responded by forming their own institutions. By the early 1950s, when Barry was approaching his teens, the gentile country clubs still would not admit Jews, although the Jewish clubs did let an occasional gentile in. Danny Thomas, the Lebanese-born Roman Catholic comedian, was the first gentile to apply for membership at the Jewish Hillcrest Club. When he was turned down, he complained angrily to the club's admissions board.

"Danny," the chairman told him, "we *do* want to let a gentile in, but we want one who *looks* like a gentile."

Thomas could do nothing about his Semitic appearance, but the next time he applied, he was accepted. To its credit, Hillcrest demanded that all members contribute five percent of their income to charity, and the club demanded proof of contributions each year before renewing memberships.

The Dillers favored tennis over golf, so they were more attracted to the Beverly Hills Tennis Club. Others who joined that club at various times were playwright Neil Simon, actors Walter Matthau and Wayne Rogers, talk show host Johnny Carson, and singer Frank Sinatra. Young Barry learned to play a creditable game of tennis by the time he was twelve.

Tired of all the snobbery and ethnic bickering between gentiles and Jews, Dorothy "Buffy" Chandler of the *Los Angeles Times* launched a campaign to unify the town by soliciting donations for the common good. With huge contributions from Johnny Carson, Frank Sinatra, real estate billionaire Mark Taper, banker Howard Ahmanson, the Dillers, and dozens of others, she built the lavish music center, which incorporates the Dorothy Chandler Pavilion in one of its wings. Chandler followed up with other projects that eventually created an atmosphere of mutual tolerance, if not undying love, among the various groups that made up this glitzy and ruthless but curiously warm-hearted town.

Many prominent Beverly Hills Jews sent their offspring to any number of private schools in the area, such as the Buckley School or the Westlake School for Girls. Michael and Reva Diller would have done no less for Barry, except that it became apparent early on, as gifted as their boy was, he was no scholar.

Barry was a dreamer. Even at an early age, he marched to a different beat from the sons and daughters of the other wealthy families in the neighborhood. Both physically and mentally, he loved speed: His mind was quick, and he later developed a fondness for fast cars, motorcycles, blinding runs down the ski slopes, and aggressive play on the tennis court. He was quick and alert in every way, but he could not motivate himself to pick up a book and study.

Both of his parents were disappointed at first. Jews tended to revere education, learning, and scholarship above everything else, but Barry cared for none of it. Not that he lacked curiosity. He had an insatiable appetite for *facts*. He needed to *know* things, and he amassed an almost encyclopedic repertoire of data and information, seemingly by osmosis. He did not so much read books and magazines as scan and devour them instantaneously. The problem was that he would spend time doing this only for subjects that interested him, which did not include geography, math, physics, and other disciplines required in school. Barry's interests were centered almost exclusively on the entertainment business, which was not an area that earned anyone high grades in the classroom, not even in Beverly Hills.

Barry's speech was nearly as rapid-fire as the cars and motorcycles he drove as soon as he was able to. His thoughts far outpaced the ability of his mouth to spit the words out, and his parents constantly yelled at him to slow down and think before he spoke. They missed the point. He had *already* thought things through; he simply lacked the patience to speak his thoughts slowly, and he also lacked patience with anyone who was not quick enough to understand him the first time. You either got it or you were history, checked off his list, written out of his life. Barry Diller rarely repeated himself, a trait he carried with him into his adult life.

Barry's older brother was a different story entirely, and he would remain a well-kept family secret. Donald Diller knew nothing but trouble from the day he was born. Reva and Michael Diller's marriage evolved into a rancorous affair that nearly ended in divorce shortly after they moved to Los Angeles. Barry and Donald were raised in a cold, harsh environment that affected them in different ways. Their father had lashed both his sons with barbed taunts from the time they were children.

"Whatever you do in life, make sure you're the best at it. The worst thing is to be a failure." Whenever they displeased him, Michael Diller lacerated his sons with the cruelest jibe he knew, "You're a failure! You'll never amount to anything!" Barry stood up to the old man, but Donald was crushed by him. Barry grew stronger and somewhat ruthless as a result of his constant clash of egos with his father, while Donald was crippled by the experience and turned to drugs for support. Later in life, Barry would question why he was the one with the strength to overcome his inner demons while his brother Donald was weak. They were products of the same gene pool, yet in many respects as different as Cain and Abel.

Donald Diller developed a pretty serious marijuana and heroin habit by the time he was seventeen. At eighteen he was arrested for bouncing a bad check, not the first time he had done so, and spent six months in prison. Throughout his twenties, Donald Diller was jailed several times for dealing in drugs, and then he was arrested for burglary when he was thirty-one. Over the years, he unsuccessfully attempted to support himself as a musician and wound up falling back on menial jobs to pay his rent.

Donald drifted into a fruitless marriage with a Hispanic woman named Teresa Mendoza, a marriage that would end in divorce in 1971 when Donald was thirty-three. He was arrested once again for dealing drugs and released in August 1975. Shortly afterward, he arrived at his ex-wife's apartment with an automatic pistol, which he claimed he had stolen from his parents' Beverly Hills home. Two days later, the police discovered his body in a cheap motel room outside of San Diego with a bullet wound in the forehead, a homicide victim in an apparent drug-related death. Barry Diller would end up paying for his brother's cremation and arrange to have his ashes scattered in a grove of oak trees not far from the murder scene.

But all that was far in the future, something Barry would never discuss with anyone except his closest friends. Considering his attitude toward formal education, it was inevitable that Barry was destined to be a part of the public school system rather than enroll in private schools. He was fortunate in that the public schools of Beverly Hills were not even remotely like the urban public schools mere mortals went to. By comparison, not even Greenwich, Connecticut, another bastion of wealth located 3,000 miles across the country, could boast of a public high school like Beverly Hills, aside from their high academic standards.

Most residents of Greenwich measured their wealth in mere millions of dollars. The cars in the high school parking lot were late-model BMWs and Mercedes Benzes, with an occasional clunker mixed in. Beverly Hills inhabitants measured *their* wealth in tens and hundreds of millions, sometimes billions, of dollars, and their kids drove to school in Porsches and Mazeratis, with nary a clunker to be found anywhere in the parking lot. Mercedes Benzes and BMWs were at the *low rent* end of the spectrum.

CHAPTER 3

SCHMOOZING HIS WAY INTO THE WILLIAM MORRIS AGENCY

BARRY DILLER WAS already two years behind his fellow students by the time he entered Beverly Hills High School. His reputation as a slow and reluctant student, who was old enough to drive in his freshman year, preceded him. His teachers sized him up immediately and decided it was better to have him out of their classrooms than in them. "Slow" students were often assigned to work with the stage crew on school theatrical productions, and Barry quickly discovered that was where he would rather be.

Small and compact, already visibly balding, with a wide gap separating his two front teeth and large jug-handle ears protruding from his head like cup handles, Barry Diller did not possess the kind of California-style good looks that other teenage kids found appealing.

Sweet sixteen and graduation parties were often held at the Chestnut room at Chasen's, a fashionable and extremely expensive Beverly Hills restaurant. How expensive? If you had to ask, you couldn't afford to eat there.

A typical shindig would include a six-piece orchestra, a male stripper for the girls, and female stripper for the boys, and a menu of caviar, filet mignon, and asparagus, with the guests dressed in formal attire. Transportation to and from was usually conducted in forty-foot stretch limousines, preferably white. One party that Diller attended also featured a three-foot tall midget who walked on his hands. The price tag for these lavish—some might say extremely ostentatious—affairs was far more than most people outside of Beverly Hills spent on their children's weddings.

All this was merely the mundane side of life. The family that needed to skimp on vacations to pay for daily existence did not belong in Beverly Hills. Families religiously spent Christmas in Hawaii and summered in Europe even in *bad* years, merely to avoid the worst Beverly Hills stigma of all: the appearance of being impoverished. Jews sent their children on their first trip to Israel at age fourteen, and everyone made their first Grand Tour of Europe at age sixteen, following the obligatory bash at Chasen's. When a fourteen-year-old friend of Diller asked her father for her first mink coat, Barry asked her why she couldn't wait until she was eighteen like everyone else.

"Better too soon than too late," she told him without cracking a smile.

Like most country clubs, the Hillcrest Club and Beverly Hills Tennis Club were even more important for cementing business relationships than for socializing. It was at the Hillcrest Club that Barry Diller, still in high school, met Norman Brokaw, the first trainee in the mailroom of the William Morris talent agency. Brokaw was a nattily dressed ball of perpetual energy who lived for the "Art of the Deal"—before Donald Trump popularized the term many years later. His agency represented some of the biggest stars in Hollywood. "Dress British but think Yiddish" was the philosophy that guided the agency and all the agents who worked for it, according to Norman Brokaw. In other words, dress like a lord of the manor and use your brain like an adding machine.

Diller took to the older man immediately. Ever in search of a mentor who could teach him something he did not already know, something valuable and important that he could use to make money, Diller found the perfect role model in Brokaw. Brokaw's clothes, from his business suits to his tennis outfits, looked as though they had been tailor-made for him—which they were. More important, Brokaw's brain raced in the fast lane, well ahead of everybody else's. Business was life, and life was war, or at least a fierce game of chess. The only way to win was to think faster than your adversaries who, in his case, were the heads of the major Hollywood studios. Diller knew immediately that he wanted to work with Brokaw at William Morris—even more, he knew that he wanted to *be* Norman Brokaw.

People who divided their time between the two clubs eventually met everyone who was anyone in the world of show business, and Diller was no exception. At Hillcrest, he ran into Frank Sinatra; Burt Lancaster; Jack Lemmon; Jerry Weintraub; power attorney Paul Ziffren; movie czar Marvin Davis, with whom he would work later at Fox; Jack Benny; George Burns; Don Rickles; Milton Berle; Groucho Marx; William Wyler; Danny Kaye; George Jessel; and scores of others. Hillcrest rules stated that members could not appear on the golf course without their shirts. Groucho Marx tested the rule one afternoon by showing up with his shirt on but without his pants.

At the Beverly Hills Club, young Barry Diller perfected his skills against the likes of high-powered lawyers Greg Bautzer, Louis Blau, Henry Bushkin, and Michael Fasman; movie titans John Huston, Jack Warner, and Billy Wilder; actors Gary Cooper and Clark Gable; and novelist Irwin Shaw.

Groucho Marx was a member of the Tennis Club as well as Hillcrest, and he played tennis the same way he did everything else: strictly for laughs. When Diller was still in high school, the club featured a no-holds-barred doubles match to celebrate the grand opening of the remodeled clubhouse. On one side of the net were Groucho and U.S. tennis champion Ellsworth Vines, representing the American contingent; opposing them were Charlie Chaplin and director Frank Perry of Great Britain.

Chaplin took his tennis seriously—a fatal mistake when playing with Groucho, who was an expert at putting people off their game. Chaplin was notorious for having little or no sense of humor off-screen, particularly when the humor was directed at him. Groucho made his entrance on the court carrying twelve tennis rackets and a suitcase.

"What's in the suitcase?" Chaplin asked, already disgruntled.

"Never mind what's in the suitcase. Do I go around asking you what's in your suitcase?"

"I don't have a suitcase," Chaplin spat between clenched teeth.

"Why the hell didn't you bring one?" Groucho spat back.

Chaplin's game fell apart completely. Groucho stood off to the side commenting on every shot Chaplin made, while Groucho's partner single-handedly demolished their opponents. Eventually, everyone at the club, onlookers and combatants—with the exception of Chaplin—was weak from laughing. Finally, Chaplin threw his racket down and shouted at Groucho, "I didn't come here to be your straight man, Groucho!"

"Well, you certainly didn't come here to play tennis either," Groucho said deadpan. He then opened his suitcase at mid-court and spread out a picnic lunch from Nate 'n' Al's, a popular Beverly Hills delicatessen. "C'mon, Charlie. Sit down and have a pastrami sandwich."

The clubs were Barry Diller's classrooms, the places he learned everything he needed to know about the only life that interested him. It was there he learned what restaurants to have lunch in and where to go for dinner, and how to get on the "A" lists for the important parties.

The trick of successful dining in Beverly Hills went far beyond securing reservations to the right restaurants, such as The Grill, Ma Maison, Chasen's, Spago, The Polo Lounge, or Morton's. Where you were seated spoke volumes about your standing in the power structure.

Beverly Hills dining was counterintuitive. While the average diner normally tried to get a quiet table in a corner with lots of privacy, in Beverly Hills the object was to be seen. Morton's, for example, was a power broker's dream. You either sat up front at one of the *right* tables, or else you were sitting in Siberia. Morton's had only ten or eleven important tables—five round tables near the door, and about six visibly displayed along the wall. Super agents Lew Wasserman and Norman Brokaw, promoter Jerry Weintraub, and later Barry Diller were among the chosen few allowed to dine up front.

Diller also learned early on how to get to the top parties. The list at a dinner hosted by actor Laurence Harvey and his wife Pauline included Rex Harrison and his then wife, Rachel Roberts. After cocktails and vats of wine with their meal, Harrison and his wife began to quarrel loudly. Finally, Harrison turned to Rachel and said, "You're just a fucking bore!"

"And you, my darling, are a boring fuck!" she replied without missing a beat.

Marvin Davis, Diller's future boss at Twentieth Century-Fox many years later, was at a party one night with his wife Barbara. Davis complained to the entire assemblage that his wife had no enthusiasm whatsoever for his hobbies, tennis and skiing.

"You don't share my hobbies with me either," she said.

"What hobbies?"

"Plastic surgery and shopping."

Beverly Hills, Diller learned, was one of the only places on earth at the time where people openly discussed—actually bragged about—their face lifts and tummy tucks. After listening to Kirk Douglas talk about his bout with the plastic surgeon at a party one evening, someone remarked that "if he has anything else lifted, he'll be wearing his dick for a necktie."

All these contacts were important for a young man on the make who was not yet out of his teens, but none were more critical than Norman Brokaw, Diller's link to the William Morris Agency. Barry Diller may not have been a scholar, but he was fortunate in knowing at an early age what he wanted to do with his life. Money was important, of course; nothing in the world he grew up in was possible without it. More important than money, however, was the power that went with it—the power to run your own life and forge your own destiny. Power and money, and what better way to get both of them than by working for the agency that represented the major stars.

Getting an interview at William Morris was not easy, however. Marlo Thomas, daughter of Danny Thomas, one of Hillcrest's token

Christians, was Barry's high school classmate. Once Barry decided it was show business or nothing, he did everything short of begging on his knees for Danny to intercede for him. Barry had already graduated from high school and had started classes at UCLA, but only to mark time until he got his break. After repeated entreaties by Barry, Thomas finally relented and arranged an interview for the fast-talking, ambitious young man with Sammy Weisbord, West Coast head of television for William Morris.

Thomas relented primarily to please his daughter, but also to get rid of this aggressive kid who would not leave him alone. Secretly, however, he never dreamed that Diller had a chance. Weisbord had a reputation for favoring young girls whom he hired to pick up his laundry, keep the refrigerator stocked with cranberry juice, and for whatever else he could get out of them. Occasionally, he would hire a boy, usually an athletic kid who could run fast, to trot over to the Hillcrest Club and fetch him a container of matzoh ball soup.

Reporting directly to him was Phil Weltman, who was responsible for developing agents for William Morris from the best talent in the mailroom. Weltman met Diller, recognized his potential, and fought with Weisbord to hire him. At first, Weisbord refused.

"Why not?" Weltman asked, exasperated. "Why don't you do for somebody else what Abe Lastfogel did for you?" He was referring to the man who hired Weisbord. Finally, Weisbord relented.

The agency that Diller joined when he was nineteen years old had been founded in 1898 by a young German-Jewish immigrant who adopted the name William Morris. He originally set himself up as a booking agent across the street from Luchow's Restaurant, on the second floor of a building on Fourteenth Street in New York City, which looked as though it had been transported from the Bavarian Alps.

In an age before radio, television, and talking motion pictures, vaudeville was the major form of entertainment for the masses. A few years later, Morris moved his fledgling operation uptown to Times Square, near the restaurants and bars in the theater district where the performers liked to hang out, then eventually expanded across the country to Los Angeles.

The story of William Morris is pretty much the story of show business itself. Before World War I, Morris was already booking some of the biggest names in entertainment. He made stars of Harry Lauder and Will Rogers, lured Maurice Chevalier to the United States in the 1920s, and put the Marx brothers in the movies. During the Great Depression, he turned Jimmy Cagney into the country's favorite celluloid gangster and Mae West into a leading sex symbol. A decade later, Rita Hayworth became a love goddess under his tutelage, and a young, vulnerable blonde named Marilyn Monroe captivated male audiences for the first time.

In the 1950s, Morris took a big chance with a down-on-his-luck saloon singer named Frank Sinatra, whose once-high-flying career had nosedived after his divorce from Ava Gardner. Morris got him an Academy Award–winning role in *From Here to Eternity*, a role that propelled Sinatra's star higher than ever before. This was the decade that Morris also discovered a quirky country singer named Elvis Presley and turned him into a legend. Around the time Diller joined William Morris, the agency was in the process of landing television roles for Dick Van Dyke and Bill Cosby, launching them as international superstars.

The oldest employee at William Morris was Abe Lastfogel, who was born the year Morris founded his agency and joined it at age fourteen. Lastfogel set out from his Third Avenue tenement apartment on a rainy day in 1912 with a slip of paper in his pocket. On it were the names of two places that he heard were looking for an office boy: a tailor shop on Thirty-Sixth Street and the William Morris Agency in Times Square. Since the talent agency was closer to home, he decided to try there first.

In his youth, Lastfogel was a small, cherubic boy with a thick shock of curly, almost kinky blond hair. Already in his sixties by the time Diller arrived, Lastfogel still had all his hair, which he swept straight back from his forehead into a helmet-like mat of tight curls. Impeccably dressed in tailor-made double-breasted suits, always buttoned, and a silk tie tightly knotted at the collar, Lastfogel and Morris set the dress code for agents at the agency.

Sammy Weisbord, a taut, wiry, pugnacious bantam cock, joined the agency in 1929, when he was nineteen years old. William Morris was his escape from his parents' corner store in Brooklyn to a penthouse office high above Beverly Hills overlooking the Pacific Ocean. For a poor kid from a New York City tenement, this was better than finding the Holy Grail—whatever that turned out to be. Lastfogel became Weisbord's surrogate father, the man who taught him everything he needed to know to succeed in the business. They ate lunch and dinner together every day while "Uncle Abe" showed Weisbord the ropes.

Morris Stoller was another major figure at William Morris when Diller arrived. Trained as an accountant, Stoller was a benevolent uncle-type who had joined the agency in 1937, while studying for his law degree at night at Brooklyn College. But perhaps the most polished bigwig at the agency was Stan Kamen, who was shy but aggressive in a low-key way. Unlike Lastfogel and Weisbord, Kamen grew up on the right side of the tracks in the exclusive community of Manhattan Beach, attended Washington and Lee in Virginia, and went on to head the flagship of the agency, the motion picture department. Barry Diller, raised in affluence himself as the son of wealthy parents, saw in both Kamen and Brokaw role models with whom he could identify.

Diller had stars in his eyes before his twentieth birthday. His ambition was boundless and his ego enormous. Starting at the bottom of the heap for starvation wages in the William Morris mailroom may have been demoralizing to some. For Diller, however, it was a revelation. He was an oddball kid, a rebel and a renegade, who was determined to do things his own way or not at all. Diller did not view the mailroom as the bottom rung of the ladder at William Morris, but rather as his entrance to the world he was born for.

It was going to become his ticket to the top.

CHAPTER 4

LEARNING TO DEAL WITH
A HOMOPHOBE ON A MOTORCYCLE

THE MAILROOM WAS a jungle. Diller, a UCLA dropout, was up against MBAs and law school graduates who had turned down enticing salaries on Wall Street. They all worked for a pittance at the agency in an effort to make their mark in show business. It was a dog-eat-dog atmosphere as the trainees did everything they could to catch someone's eye and get out of the mailroom first.

The so-called training program was little more than a hazing ritual. Besides fetching matzoh ball soup from Hillcrest for Weisbord, the trainees spent a year or more sorting mail and delivering scripts before they were considered seasoned enough to even answer the phone for a junior agent. The work was humiliating for ambitious young people, boys mostly, whose impatience to become agents sometimes got the best of them. Yelling matches were common, and tempers flared and sometimes erupted into fist fights.

On one memorable occasion, one of the agents summoned two trainees into his office, handed them a paper bag, and told them to deliver it immediately to his doctor. On their way over, they opened the bag and peered inside, stupefied at the sight of a stool sample at the bottom of the bag. The bag of warm shit they had been ordered to deliver said it all; it told them more than words ever could about their precise standing at the agency. Their only comfort was the knowledge that if they survived "boot camp," they might go on to become some of the highest-paid people in the entertainment business. Tenure at William Morris spelled respect and stability. It meant you would enjoy a powerful niche in the industry and the financial security that went with it.

Diller was handed his exit visa from the mailroom by Weisbord's chief subordinate, Phil Weltman. Weltman had stepped off the Super Chief in 1947 in Los Angeles, where Sammy Weisbord was waiting to greet him. Weisbord drove him right away to his new home at the Chateau Marmont. At the time, the lights of Ciro's and the Mocambo, the most glamorous nightclubs in town, were still ablaze on Sunset Strip. The bungalows of the Garden of Allah with their red tile roofs were still fashionable; by the time Barry joined William Morris, the bungalows had long ago fallen to seed before being bulldozed away to make room for a shopping center.

Weltman and Weisbord lived in adjacent suites at the Chateau Marmont, Phil in 4H and Sammy just above him in 5H. Both were dyed-in-the-wool bachelors who enjoyed trips to the beach where they could cultivate their tans and eyeball young women in scanty bathing suits. They spent weekends together in Palm Springs, vacationed in Hawaii and Europe, and walked the Strip at night while discussing the events of the day, occasionally stopping off at one of the many nightspots along the way.

Weisbord was friend and mentor to Weltman, as well as his boss. Hollywood had become more and more of a television town. The rule in the industry was that the agents found the talent and made the deals in New York City, then shipped the performers out to the west coast where the shows were produced. For every movie being made, two television shows saw the light of day. Packaging the deals was where the agencies made their money, and none made more than the Morris Agency. With TV generating more than 60 percent of gross revenues, Sammy Weisbord had one of the best jobs in the industry as the West Coast head of television.

Weisbord was a pit bull in an age before anyone knew what a pit bull was. Tenacious, ferociously loyal to Lastfogel and the agency, he lived to make deals and to win at everything he did. He had to have the best tan in Hollywood and be in the best physical condition. He once challenged five Morris agents to a medicine ball sit-up contest and outlasted all of them, turning his back into a black-and-blue lunarscape in the process.

Weisbord was fanatical about his diet and convinced himself that cottage cheese, wheat germ, and cranberry juice were the keys to a long and healthy life. Cranberry juice in particular, according to Weisbord's prescription for longevity, would preserve his urinary tract, which he placed right up there with Moses and the Pentateuch in the grand scheme of things. He preferred to have his juice poured by pretty young women, which was the only reason he relented on occasion and hired a female for the mailroom. The subject of his urinary tract was paramount in his mind at all times, even when discussing business with agency clients.

"I don't really care about his urinary tract," the actress Dinah Shore fumed to Diller after leaving a meeting with Weisbord. "I came here to talk about *my* career."

Weisbord was a company man, from his William Morris cuff links and tie clasp to the initials "WM" on the custom license plates adorning his black Cadillac. Weltman learned everything he knew about the business from Weisbord, but he regarded Sammy's personal life as a touch on the bizarre side.

Weltman was more easy-going; his feet were planted more firmly on solid ground. He regarded the trainees in the mailroom as something more than chattel, more than mere automatons who existed only to run personal errands. To Weltman, the mailroom was a testing ground for talent, where the best of the unseasoned young men might rise above the pack and eventually assume the role of agent. Weltman was quick to realize the potential of young Barry Diller and tapped him to be his secretary after Barry's obligatory year of paying his dues.

After many years of bachelorhood spent in Weisbord's company, Weltman met a former beauty queen at poolside during one of their Palm Springs weekends and decided she was the one he wanted to marry. Sammy listened to the news in silence and then reacted in a way that summed up his character better than anything else.

"Have you told Mrs. Lastfogel?" he demanded more than asked.

"Are you saying I need to get her permission?"

After a heated debate about Weltman's "loyalty," Weisbord relented and agreed to be his friend's best man at the wedding. Phil Weltman and his bride set up housekeeping in a secluded section of Bel Air, and Sammy Weisbord gave up his suite at the Chateau Marmont and moved into a penthouse apartment in the Sierra Tower. From his balcony, Weisbord could look out across the broad expanse of Beverly Hills and see the Beverly Wilshire Hotel where Mr. and Mrs. Lastfogel lived. Abe Lastfogel was the man Weisbord worshiped, the man to whom he owed everything. The last thing in the world he would ever do was show disloyalty to the Lastfogels and to the agency by taking a wife.

Barry Diller owed his own good fortune to Phil Weltman. During his year in the mailroom, he learned the ropes the same way Norman Brokaw had twenty years earlier. By keeping his eyes and ears open, he figured out who the movers and shakers were at the agency, he ran around town delivering scripts, contracts, and checks, and most important, he studied the confirmation memos that went out detailing the terms of the deals the agency had worked out.

Working for the princely sum of $40 a week, Diller spent his spare time learning typing and shorthand. He knew he would wind up back on the street in a hurry if he screwed up once by having an accident on the way and showing up late with a delivery. His colleagues in the mailroom would have been happy to see him go; his departure would mean one less trainee for them to compete against. They were all in a contest to make it out of the mailroom first by being tapped as someone's secretary.

As secretary to Weltman, Diller typed up memos, answered the telephone, took notes at meetings, and kept the details of those meetings straight so Weltman could refer to them later. Diller was nothing if not a quick study. Adapting to the business like a duck to water, it did not take him long to figure out the best way to structure a deal, how to give up minor points to appease the other side while locking up the important issues for the client. The immediate goal of former trainees who had advanced to secretary was to learn the business thoroughly enough to be promoted to junior agent.

Weltman was a strait-laced disciplinarian who believed in playing by the rules, and Diller respected him both as a boss and a mentor. Other secretaries learned more about some of the "fringe benefits" of the business working for flamboyant agents like George Wood. Known as "Mr. Show Business," Wood expected his secretaries to work harder than anyone else and stay late into the evening. However, he compensated for his demands by leaving his intercom on so his secretaries could listen in when he was screwing somebody in his office.

Weltman was tough and demanding in his own way, which was that of a drill instructor riding herd over his troops. You either quickly learned the business inside and out under his guidance or you were out the door. Working for Weltman, Diller learned to be tough, even ruthless, during negotiations, but scrupulously honest as well. Do everything you had to in order to get the best terms for the client, but once the deal was done, you honored it down to the last detail. After a deal was agreed to verbally, Weltman—and Diller—stayed as late into the night as it took to prepare and deliver a confirmation letter. That way, there was no time for the buyer to reneg on the deal, and no room for misunderstanding.

As Weltman counseled Diller, "Get used to wild rantings from the buyer and don't be intimidated. You can always come down if you have to, but you never know what the traffic will bear until you mention a price."

William Morris was more than just a place of employment for Diller and the others who worked there; it was family. The tone was set by Abe Lastfogel who taught everyone that the client and the agency came first, not the agent. Everyone pulled together as a team, and that way everybody prospered. As different as Weisbord, Weltman, Wood, Brokaw, and the others were in their personal quirks and idiosyncrasies, they all worshiped Lastfogel and subscribed to

his credo. The agency had made them all rich. They owed everything to William Morris—their expensive homes and cars, their memberships at Hillcrest and other clubs, all their other luxuries,

and their enviable contacts in the most glamorous industry on earth.

Loyalty meant that you did not leave William Morris for any reason short of death. Young Barry Diller cringed in fear one day when George Shapiro, another of Weltman's secretaries, told Weltman that he made his army drill sergeant look like Mary Poppins. Shapiro had gotten into William Morris through his cousin, the comedian and writer Carl Reiner, who had launched his own career with Sid Caesar on *Your Show of Shows*. Weltman brought Shapiro out of the mailroom to work with him on *The New Steve Allen Show*, which had just been bought by ABC.

After telling off Weltman, Shapiro screamed "I quit!" and ran out of the office. There was silence in the agency for almost a minute, when Shapiro came running back blubbering, "I'm sorry. I don't know what got into me." Weltman laughed heartily, threw his arm around Shapiro's shoulder, and welcomed him back to the flock.

Perhaps the most demanding client at the agency during Diller's tenure was a young, insecure hothead named Steve McQueen. McQueen was a latter-day James Dean, with the same passion for fast cars and motorcycles. Unlike Dean, who was vulnerable and somewhat androgynous,

McQueen walked around with a chip on his shoulder and was always spoiling for a fight. Short and wiry, with a perpetual pout on his face, he was openly and violently homophobic, terrified that somebody might take him for "a queer," as he invariably referred to homosexuals.

Stan Kamen, McQueen's agent at William Morris, walked on eggs every time he was in McQueen's presence. At least half the boys in the mailroom and a good percentage of the agents were gay, according to several sources, but they kept their private lives to themselves for fear of antagonizing their socially conservative boss, Abe Lastfogel. For Diller, Kamen, and many of the others, putting up with McQueen's savage rantings about "queers" was like humoring Hitler while he foamed at the mouth about Jews. McQueen liked to get into fights to prove his "manhood," and he was not beyond bashing gays to convince the entire world that he was not one of them. All of them quivered when McQueen was around, but Kamen caught the brunt of his abuse since he had to deal with McQueen regularly.

Steve McQueen had already earned a reputation as the star of a popular television series, but he was determined to make it in the movies as well. Since Lastfogel wanted to keep him as a client of the agency, it fell to Kamen to make sure it happened. Kamen confided to Barry Diller about the impossible position he was in—turning a surly, snarling, homosexual-hating television hero with limited acting ability into a major movie star.

Not least among the problems of landing McQueen a suitable movie role was that he was not very literate. He refused to read scripts and confined his literary endeavors to perusing automobile and motorcycle magazines. McQueen's wife at the time, a young beauty named Neile, took on the job of approving movie scripts worthy of her husband's consideration. Neile McQueen had given up a promising acting career of her own to assume the full-time occupation of wife, nursemaid, business manager, and amanuensis to her ever-brooding husband.

Finally, a role came along that seemed to hold great promise. Kamen saw the possibilities for McQueen in the character of Captain Virgil Hilts in a new movie about to be filmed, *The Great Escape*, about POWs in a Nazi concentration camp. He passed the script along to Neile, who agreed with him. The big movie project for the agency in 1962 was *It's a Mad, Mad, Mad, Mad World*, which was being filmed in the blistering desert outside of Palm Springs, starring a long roster of William Morris clients. Kamen saw the potential for *The Great Escape* to become a major feature film as well, and he was determined to secure one of the leading roles for an agency client.

McQueen agreed reluctantly to take the part and flew over to Bavaria to begin shooting. Hilts, the character he was to portray, was a brooding, ill-tempered, vague, undefined loner—a perfect description of McQueen himself. All he had to do was walk in front of the camera and be himself without even attempting to act. McQueen, however, was unhappy with the role from the beginning. He complained constantly that others in the movie, including James Coburn and James Garner, had bigger roles than he did. He wanted his part expanded, more lines added, more action sequences added for his character. Eventually, he talked the director, John Sturges, into writing in a long motorcycle escape scene for him.

Sturges agreed, but McQueen was still unhappy, demanding that his role be made even larger. He was particularly annoyed with Garner who, oddly enough, idolized McQueen and adopted some of his eccentric mannerisms in an effort to give more substance to the character he was playing. The more Garner imitated McQueen, the more McQueen came to hate him. He accused the director of fleshing out Garner's role at the expense of his.

When the camera finally rolled, McQueen vented his dark, feral frustrations by charging across the countryside on his motorcycle like a demented animal just let loose from a cage. He scattered chickens, geese, and other livestock—everything that stood in his path—in his mad fury, ignoring the demands of the script. Sturges tried to rein him in, asking him to do the shot the way it was written. McQueen responded by walking off the set and refusing to cooperate unless he got his way.

At an impasse, Sturges called Kamen in Beverly Hills and asked him to fly over and do something about his impossible client. Kamen asked Barry Diller to join him for moral support, and both of them set off on the trip across the Atlantic. When they arrived on the set, they found the entire cast and crew, except for McQueen, standing around drinking beer and partying. McQueen was sulking alone inside his trailer.

"What's wrong?" Kamen asked.

The best excuse for his actions that they could elicit from their semi-literate client was that he was tired of being pushed around by "a bunch of queers." Either they would rewrite the scene and let him do it his way, or he was walking off the set. Kamen and Diller conferred with Sturges, who was equally adamant. He had reached the end of the line with the agency's prima donna, he said. Unless McQueen was back on the set ready to work the following morning, Sturges said he would take him out of the picture.

"What's he gonna do?" McQueen asked when they returned.

"Nothing," Kamen said. "You'll just have to trust Sturges."

Kamen and Diller got on the next plane and headed back to California, and McQueen shrugged his shoulders and returned to work the following day. This time he projected his fury into the camera instead of at his fellow actors and the livestock that inhabited the German countryside. The rest is film history. McQueen skidded and fishtailed on his motorcycle like a man who had nothing left to lose—precisely the image Sturges wanted to capture.

McQueen did all his own stunt work in the scene, except for the final leap over the barbed wire fence to freedom in Switzerland. The legend grew that McQueen performed that last stunt as well, but it was actually made by a motorcycle mechanic named Bud Ekins whom McQueen had befriended and brought with him to Germany. Ekins had tutored his buddy in the techniques of stunt driving, and McQueen could not wait to try out his newly learned skills in front of the camera.

In one of Hollywood's many ironies, Steve McQueen's motorcycle scene turned *The Great Escape* into a popular classic, and the William Morris Agency added a brand-new movie star to its roster of clients—a charismatic, homophobic biker from Los Angeles' San Fernando Valley, by way of Beech Grove, Indiana.

CHAPTER 5

THAT GREAT MARQUEE IN THE SKY

BARRY DILLER'S EDUCATION was progressing at a rapid pace. While he had grown up surrounded by some of the leading figures in show business, working at the William Morris agency showed him how the deals that turned his neighbors into superstars were made. Diller was more fortunate in his upbringing than most of the other agents at William Morris, who were largely working-class Jewish boys from Brooklyn or the Bronx. For them, show business had transformed their previously drab existences into a rarefied life of glamour and excitement. They came to think of the agency and its clients as family. Even some of the clients developed the same feeling.

At a party to celebrate his twenty-fifth anniversary as a William Morris client, comedian Abe Burrows proclaimed, "I don't think of my commission as a commission. To me it's like sending money home to my mother."

Abe Lastfogel's wife Frances agreed without hesitation. "You bet your ass, and you'd better keep sending it, too."

Burrows laughed along with everyone else. They all realized that, while money was the grease that kept the William Morris family on track, loyalty was the glue that held their mutually dependent careers together. Loyalty and food, particularly a good pastrami sandwich from Nate 'n' Al's. Carol Channing once walked into Abe Lastfogel's office with a heavy bag slung over her shoulder.

"What's in there?" Abe asked her.

"Diamonds, negotiable securities, and sandwiches."

"What kind of sandwiches?" he asked, his eyes lighting up with hungry curiosity.

The agency boasted a roster of clients that was the envy of the industry. Following Steve McQueen's great success in *The Great Escape*, William Morris propelled Bill Cosby's star into orbit in the fall of 1963. Sheldon Leonard was the hottest producer in television, and his relationship with William Morris was largely responsible for the agency's clients appearing twenty-seven hours a week on television, more than three times the hours of its nearest competitor. Leonard had a deal with NBC to develop an adventure series called *I Spy*. He had already signed Robert Culp as one of the leads and was looking for a contrasting type to costar with him.

Cosby supplied about as much contrast as anyone could ask for at the time. He was overtly funny in contrast to Culp's more whimsical humor. He was also black, which posed a great risk for Leonard and for the agency. Would white America tune in each week to watch a series featuring a black hero? It had never been done before, but if anyone could pull it off, it was Bill Cosby. Or so argued Barry Diller, Stan Kamen, and others at the agency after catching Cosby's standup comedy act on television one night.

Cosby belonged to a new generation of comics. They differed from the comedians of the past like Milton Berle ("The Thief of Bad Gags," as he called himself) and Henny Youngman, who depended a lot on verbal slapstick and outrageous puns. Cosby and his ilk employed humor that was personal and irreverent, but not as biting as the comedy of Lenny Bruce, Dick Gregory, or Mort Sahl. Cosby and others like him took their lead from groups like the Kingston Trio and the Smothers Brothers, who thought of themselves as intellectually provocative without being threatening in the eyes of middle-class America. Thirty years later, their style would best be described as "Satire Lite." Cosby was quintessentially middle class himself, the first African-American actor to project that image. Sheldon Leonard threw caution to the wind and followed his instincts. He signed up Cosby as Culp's costar for the new show, and the William Morris agency had another major star on its roster of clients.

Barry Diller's role as Phil Weltman's secretary increased his visibility at the agency. Weltman learned to trust Diller's judgment and brought him in on more and more of the deals he was working on. Diller was a quick study. He was shrewd and had a natural instinct for the business. Weltman saw from the beginning that Diller possessed a trait that could not be learned in business school no matter how intelligent the student—a knack for dealmaking. Like many great negotiators who came before him, Diller could smell blood as it was beginning to float in the water. It was a killer instinct, a random gene that turned people into sharks when they sat across from their opposite number at the negotiating table. Weltman noticed that Diller also had integrity, another quality that Weltman and his bosses at the agency regarded as essential. The young son of a Beverly Hills real estate developer was on the fast track toward success.

So was David Geffen, a twenty-two-year-old kid fresh out of the mailroom himself. Geffen's background was more typical of the other youngsters hired to work in the mailroom and was a world apart from Diller's. He had grown up in a working-class Jewish family in Brooklyn. His mother Batya ran a shop called "Chic Corsets by Geffen" that made ladies' underwear in Boro Park, a bustling Brooklyn neighborhood. David's father was a mostly unemployed pattern worker who could barely afford to house his family, including David's older brother, in a walkup tenement apartment.

David wanted to be a dentist but after graduating from high school, he decided to drive across the country first to visit his brother, who was studying law at UCLA. Seeing Beverly Hills for the first time was like achieving Nirvana for a poor kid raised in the congested streets of Brooklyn. The luxury, the glamour, the weather, the sheer unreality of it all made an impression that would never leave him. After visiting with his brother, he enrolled at the University of Texas before transferring to Brooklyn College, but the lure of California proved too difficult to resist. A lie earned him his way into the William Morris office in New York City. Believing that he needed a college degree to work there, he put down on his application that he had graduated from UCLA. The mailroom gave him the opportunity he needed to complete his deception. When a letter arrived from UCLA stating that the first name on the application did not tally with the Geffen who had graduated from the university, David inserted his own letter and forwarded it to personnel.

Once his position was secure, Geffen headed out to the Beverly Hills office on his vacation, where he met and immediately became enamored of a fellow employee named Barry Diller. Young Diller was everything that Geffen was not: self-assured and socially adept. He knew his way around the Beverly Hills watering holes and introduced Geffen to a nightlife the youngster from Brooklyn had only heard about before. David Geffen had known since high school that he was gay, but he felt inhibited in Manhattan because it was too close to home. However, being three thousand miles away, particularly in a city where nothing was shocking and all things seemed possible, was a liberating experience. Diller was already making a name for himself working for Weltman, and he helped arrange a transfer to the West Coast for his buddy from Brooklyn.

Jerry Brandt, a young agent in William Morris's music division, asked rhetorically, referring to the film and TV agents. "Schmuck! You think these guys are gonna listen to you? They don't care what you've got to say. They're older than you are. Deal with people your own age. Go into the music business. Nobody knows what you're doing there, and nobody knows how to do it."

The education of Barry Diller and David Geffen progressed further under Brandt's tutelage. Diller, Geffen, and most of the other secretaries recently out of the mailroom had been struggling to make their way and put their own deals together. Brandt was a standout in that he had developed his own niche and was raking in piles of cash. Tall and slick, Jerry Brandt was a born salesman. While Diller and the other aspiring agents were still surviving on starvation wages, Brandt wore finely tailored mohair suits and gold watches. Diller jetted across town on his motorcycle, while Brandt had a chauffeured limousine at his beck and call whenever he stepped outside the office. Diller and Geffen often ate together, but Jerry Brandt wined and dined with Mr. and Mrs. Lastfogel at the Hillcrest Club. Clearly, the fastest route to success at the agency was on the music side of the business, putting together deals for leading pop singers like Bobby Vinton, Bobby Darin, Steve Lawrence, and Eydie Gorme, and Brandt had staked out the post position for himself.

Diller, Geffen, Michael Ovitz, and some of the other quick studies at William Morris caught on fast. Their big break came when the Beatles turned rock 'n' roll from a well-paid cottage industry into an international mania. Suddenly, working-class Brits were in a position to command stratospheric fees to appear on American television shows for six or seven minutes at a time. The young Turks at William Morris searched the working-class pubs and alleys of England for shaggy-haired Beatle clones who could carry a tune.

And so the British invasion became a full-blown infestation, with groups like the Animals, Herman's Hermits, and the Dave Clark Five filling the airwaves with their jarring Cockney howling, not only in the United States, but throughout Europe and Japan as well. The biggest catch of all in dollar terms was a sinister-looking pub band headed by the scabrous Mick Jagger that had just come out with a song called "Satisfaction." Thus did five cadaverous misfits, who went by the name of the Rolling Stones, propel Jerry Brandt, Barry Diller, and David Geffen several rungs higher on William Morris's ladder on their way to the top.

"I can't get no satisfaction, I can't get no satisfaction, 'cause I try and I try and I try and I try. I can't get no, I can't get no . . ." Who would have believed that lyrics such as that delivered by a group of prancing, hyper-kinetic wild boys would go on to make tens of millions upon millions of dollars for them and their agents over the decades?

This end of the business was so new that they simply made it up as they went along. When a musical group's business manager wanted the agency to trim its commissions below the sacrosanct 10 percent, the young Turks simply lowered the tariff to 7 percent—a sacrilege at the time. At first there was resistance from the agency's accountants.

"We don't do business with riffraff like that," Diller was told.

"Oh yeah? Do you know how much they get for a night?" Diller asked. "Twenty-five thousand dollars."

The accountants' jaws dropped and the eyes opened wider. Twenty-five grand was an incredible sum at the time for a couple of hours work in front of an audience.

"Seven percent of a twenty-five thousand-dollar advance against 60 percent of the gross in arenas and stadiums in city after city for days and weeks at a time adds up to . . . well, you figure it out."

Suddenly, William Morris was representing street-wise urchins—descendents of Oliver Twist on steroids howling the lyrics to their songs—for a mere 7 percent. Steve McQueen was cute, but this was real money that the William Morris upstarts were talking about. By 1964, the music department, once an adjunct of the agency that none of the older agents wanted to bother with, had become the tail wagging the dog. The agency's roster of musical talent grew to include the Beach Boys, who were back on the charts for the third year in a row with "California Girls" and "Help me, Rhonda"; Chad and Jeremy, whose electrified version of Bob Dylan's "Mr. Tambourine Man" paved their way to a platinum record; and Sonny and Cher, the Romeo and Juliet of the bell-bottom set.

None of this was lost on Abe Lastfogel. Dining one night at Hillcrest with Colonel Tom Parker, Elvis's Svengalian manager, Lastfogel asked him how he had become so successful.

"Merchandising! That's the secret. You give me all the popcorn at all the movie theaters across the U.S.A., and you can shove Elvis up your ass."

Merchandising and marketing! Tastes change over time, and with the passage of the seasons comes a changing of the guard as the stars of yesterday pass on and surrender the stage for the latest generation.

The passing of Sophie Tucker in February 1966 marked the end of an era, both for show business and for the William Morris agency. At eighty-two years of age, she was the agency's oldest client, having signed with William Morris himself in 1910, and she was also one of Abe Lastfogel's oldest living friends. The woman who had wowed audiences with her beads and feathers and sequined gowns, and who characterized herself as the "3-D Mama with the Big Wide Screen," had come to the end of a long, productive life, a victim of lung and stomach cancer.

Lastfogel took charge of the funeral arrangements. Sophie Tucker had done everything in grand style, and Lastfogel wanted to be sure she went out in style as well. The memorial service took place in Riverside Chapel in New York City, the red brick funeral home around the corner from the Ansonia Hotel where Sophie had been maid of honor at Lastfogel's wedding almost forty years earlier. A thousand mourners squeezed inside, while 3,000 more crowded behind police barricades set up in the street.

George Jessel gave the eulogy, ending in his typically schmaltzy style, "In that Great Marquee up there, Sophie's name is a most shining adornment."

Lastfogel and company were mourning more than the death of a long-time client and friend; the names of an entire generation of yesteryear's top performers, many of them agency clients, adorned that Great Marquee in the Sky. Among them were Al Jolson, Fanny Brice, Eddie

Cantor, and Joe E. Lewis—who was not yet officially deceased, but his liver was already well pickled in copious vats of booze.

The end of an era was also reflected in the death of cafe society. No longer could the El Morocco, the Stork Club, the Latin Quarter, and other brassy supper clubs compete with the deafening clamor and dazzling lights of Las Vegas casinos and rock 'n' roll emporia. The cafés gave way to a new generation of eardrum-splitting watering holes with names like Arthur and Le Club. Jet-setters breezed in for a few hours or so to take in the latest bands of the hour, then whisked themselves off to the next stop on their frenetic itineraries, sometimes hitting four or five clubs in a single night. The old style may have been corny, but it possessed a certain civility, if not elegance, that had been replaced by a new wave of hedonism and obsession with youth.

The Hollywood studios themselves had begun to take on the aspects of geriatric wards. The last of the original Warner Brothers, Jack, was in his mid-seventies. Paramount's chairman, Adolph Zukor, was ninety-three. Twentieth Century-Fox's leader, Darryl Zanuck, was a mere youngster of sixty-four. Abe Lastfogel and most of William Morris's top agents were in their sixties, and the agency's luster was beginning to be overshadowed by a tenacious competitor named Creative Management Associates, headed by a forty-two-year-old dynamo named Freddie Fields.

Fields operated more in the style of Barry Diller, Michael Ovitz, and the other up-and-coming youngsters at William Morris. Debonair and charming when he needed to be, Fields was married to the glamorous, ever-youthful actress Polly Bergen, who was like a female version of Dorian Grey. Jerry Brandt may have been chauffeured around town in stretch-limos, but Fields gadded about in a white Bentley outfitted with a bar and telephone.

While many of William Morris's clients were either dying or exhibiting the early stages of rigor mortis, CMA was signing up the hottest acts in the business: Dean Martin and Jerry Lewis, Jackie Gleason, Phil Silvers, George Burns and Gracie Allen. Fields even managed to steal Judy Garland from William Morris after her triumphal performances at the London Palladium and the Palace in New York. It was not volume he was after, but rather the highest-paid entertainers in the industry. He operated under the philosophy that 7 percent of the highest-paid talent in the business was better than 10 percent of the lower paid.

"There are too many old fat cats at William Morris," Diller told Geffen. "But we're young and hungry, and so is Freddie."

By 1966, the seismic shift in show business away from the old toward the new and young had passed the point of no return. Barry Diller grew increasingly restless. He was anxious for his agency to either change its priorities or at least recognize the contribution he and the other young agents were making. Until now, none of them had complained about the $15,000-to-$20,000 salaries William Morris paid its junior agents. But the yawning gap that separated their incomes from the incomes of the lean and hungry CMA agents could no longer be ignored. More and more, accountants were running the firm.

"Forty dollars for lunch!" Nat Kalcheim screamed at Diller one day. "In my day we ate at the cafeteria."

"In your day you didn't book twenty-five-grand-a-night rock 'n' roll bands."

The generational divide grew wider and wider. Diller and the other junior agents started to complain that they were being cheated. Their salaries and bonuses did not begin to match a reasonable share of the commissions they brought in. The youngsters could make deals and sign clients, but they were not going anywhere because too many well-fed geezers at the top refused to give up their meal tickets.

Jerry Brandt was the first of the young Turks to leave. He made his decision after learning that his 1965 bonus was going to be only $6,000.

"I think you made a mistake," he said to the accountants.

"How much were you expecting?"

"Twenty-five thousand."

"But it's already in the books!" they protested.

How typical, Brandt thought. "It's in pencil," he pointed out. "You can erase it."

In the end he settled for $14,000. He quit the agency and used his money to open a discotheque on the Lower East Side of Manhattan called the Electric Circus, which became a popular hippie hangout.

David Geffen's patience also ran out. He quit and took a job with the Ashley Famous agency for $50,000 a year, more than twice his salary at William Morris. The final straw for Barry Diller was when he approached Sam Weisbord one day and asked if he could hire his own secretary to help lighten his workload. No matter how much Diller pleaded with the older man, Weisbord refused to budge. In frustration, the aggressive twenty-four-year-old put the word out that he was looking for a change. He had learned everything that William Morris could teach him, and it was time to move on.

Diller did not have to wait long. ABC programming chief Leonard Goldberg had had his eye on Diller for some time. When he extended an offer in 1966 for the young man to move over to the junior network, Barry Diller agreed, after some initial hesitation.

CHAPTER 6

DON'T CALL HIM A *PUTZ* ANYMORE

IT WAS A warm spring evening in Beverly Hills when Leonard Goldberg first met Barry Diller. Goldberg was dating Marlo Thomas at the time, and he ran into Barry at a party at the Thomases. The Dillers lived down the street from the Thomas home, and Barry was friendly with both Marlo and her sister Terry. After serving his apprenticeship at William Morris, Diller was full of ideas and had just been promoted out of the mailroom. Goldberg was amused by the cocky youngster who already knew a lot about the business and who flaunted his knowledge. It was immediately apparent to Goldberg that the younger man was seething with ambition.

Goldberg liked him right away. He had assembled a team of "killers," as he put it, at ABC. "I wanted guys around me who were smart and tough." Barry Diller seemed to fit the mold, but Goldberg could not be entirely sure, so he went out of his way to provoke a fight.

"You don't know shit about the business. You think you do, but you're still a young *putz*. You've got a lot to learn."

When Diller got mad, it appeared as though his ears were twitching and his pale blue eyes were emitting sparks. He tightened his compact body until it resembled a giant fist, stood on his toes, and thrust his face within inches of Goldberg's.

"Don't call me a *putz*, you silly fuck! Who do you think you're talking to?"

"Where do you think you're going at William Morris? Smart guys, tough guys are tripping over themselves to become agents there. What makes you think you've got what it takes?"

"It's the best agency in the business, and it takes care of good people. I'm already on my way up the ladder."

Goldberg defused the situation before it got out of hand. He shook Diller's hand and set up a meeting with him the following week. Over lunch, Goldberg extended an invitation.

"I think you've got what it takes. I'd like you to come to New York and be my assistant at ABC."

"And forget about being an agent?"

"Nobody really wants to be an agent. I mean, if you can't do anything else, you become an agent."

"I don't agree. I like William Morris, and I want to be an agent there. It's the right place for me."

Diller stayed at William Morris a few years longer and continued his climb up the agency's ladder until he ran into a roadblock in the person of Sam Weisbord, who was reluctant to pave the way for Diller's further advancement. In the summer of 1966, not long after his twenty-fourth birthday, Diller decided to accept Goldberg's offer and move across the country to New York City.

The move was a giant step in more ways than one for Barry Diller. It involved reversing roles by leaving the agency side of the business, the selling side, for the customer or buying side. It also meant giving up "paradise"—perfect weather in one of the most beautiful settings on earth—for the filth, grit, humidity, and generally unpredictable climate of New York.

The network Diller joined in 1966 was still a struggling enterprise. It was the youngest of the three major networks, a spin-off from RCA's Blue Network of 1943. The same year it was sold again to LifeSavers candy promoter Edward J. Noble, when the FCC prohibited any company from owning more than one network.

Throughout the 1940s and 1950s, ABC remained a far-distant third among the networks as it had only five television stations and no daytime programming. Both CBS and Twentieth Century–Fox failed in their attempts to buy the company, but United Paramount Theaters forced a merger with ABC in 1953. Leonard Goldenson of Paramount presided as chairman of ABC, patching together a few affiliated stations and substituting creativity for money when it came to programming. He put together crucial programming deals based more on his personal tastes than on any bold master plan. Like the general of an undermanned army, Goldenson knew he had to outmaneuver the opposition rather than try to outgun it.

Goldenson began by hiring Disney Studios to produce a series for ABC's 1954–1955 season. Other studios joined in, including Warner Brothers, producing shows like *Ozzie and Harriet* and *Wyatt Earp*, starting in 1955. Goldenson also scored a news coup by televising the complete Senate hearings staged by Senator Joseph McCarthy for thirty-six straight days in 1954—unheard of at the time. Throughout the remainder of the decade, and into the 1960s, ABC under Goldenson challenged the broadcasting media by ignoring many of their major assumptions.

"Hey, this is crazy," Goldenson told novelist Roy Huggins, the author of *77 Sunset Strip*. "They are doing radio with pictures, and this is not what TV is." He was talking about TV's capacity for dramatization rather than mere video clips of people reading scripts. TV was a wholly different medium than radio, and the early pioneers of television had failed to understand the distinctions.

Goldenson forged a marriage between broadcasting and the movie industry, running one-hour shows that told stories in the same manner movies did. One of his first big hits was the series *Cheyenne* starring Clint Walker, an out-of-work actor earning his rent money as a security guard in Las Vegas. The series was a watershed for ABC, television's first hour-long western that ran for seven years, prompting CBS and NBC to counter with westerns of their own, such as *Gunsmoke*.

Goldenson initiated other revolutionary changes. He was the first to wrest control of programming and scheduling away from the advertisers. He established ABC as the first network to turn the viewing of sporting events into a national pastime. Goldenson also popularized televised news by delivering it nightly into living rooms across the country for the first time. While not as well known as David Sarnoff or William S. Paley, Goldenson was one of the pioneers who set the stage for the expansion of network telesion.

Goldenson's personal preference for music immortalized schmaltz in a way it had never been done before. A band leader named Lawrence Welk and his group had established themselves locally, appearing live at the LaMonica Ballroom in Santa Monica. Their music was broadcast on Saturday nights at nine o'clock by KABC-TV, an affiliate of Goldenson's network. On a whim, Goldenson decided to televise the show nationally in the summer of 1955, and the response was overwhelming. The *Lawrence Welk Show*, sponsored by Geritol, which was introduced as an alcohol-based, iron-and-vitamin B tonic in August 1950, became one of the most successful programs on television, thanks to Goldenson's genius for programming according to reviewers at the time.

"What genius?" Goldenson said later. "I put him on because I liked his music. It was as simple as that."

Another intuitive move that met with astonishing results was Goldenson's decision to put religion on the air. Bob Weitman, one of his executives, approached him with the then-controversial idea in 1955.

"I want to go after Bishop Fulton Sheen," he said. Weitman and Goldenson were both Jewish, but they recognized a showman when they saw one.

"Go," Goldenson responded.

Weitman visited the bishop at the office of the Propagation of the Faith on Fifth Avenue. When he arrived, a man wearing a fedora was sitting next to a beautiful woman, listening to Bishop Sheen play the piano.

"How would you like to be on television?" Weitman asked Sheen when they were alone in the bishop's office.

"You're going to make trouble for me and for yourself," was the bishop's initial response.

Sheen was a born ham, however, and could not resist the appeal of a nationwide television audience for himself and his beliefs. He soon accepted Weitman's offer.

"It's none of my business, Bishop," Weitman said, "but who is that gentleman sitting out there with the fedora, and who is the beautiful lady with him?"

"That's Clare Boothe Luce."

She was there for a session with Sheen, who was in the process of converting her to Catholicism. The man in the hat turned out to be Fritz Kreisler, a friend of Sheen and one of the world's finest violinists. Kreisler wrote Sheen's entrance music, and the bishop walked out on the set in simple garb and no props. He looked at the camera and talked for thirty minutes straight, with no interruptions for commercials or station breaks. He offered plain talk with no bells and whistles, no pizzazz. The following week the network was bombarded with letters, most of them stuffed with checks made out to Sheen's organization. Catholics, Protestants, Jews, and those of no persuasion sent letters of praise as well as money, the best endorsement of all.

"What is all this?" Goldenson asked Weitman in astonishment.

"It's for the bishop. We've got to keep this guy on."

"You're right," Goldenson said, and a new hit show was born.

Weitman left ABC to accept an offer from CBS that he couldn't refuse, and Goldenson replaced him with Bob Lewine, who had been successful in getting good programming from Disney and Warner Brothers. In 1958, ABC was still a distant third in network ratings even under Lewine's guidance, however, so Goldenson was forced to do a complete management overhaul.

"Everyone kept insisting that nothing could be done," Goldenson said.

"I was worried to distraction. For months I had sleepless nights of tossing and turning, wracking my mind for answers."

The arrival of thirty-eight-year-old Ollie Treyz was Goldenson's salvation. Treyz was a human buzz-saw full of ideas, energy, and unpredictable enthusiasm. "I gave him his head," Goldenson said, meaning that he gave Treyz enough rope to either hang himself or succeed brilliantly. Goldenson decided to go for broke on the strength of Treyz's instincts. At this point, Goldenson had nothing to lose.

With the volatile and somewhat eccentric Treyz in control of programming, ABC aired a series based on Roy Huggin's novel *77 Sunset Strip*. The show starred a young actor named Edd "Kooky" Byrnes, who was a somewhat slicker version of the deceased megastar and teenage icon James Dean. Byrnes developed the affectation of running a comb through his lank blond hair throughout each episode, and teenagers went wild. Teenage boys related to his rebellious, devil-may-care demeanor, and teenage girls fell for his boyish good looks and bad-boy attitude. From the first episode, it was a must-see show for teenagers across the country.

Treyz's forte was research. He commissioned a professor at Columbia to conduct a study on TV audiences to see if there was a way ABC could narrow the divide with CBS and NBC. Professor Paul Lazarsfeld, a leading expert in the field of crowd behavior, discovered that the top programs at the other networks featured former radio performers who were popular with older audiences. However, Lazarsfeld also learned that advertisers were interested in targeting young viewers who were more likely to switch both product brands and the shows they watched than older people, who tended to be victims of habit. Even more important, people between eighteen and forty-nine years of age spent more money on consumer items than older folks.

In effect, Treyz had commissioned the first demographic study for television, and he pitched his findings to the advertising community. Treyz recommended that ABC adopt programming geared for the young and active set, starring handsome men and beautiful women in stories dealing with the problems of youth. Coming up with the right stories meant hiring a new generation of programming executives who were both young and smart enough to know what appealed to their age group.

One of the first of this new breed of executives to join the ABC team was a young man with prior experience at CBS named Dan Melnick. Treyz, with Goldenson's blessing, was searching for youngsters with belly fire, willing to experiment and take risks in an effort to make a name for themselves in the business. By his own admission, Melnick was "a wiseass, arrogant kid"—just what the network needed.

Melnick decided that the only way to make his mark was to air shows that the other networks would not even consider. It was not so much a question of counter-programming—running a comedy against a drama, for example—as it was of adopting a lineup of youth-oriented shows against the major networks' geriatric format. In today's culture, the programs ABC put on seem tame, but in the late 1950s they were the equivalent of the types of shows that put Fox on the map thirty years later.

Ben Casey, for instance, starred a dour Vince Edwards as a counter-culture doctor with a talent for infuriating almost everyone, including members of his own profession. *The Fugitive* starred David Janssen as a middle-class man on the run because he was unjustly framed for a crime he did not commit. *Maverick* featured James Garner as the antihero who always gained the upper hand over crooks in the establishment.

ABC's progress was not immediately discernible, but by 1960 the network was beginning to close the gap with CBS and NBC. By the mid 1960s, Goldenson had elevated ABC from a collection of stumbling radio and television affiliates into a strong third-place contender. By this time, ABC had grown into an appealing entertainment franchise that attracted the attention of potential suitors. Goldenson, who had succeeded so far through hard work and crafty corporate generalship, marshaled his forces to fight repeated takeover attempts by Norton Simon, General Electric, and a bizarre, recluse billionaire by the name of Howard Hughes.

When Ollie Treyz and Dan Melnick left ABC for greener pastures, Goldenson was confronted with the dilemma of replacing them with a new team of young, motivated, highly talented people. It was at this point that he brought in Len Goldberg, who would tap Barry Diller to be his aide and chief amanuensis. ABC was still not turning a profit, despite its programming successes, and Goldenson informed his staff that he was thinking of exiting daytime programming altogether and concentrating on the more lucrative prime time hours. In 1965 Goldenson offered Goldberg a promotion of sorts, loaded with pitfalls—the job of vice president of daytime programming.

"I understood it would probably be a one-year job," Goldberg said, "because, if we didn't substantially improve, the department was out of business. Much to everyone's amazement, I took it."

Goldberg took his first big gamble in the summer of 1965. He ran an hour of rock 'n' roll at two o'clock in the afternoon, with Dick Clark serving as host. The initial exposure of Clark to mid-afternoon viewers met with moderate success, thanks largely to teenagers who rushed home from the beach early enough to watch the show. Goldberg was encouraged enough to launch another daytime program called *The Dating Game*, which featured ordinary guys competing with one another to land a date with attractive young girls. Teenagers of both sexes, fighting their own battles with zits and other pubescent maladies and insecurities, immediately identified with the participants.

If dating worked so well, why not try mating? Goldberg extended the logic of his early success a step further with *The Newlywed Game*, featuring contestants only a few years older than the daters discussing their marital problems. "Now that you landed the date and won a mate, see what you've got to look forward to!" This formula worked well, drawing a slightly older audience. Just about everyone in his or her twenties and thirties who had been married for a few years was battling financial insecurity, anxiety over dripping stockings in the bathroom, caps left off toothpaste tubes, snoring, and other annoying minutiae of daily cohabitation. ABC had tapped a lucrative vein, and Goldberg's job as chief of daytime programming was secure.

By the time Len Goldberg asked Barry Diller to join his team at the network, ABC's franchise was gaining in value thanks to its emphasis on programming for the young and active set. Diller would apply this formula successfully twenty years later, when he helped Rupert Murdoch turn Fox into the fourth network based on the strength of its irreverent, counterculture programming. In the beginning, however, he had some misgivings about taking the job in New York City, which he expressed to Goldberg.

"People say I'm your secretary. They make fun of me."

"Don't worry. In a very short time no one will ever make fun of you again," Goldberg told his young assistant, a statement that turned out to be far more prophetic than either of them realized at the time.

CHAPTER 7

GIVING BIRTH TO
MOVIE OF THE WEEK

MICHAEL EISNER WAS the next to join Goldberg's team at ABC. Eisner had sent out over one hundred resumes in his job search but received only one response. Eisner's resume landed on Barry Diller's desk, and Barry invited him in for a meeting. Diller was impressed by Eisner's intelligence and toughness and passed him along for Goldberg to interview.

"I like him," Goldberg told Diller. "He doesn't know any of the rules, which is great because he won't feel bound by them." Another member of Goldberg's "Youth Squad" who was not bound by the rules was Marty Starger, who had worked for Goldberg at an advertising agency and eventually succeeded him as head of programming at ABC.

The cheapest way for ABC to advertise its new lineup of shows was to promote them on the air. However, since ABC had far fewer affiliated stations than CBS and NBC, this type of on-air promotion reached a relatively small viewing audience. The alternative was to come up with shows that could be advertised successfully in other media because of their youth appeal.

With this in mind, *Mod Squad* was successfully launched. The show featured a hip young group of crime-stoppers that appealed not only to kids, but also to older viewers searching for some mindless escapism. Goldberg and his team followed this hit with *That Girl*, starring Diller's friend and neighbor from Beverly Hills, Marlo Thomas, which also became an instant success.

Next, Barry Diller discovered a script for a series that had been developed for another network and then rejected. The story centered on a folksy, affable doctor named Marcus Welby—the kind of doctor who has long since vanished into the ether. Doctor Welby actually made house calls, got involved with his patients' family situations, and followed up to see how everyone was doing. Sending bills or collecting the money due him from insurance companies seemed to be the last thing on his mind. Money was never mentioned, although he apparently got paid for his services since he lived as well as most doctors do. He was always neatly dressed, drove a late-model car, and lived in a house that was the envy of his neighbors. Most of all, he was lovable; his patients couldn't wait to see him no matter how sick they were.

Diller showed the script to Marty Starger, who also fell in love with Dr. Welby. Both of them wanted to hire Lee J. Cobb to play the lead, following his big success in *Twelve Angry Men*, but when Cobb was unavailable they showed the script to Robert Young. Young had enjoyed a major success with *Father Knows Best* some years before but had been unable to find suitable work since. He was more than eager to play Dr. Welby.

"That's a terrible idea," Goldberg told Diller and Starger when they approached him about using Young. "He's just wrong. He's good-looking and charming. He's a leading man. This is not written for a leading man."

When Diller sent word back to Young that he had been turned down for the role, Young called Goldberg directly. "Mr. Goldberg, I understand you don't want me to be in *Marcus Welby*," he said.

"You're just too handsome for the part. And you look rich and successful. This guy is struggling."

"I don't think I'm handsome. Maybe I'm charming," Young replied. "But why can't he be successful? Why can't he drive a nice car? There's nothing wrong with that."

"That's just not the character."

"I wish you'd reconsider."

Through sheer persistence, Robert Young eventually convinced Goldberg to let him play the role, and *Marcus Welby, M.D.* became one of ABC's greatest hits—an early coup for Diller, who had discovered the script and pushed hard for Young to star in the series.

Diller's next big breakthrough occurred early in 1968. It started as the brainchild of Roy Huggins, who thought of the idea as he was walking off the effects of a hangover on Malibu Beach on New Year's Day. ABC had been trying to launch full-length movies for television following the early success of its one-hour westerns. The problem was money. The network lacked the capital to finance the purchase of feature films long enough to fill a two-hour spot.

"Why must we do two-hour movies on TV?" Huggins asked himself when the vapors of New Year's Eve began to dissipate. In the old days, many movies ran seventy-five or eighty minutes. Huggins himself had produced feature films as short as that. One of those epiphanies that sometimes strike in the early hours of the morning when you can't sleep—or when you are suffering the effects of too much booze—suddenly flashed before Huggins's eyes. *Movie of the Week,* the vision read. How about a seventy-minute movie with twenty minutes of commercials running from eight-thirty to ten o'clock one night a week? Like Saul on the road to Damascus, Huggins was thunderstruck by his serendipitous discovery and could not wait to share it with a potential buyer.

"We don't want anything to do with this. You are on your own," said Sid Sheinberg, vice president in charge of television at Universal Pictures when he heard Huggins's proposal.

Down but not out, Huggins next approached Fred Silverman and Mike Dann at CBS with his concept.

"Roy, that is the worst idea I've ever heard in my life," said Dann, who stood up and abruptly walked out of the meeting.

Woozy from two head blows in a row, Huggins managed to get up off the proverbial canvas and pitch his idea to Herb Schlosser at NBC. Schlosser was more polite than the others but equally to the point. "We already have a two-hour movie series. Can't use it."

Huggins was almost ready to throw in the towel when he got a call from Len Goldberg, who had read about Huggins's idea in *Variety*. "Are you interested in presenting it to us?" Goldberg asked. Was he interested? He had begun to feel like Lazarus in the tomb, and now Goldberg had let a glimmer of light shine into the crypt.

Huggins arrived at ABC's offices and found himself staring across the table at Goldberg, Barry Diller, and a few other members of Goldberg's team. He made his pitch and waited uneasily as his listeners silently exchanged glances. Then the questions erupted, first from Diller.

"What kind of stories would you tell?"

"You must start with hard-hitting melodramas and mysteries until you've got your audience. Then you can branch out and tell character stories or war stories or anything you want. It's an anthology series."

"How many shows would you run?"

"One a week for six months. Twenty-six in all."

"Okay, Roy. We'll get back to you," they said. The meeting was over. Nothing had been decided, but it was the best reception Huggins had yet received for his proposal. A few weeks passed, and Huggins picked up *Variety* one day and read that ABC was planning to launch a ninety-minute weekly series called *Movie of the Week*. This was his idea, and nobody had even checked with him about it. He called Goldberg immediately.

"We are going to do this ourselves," Goldberg said. "It's too big for any one person."

"How can you do that? I brought you this concept!" Huggins was upset, but legally he had no solid footing. All he had was a concept, which could not be copyrighted. Ideas are in the public domain. Goldberg knew this as well as anyone, but he was not out to screw Huggins. He merely wanted to use his advantage for bargaining power.

"We're going to do twenty-six of these, and we think it's too much for any one producer. How many would you like to do?"

"Twenty-six."

Goldberg laughed. "The network has to control a show of this importance. How would you like to do eight?"

It was a good compromise, Huggins later realized. Goldberg did not have to cut him in on any of the movies. But Goldberg and his team of "killers" were not thieves, just tough, hard-nosed negotiators. Huggins let his pride get the best of him, however, and turned down the offer. So the concept was given to Barry Diller to execute, and Diller developed it into one of ABC's most successful programs. It was nothing short of a godsend for the network.

Diller's career at ABC, and in the industry, accelerated considerably as a result. Over the years, the myth would develop that *Movie of the Week* was Diller's baby, that he saved ABC and propelled its star skyward with his stroke of genius. Diller never claimed credit directly, but still the belief took hold that he invented *Movie of the Week*. He would have been crazy to deny it too vehemently.

With Goldberg's blessing, Diller and Marty Starger approached ABC's board of directors with a request for $14 million to launch the series.

"Maybe we should just try one or two first," was the initial response.

"No, it's got to be a series," Goldberg said, backing up Diller and Starger.

Largely on the strength of Diller's salesmanship, the board agreed to finance the project for the full amount without so much as a pilot or a script. Then the hard work began. All they originally had was smoke and mirrors—a vague concept with no substance to back it up. Diller needed stories, not ideas, to make the series work, and stories that were good enough to hold the viewers' attention for ninety minutes week after week did not grow on trees. Diller had to develop them.

Miserable as he was living in New York, Diller welcomed the opportunity to return to his old stomping ground on the West Coast to meet with studio heads. In the beginning he was greeted by blank stares. The studios were used to developing either full-length feature films or half-hour television shows—even one-hour programs. But seventy minutes? It sounded like a freak to them, some sort of a mutant. Something not fully developed, almost deformed.

Diller and Goldberg realized that if they wanted to get this project off the ground, they would have to jump-start it themselves. They contacted a producer named Harold Cohen who had previously approached them with a series about a spy based on an already published novel. This was a start. Adventure. Intrigue. A property they could pick up cheaply. They hired Jimmy Sangster to write the script and cast Robert Horton of *Wagon Train* fame, Sebastian Cabot, star of *Family Affair*, and actress Jill St. John to star in the first two back-to-back movies.

After ABC announced what it was doing in *Variety* and the other trades, the phones started ringing off the hook. All the studios that had previously turned down the idea now wanted to participate in the new venture. Diller learned a lot about human nature in the process. You can pitch a new idea until you're hoarse, but no one wants to run the risk of failure on an untried concept. As soon as it becomes a reality, however, everyone wants to get in early. The risk then shifts to being left behind at the station when the train is taking off. It was an amazing revelation in the subtleties of human psychology. The illusion of success becomes its own reality.

By this time, Barry Diller had evolved into a tough, seasoned business-man as well as a shrewd negotiator. One of his major strengths was securing the rights to stories from the studios at a favorable price. The going rate for everyone else was $400,000 per film, but Diller managed to obtain stories for *Movie of the Week* for $350,000, largely on the prospect of offering the studios a steady stream of business down the road.

According to Diller, "The wonderful thing about ABC was that it allowed people like Michael Eisner, me, and an endless list of others to take all the responsibility we wanted. It was never a question of waiting for someone to give us responsibility."

ABC supplied Diller, Eisner, and the other killer kids with enough rope to either hang themselves or to secure their careers if their projects were successful. Diller was permitted, at the tender age of twenty-four, to deal directly with studio heads and to make his own deals for the network. This authority brought him into direct contact with entertainment titans like Lew Wasserman, Arthur Krim, and Charlie Bluhdorn, the former industrialist who would later become Diller's boss at Paramount.

"I was responsible for ABC's movie inventory, buying movies and scheduling them. That's a remarkable load to put on a kid," said Diller.

After turning down Diller when he originally approached the studio, Universal chairman Lew Wasserman became personally involved and agreed to everything his company had said no to the first time around. More studios quickly fell in line, and others—Lorimar among them—came into existence on the strength of ABC's seed money used to fund stories for *Movie of the Week*.

"By controlling production of the movies ourselves and contracting with several production companies," said Leonard Goldenson, "Barry let competition work in our favor. We stayed within his original three-hundred-and-fifty-thousand-dollar budget per film. Thereafter, in all the years he worked for ABC, Barry was uniformly successful in meeting fiscal targets."

The 8:30 to 10:00 p.m. slot proved to be an effective bridge, sandwiched as it was between other popular ABC shows and the news, which allowed it to hold viewers' attention throughout the evening.

During the next few years, Diller cloned *Movie of the Week* and created copycat programming, such as *Movie of the Weekend* and *ABC Suspense Movie*. His success with this format gave birth to a brand new made-for-television movie genre. It emboldened Diller to produce movies tackling subjects that were previously considered too controversial for television. Among them were *Brian's Song*, the story of football player Brian Piccolo, whose career was shortened by cancer, and *That Certain Summer* starring Martin Sheen and Hal Holbrook, one of the first films in the United States to deal explicitly with homosexuality.

Diller was jolted in May 1969 by the departure of Len Goldberg for Screen Gems, a Columbia subsidiary. Until then, Diller had enjoyed working for Goldberg and regarded him as both a mentor and a father figure. The search for the mythological father, the older man who was smarter than he was, whom he could respect and look up to, would pre-occupy Barry Diller all his life. His own father was financially successful but hardly a man of towering intellectual gifts. Michael Diller was also socially conservative and narrow-minded about issues such as homosexuality. In Goldberg, Barry Diller found a boss with a *laissez-faire*, live-and-let-live perspective on life, a man who regarded others with a measure of understanding and acceptance, if not approval.

Marty Starger was tapped to be Goldberg's replacement as the new head of programming at ABC. Diller and Starger had gotten along and worked well together for the past few years. At twenty-seven years of age, Diller could not really expect the top job to go to him. He was pleased by Starger's success but somewhat resentful at the same time. Even though he may not have been quite ready to fill the position himself, he knew he would have been capable of growing into it had it been offered to him.

CHAPTER 8

LIFE IN THE SHARK TANK

IN 1970, THE FCC rocked all three networks with a ruling that as of January 1971, they would no longer be able to carry commercials for cigarettes. Tobacco advertising had provided a large portion of network revenues since the advent of television. For ABC, the end of cigarette advertising amounted to a loss of 7 or 8 percent of primetime revenue just as it was beginning to challenge CBS and NBC as a strong third-place contender.

ABC needed something close to a miracle to keep it from going down for the count, and the network received it in the form of another ruling from the FCC on the twin subjects of "network dominance" and "control of programming." In effect, the government snatched away precious revenues with one hand, then restored ABC to health with the other through a complicated ruling that affected prime time programming in a way that hurt the two major networks and indirectly benefited ABC. The ruling restricted programming at CBS and NBC while allowing ABC to introduce more innovative shows in an effort to give ABC more equal footing on the playing field. The net result was that ABC was able to charge advertisers additional money for prime time slots for their more imaginative programming, more than making up for lost cigarette revenues.

ABC pursued its advantage by focusing on its core strength: finding and developing good stories for television movies. As Diller put it, "When you have a really big novel, it takes the right forum to tell the story. What better place to do that than on television?"

Diller secured the rights to Leon Uris's powerful novel *QB VII*, dealing with two subjects controversial to television at the time: castration and the Holocaust. "I wanted to test the form with something tough, not something easy," Diller said. "We got remarkable results. Then I bought *Rich Man, Poor Man*, the Irwin Shaw novel, simply because I thought it was a good, good read."

Because the novel was too long to telecast the story in a single night, it was spread out over six two-hour segments—the first time this approach had been introduced to the public. Reviewers were generally upbeat about ABC's latest innovation and referred to it as a "miniseries." Thus, another new format came into existence thanks to Diller's willingness to take risks and test the limits of the medium.

Michael Eisner also made a huge contribution to ABC's success during this period. Diller, Eisner, and Starger spent countless hours brainstorming at a retreat in New Hampshire and at Starger's house in Malibu, tossing ideas in the air to see how many of them would fly.

"Mike would come in with ten ideas, seven of which were absurd," said Starger. "But three would be crackling good ideas. He was the ideal development person. You want somebody who's totally free, not somebody who edits himself."

The three of them and other members of their staff were discussing new program ideas at Starger's Malibu home when Eisner said, "We all remember our high school days with nostalgia. What if we take some people in their late twenties and early thirties, our target age, and do a show based on when they were in high school?"

Diller and Starger were both receptive to the idea. The outcome of this meeting was a new sitcom called *Happy Days*, featuring Henry Winkler in the role of the Fonz.

Barry Diller's professional life could not have been going better, but his personal life left much to be desired. He missed Southern California and had a lot of trouble adapting to New York City. The weather was abominable by comparison, and culturally he felt like a fish out of water.

Like most successful young professionals, Diller lived in a modern high-rise apartment building on the East Side. A compulsive workaholic, he put in long days at work that more often than not spilled over into the weekends. One of his favorite places to unwind after work was the Ginger Man, a bar and restaurant owned by actor Patrick O'Neal, who is now deceased, located a block away from ABC's offices on West Sixty-Sixth Street, a few blocks north of Lincoln Center. O'Neal had opened the popular establishment in the 1960s following his off-Broadway stint as Sebastian Dangerfield in the play *The Gingerman*, based on J.P. Donleavy's novel of the same title. His West Side watering hole was modeled along the lines of the Dublin pubs where Dangerfield did most of his Rabelaisian drinking and carousing.

Diller would also stop for a drink with Eisner and Starger in another of O'Neal's bars called O'Neal's Saloon, a few blocks south on Broadway just across from Lincoln Center. O'Neal was forced to change the name of his second gin mill when he ran afoul of New York's labyrinthine laws governing food and drink. Since saloons were considered to be synonymous with speakeasies, which were phenomena of the Prohibition era, New York had outlawed the use of the word since the 1920s. O'Neal, a true maverick himself, simply scratched out the "S" in saloon and replaced it with a "B" without bothering to add the second "L" in balloon. Both the actor and his customers gathered nightly to toast the idiocy of the state's mindless bureaucracy, laughing at his deliberate misspelling of his second bar and restaurant, which went on to rival the popularity of the Ginger Man.

Diller was quick to discover Zabar's farther north on Broadway, which was arguably the best place in the city for bagels, lox, and other Jewish favorites. Still compact and trim—as he would remain all his life—Diller kept himself in top physical condition, quick-stepping across Central Park on his way back and forth from work every day. Diller walked the length and breadth of Manhattan or jetted around town on his motorcycle when he wanted to get someplace fast. He often rode down to Greenwich Village on weekends, frequenting bars, many of which had a gay clientele, in a city that had not yet fully accepted alternative lifestyles despite its reputation as a bastion of political liberalism. Diller's leisure attire ran to black leather jackets and jeans, with a thick coating of suntan lotion smeared across his prematurely balding dome.

Diller's political leanings were decidedly left-wing, not unusual for most people in his business. At the same time, he was a fierce competitor in a business heavily regulated by the federal government, and he observed first-hand how uninformed government meddling often led to inadvisable public policy. So, while his instincts and comfort zone pulled him toward the left, in the business world Diller was a practicing free market capitalist of the highest order. Economically conservative and socially liberal, Diller met the broad definition of libertarianism—although he acknowledged a bigger role for government than most capital "L" Libertarians would have preferred.

"Diller, Starger, me, and the others, we were all in a fish tank at ABC, and the strongest fish dominated," said Michael Eisner. "Nobody cared what we did as long as we were successful and responsible, as long as we didn't do junk. If we failed we would have been thrown out."

Eisner might more accurately have called the environment in which they worked a *shark* tank instead of a fish tank. Diller and his ABC colleagues maneuvered to come out on top in a dog-eat-dog world that was as predatory as any envisioned by Nietzsche or Darwin. Diller's highly developed social conscience served to temper his nature as one of Goldberg's top killers, but he remained a super negotiator who went for the jugular first and asked questions later.

By 1971, when he was twenty-nine years old, Diller had already risen to the post of Vice President in Charge of Feature Films and Movie of the Week. He reported directly to Fred Pierce, President of Television. Pierce was a fair but tough-minded executive who stated his philosophy succinctly.

"My personal philosophy is that you first compete to be equal. Then you compete to win. Then you compete to be the best. Then you compete and be the best and put something back in."

Under Pierce's guidance, Diller helped ABC break new ground by filming novels for television, committing money to exciting new projects, and then putting something back into the medium. The final item included bringing quality drama back to television through *ABC Theater*, which began in 1973 as an occasional series.

The first in the series was David Susskind's production of *The Glass Managerie*, starring Katharine Hepburn in her television debut. Pierce and Diller followed it with other outstanding dramas, including *Elephant Man*; *Divorce Wars*; *My Body, My Child*, which was about the still controversial topic of a woman's right to have an abortion; *Women's Room*, starring Lee Remick; *Shadow Box*, directed by Paul Newman; and *Who Will Love My Children?* starring Ann-Margaret in her first major dramatic role.

Diller's role in transforming ABC into a major network attracted the attention of Charlie Bluhdorn, an industrialist who had assembled an empire that included Paramount Pictures under the Gulf + Western banner. Bluhdorn was a bit rotund and spoke with a heavy Viennese accent. He wore thick eyeglasses and swept his hair over the top of his head from the area above his left ear. Bluhdorn was extremely excitable and sprayed everyone with saliva when he spoke. His aides tried to stand back a few feet when they met with him, but Bluhdorn had a habit of thrusting his face within inches of theirs as though he were trying to use their noses for a microphone.

Notwithstanding these unattractive personal traits, Bluhdorn had a genius for multiplying stratospheric numbers in his head in seconds. He could be funny, infuriating, charming, insulting, and just plain crazy depending on the day of the week and hour of the day when he cornered his employees. His nature was nothing short of mercurial.

Bluhdorn's personal life was ultraconservative. He was a devoted family man with a gorgeous wife and obedient children. However, while he dearly loved his family, the thing he loved best in life was cutting a deal. Bernard Baruch once said that the easiest way to make a small fortune was to start with a large one, but Bluhdorn did the opposite. He began by making a small fortune in commodities, which he turned into a large fortune buying and assembling companies. A critic once wrote that his empire, Gulf + Western, should have been more accurately named Engulf + Devour.

A dealmaker par excellence, he admired this ability more than anything else when he recognized it in others. Since Barry Diller negotiated most of ABC's movie deals, Bluhdorn had the opportunity to observe the younger man's tenacity when he bought films from Paramount. Bluhdorn reasoned that if he could not best Diller at the negotiating table, he would be better off having the pugnacious little shark working for him. Paramount's bottom line was suffering at the time, and Bluhdorn had no media savvy of his own. In 1974 Bluhdorn decided to make Diller an offer he would find hard to refuse: the chairmanship of Paramount Pictures. Diller understood the movie business as well as anyone Bluhdorn knew, and Diller's business and negotiating skills would also be an asset to the company. But first he cleared it with Diller's immediate boss, Fred Pierce.

"Charlie called me and asked if I'd let Barry out of his contract. He wanted to make Barry chairman of Paramount. But before he spoke to Barry, he wanted our approval."

Pierce conferred with Elton Rule, another ABC executive, who replied, "How can you possibly stop a person from accepting that kind of an offer? If you don't let him take advantage of this, I'm not sure what his reaction will be as far as continuing to contribute to ABC is concerned. I think he can do us a lot of good as head of the studio. He might help us get a preferred position on shows they develop."

Pierce agreed and decided not to stand in Diller's way.

"Making me chairman of the Board of Paramount was a rather large leap of faith for Bluhdorn," Diller said. "When I told Goldenson, he said, 'You have to take this opportunity.'"

Diller enjoyed working for the network and was not eager to leave, but the opportunity to head up a major Hollywood studio at age thirty-two was impossible to turn down.

"I think Bluhdorn respected me because I was so young," Diller said, "and also because I wanted to prevail. Winning requires an act of will. There are moments when my exercise of will is strong, and this business is all about will."

Before he left ABC, however, Diller approached Herman Wouk about the possibility of adapting his novel *The Winds of War* for television. Wouk was understandably suspicious of the entertainment business, considering the horrible adaptations it made of his earlier works, *Marjorie Morningstar* and *Captain Newman, M.D.* Diller got Fred Pierce interested in the project, and through Pierce's efforts ABC finally consummated a deal with the author by promising to restrict the kinds of commercials the network ran with the show.

Then the fun began. Casting was the biggest problem, with the selection of the dreadfully wooden Ali McGraw to play the female lead Natalie, and Robert Mitchum to play Pug Henry, the hero of the story.

"No one's better than Mitchum in a uniform saying nothing," said Brandon Stoddard, who worked with Pierce on the show, "and Pug has nothing to say. He just walks around looking confident and makes you feel good."

There was a potential problem with Mitchum, who was a semiretired old drunk at this point in his life. If you wanted to have an intelligent conversation with him, you had to catch him before noon when his cocktail hour began.

"I'm worried," Stoddard told Dan Curtis, the director of the show.

"Let's invite him to lunch and see what's up," Curtis said.

Mitchum arrived for lunch at Jimmy's in Beverly Hills, and Stoddard and Curtis ushered him to a table outside in the sunlight where they could check out the condition of his eyes. But Mitchum was smart enough to wear dark sunglasses for the occasion, which succeeded in hiding any signs of a life given to indolence and excess.

On the best of occasions, Mitchum was surly and reticent. What you saw on the screen—a beefy, self-absorbed brawler with a mean streak running through him—was Mitchum in real life. Neither he nor George C. Scott was about to win any personality contests. Stoddard and Curtis tried everything they could think of to get Mitchum to take off his dark glasses, without success. Finally, Stoddard appealed to his vanity.

"Those are nice glasses," he said. "Are they prescription?"

Anxious to prove that he could still see clearly in his advancing years, Mitchum took off the shades and handed them over. Stoddard and Curtis checked out his eyes, which were heavy-lidded and slightly bleary, not too different from the Mitchum of old. They decided then and there that he would do.

As it turned out, Mitchum was not the problem. The show was a hit, attracting a large audience, but the critics savaged poor Ali McGraw's performance, calling her everything from a piece of furniture to a zombie. Mitchum was just Mitchum. No one expected him to be anything different.

Diller was long gone by the time the show finally aired, but his success in adapting big novels for the small screen was his legacy to the network that launched him into the major leagues of the entertainment industry.

CHAPTER 9

HOW TO MAKE
CHARLIE BLUHDORN VOMIT

LIKE THE ROMANS who pushed ever outward, beyond the Italian peninsula and into the countries of North Africa and much of Europe, Charlie Bluhdorn was determined to extend the boundaries of his own empire beyond mining, manufacturing, and the financial industries.

There was big money to be made in entertainment, and money and power captivated Bluhdorn's attention more than any other commodities. His Leisure Time Group, as he named it, encompassed book publishing with Simon & Schuster, spectator sports with New York City's Madison Square Garden, and movies with Paramount Pictures. By the time Barry Diller joined Paramount in 1974 as its chairman and Chief Operating Officer, the Leisure Time Group composed 14 percent of the Gulf + Western conglomerate Bluhdorn had built from scratch in 1957.

In 1958, Paramount turned its largest profit in nine years, and the prospect for future earnings increases seemed promising. However, the general decline in movie attendance that had begun after World War II continued into the mid-1960s, when higher ticket prices served to camouflage lost revenues from sagging attendance.

By 1965, Paramount's executive ranks had been decimated by the defections of top talent to other studios. Executive Vice President George Weltner, who had assumed control of daily operations of the company, found himself under attack by a group of dissident shareholders led by Broadway producers Ernest Martin and Cy Feuer, and chemical mogul Herbert Siegel. Just as the rebellious faction was set to launch a proxy battle to take control of the studio, Charlie Bluhdorn entered the fray with a preemptive bid of $83 per share, $10 above the market price. The deal took effect on October 19, 1966, and Bluhdorn folded Paramount into his expanding empire, the first major studio to be swallowed by a conglomerate.

Paramount soon began to contribute handsomely to Gulf + Western's bottom line. Movie attendance picked up despite higher ticket prices after a twenty-five year skid. By 1972, the revenue from movie tickets sold in the United States and Canada climbed to nearly $1 billion, after having plummeted from $4 billion in 1946 to $820 million in 1971. The ongoing war in Vietnam and the ensuing antiwar protests across the country may have contributed to the upswing, since movie attendance tends to benefit during turbulent periods.

Bluhdorn was anything but an absentee emperor presiding over his fiefdom from a distant throne. He plunged into the day-to-day operations of the studio from day one, making sure that Paramount participated fully in the industry's upturn. Bluhdorn chose his executives carefully, tapping Stanley Jaffe, Frank Yablans, and David Picker to serve as president in that order, and later Michael Eisner to fill the role after Diller took over as CEO.

Diller's predecessor was Robert Evans, who had enjoyed a quixotic career in and out of the movie industry before Bluhdorn picked him to head up Paramount when he was only thirty-six years old. Evans had been an actor and played the matador Pedro Romero in the film adaptation of Hemingway's novel *The Sun Also Rises*. He turned to a partnership in his brother's fashion business, Evan-Picone, when his acting career hit the skids. And he was first and foremost a womanizer who had competed with his friend Warren Beatty to bed the most desirable women filmdom had to offer.

Bluhdorn needed a Hollywood professional who knew his way around the movie business to help him put Paramount in the black. The man he picked had to be ambitious, dependent on Bluhdorn for his financial security, and willing to do his bidding. With the help of Martin Davis, a ruthless Gulf + Western executive with the instincts of a Doberman pinscher, he settled on Evans to fill the role.

During his first interview with Bluhdorn and Davis, Evans realized that he was up against two crafty business tycoons who had the power to make him a force to be reckoned with in the entertainment industry or eat him for breakfast, lunch, and dinner if he rubbed them the wrong way. Against his better judgment, Evans reluctantly agreed to become "Bluhdorn's Blowjob," as he was labeled by an industry magazine.

"I want twenty pictures a year from you," Bluhdorn told him right up front. "The *alte kocker* in charge of Paramount now is ninety years old. He went to see *Alfie* and he couldn't hear a thing."

Working for Bluhdorn and Davis was like holding two tigers by the tail. They refused to give Evans a minute's peace. No second of the day or night could he let his guard down. If the telephone rang at three in the afternoon or three in the morning, Evans was expected to be there to answer it. He was head of the studio in name only; in reality, he was a combination major-domo and amanuensis for two forces of nature who micromanaged every thing he did down to the last detail.

"Go by the seat of your pants, Evans," Bluhdorn instructed him, clearly relishing his foothold in the movie business like a kid running a candy factory. "Make pictures people want to see, not fancy-schmancy stuff people don't understand. I want to see tears, laughs, beautiful girls—pictures people in Kansas City want to see."

Bluhdorn slept only two or three hours a night, and he could not understand why anyone else needed more sleep. He could be charming when he wanted to be but was mostly insulting and infuriating when he did not get his way. More than sex, money, and family, getting the best of a deal was the stimulant that turned him on the most. The more he negotiated, the more excited he got.

"I want everybody to get rich, but don't rape me," was his favorite negotiating ploy.

"Hollywood—I thought it was glamorous," he said to Evans after his first business trip there. "Everyone I meet is under five feet tall."

This was a reference to the diminutive Abe Lastfogel, who stood barely over five feet, as well as to some of the other William Morris agents he encountered across the negotiating table.

Thanks to Bluhdorn's negotiating skills, Evans was able to sign up Jack Lemmon and Walter Matthau for *The Odd Couple* with extremely favorable terms for Paramount. On his own, Evans signed Jack Nicholson to co-star with Peter Fonda and Dennis Hopper in *Easy Rider* for $12,500. It was the biggest role of Nicholson's career to date, and the pay was twenty times more than Nicholson had received for any previous role. Those movies made money for Paramount, but the one bomb that almost got Evans fired was *Tropic of Cancer*, based on Henry Miller's erotic novel of the same name. The movie featured Ellyn Burstyn lying naked on a bed with her legs spread, picking crabs out of her pubic hairs.

"I want to vomit," was Bluhdorn's reaction when he saw it. It was hardly the kind of movie that would play in Kansas City. Despite its underwhelming reception by both the reviewers and the movie-going public, Evans survived the disaster and managed to hang on to his job for a while longer.

The movie that saved not only Evans's job but the studio as well when Bluhdorn threatened to sell off Paramount's assets and shut it down was *Love Story*. Paramount had been losing money on spaghetti westerns and other flops when Bluhdorn threatened to pull the plug unless Evans could come up with a miracle. Evans acquired the rights to Eric Segal's novel before it became a runaway best-seller, and Evans cast his wife of the moment, Ali MacGraw, and actor-brawler Ryan O'Neal to play the leads. The appeal of the movie confounded everyone. *Love Story* was the mother of all tear-jerkers, a twenty-tissue movie that became the highest-grossing movie in history at that time, pulling in more than one hundred times the $2 million it cost to make it.

In 1968, Evans serendipitously optioned Mario Puzo's novel, *The Godfather*, for $12,500. Puzo was in hock to the mob for ten grand in gambling debts when he walked into Evans's office with an untitled sixty-page manuscript under his arm. Like Puzo, Evans was also a compulsive gambler who had lost far more at the card table and in the stock market than he had ever made. He bailed Puzo out mostly as a favor, only to see the work-in-progress he had optioned go on to become a huge best seller.

Next, Evans signed an overweight, down-on-his-luck actor named Marlon Brando to play Don Corleone, the mafia kingpin in the movie. Brando was out of work and desperate to get a part. He agreed to work for scale plus a small percentage of the gross. The movie based on Puzo's novel was released in 1972 and became the number one box office champ up to that date, grossing more in six months than *Gone With the Wind* had in thirty-three years. Brando had his agent approach Evans for more money. Marlon needed $100,000 to pay back taxes, alimony, and child support.

"Give it to him!" Bluhdorn said immediately. "But take back his points."

And so it came to pass that Brando got his hundred grand and gave up points on the movie that would have amounted to $11 million over time. Brando fired his agent and his lawyer when he realized what they had done, and Bluhdorn practically had an orgasm pulling off one of the most lucrative negotiating coups of his life.

By 1972, thanks to *Love Story*, *The Godfather*, and a few other big hits, Evans had succeeded in transforming Paramount into the largest studio in Hollywood from the ninth-largest when he took over in 1966. On the surface he was riding high, the latest Golden Boy of filmdom. In reality, he was a mere employee, kept on a short financial leash by Bluhdorn, who refused to give him an equity stake in the company. Both Evans and Frank Yablans, functioning as president, decided it was time to make their big move when the success of *Godfather, Part II* and *Chinatown*, starring Jack Nicholson, further entrenched Paramount in the catbird seat.

During dinner with Bluhdorn at Pietro's Steakhouse in New York City, Yablans made his pitch for Evans and himself. "Charlie, there are the haves and have-nots, and Evans and I are the have-nots. Paramount reached the heights of Mount Everest, and we're two schmucks without so much as a rope to climb it."

Bluhdorn was not receptive. The ultimate deal maker, he had already gotten what he wanted out of both of them and saw no percentage in cutting them in for a piece of his empire. A young man named Barry Diller had caught his attention over the past few years, and Diller struck him as just the right person to carry on the work they started. In a stunningly swift move, Bluhdorn executed his palace coup, firing Yablans and installing Diller as the new head of Paramount.

At thirty-two years of age, Diller was four years younger than Evans was in 1966 when Bluhdorn hired him to rescue Paramount. Evans was tall and handsome with thick swept-back hair; he had a talent for driving women wild. Diller was quite the opposite: at five-feet-seven inches and balding, rumored in the industry to have homosexual tendencies, which he has denied all his life, Diller was a good match for Bluhdorn at the negotiating table. Evans was still on the payroll but suddenly found himself without a clearly defined role at Paramount. Adding insult to injury, Bluhdorn divested himself of the chairmanship of Paramount and bestowed it on Diller, a title Evans had been lusting for since he joined the company.

"Diller epitomized the new breed of Hollywood," said Evans. "Pragmatic, insightful, and focused on the future. He was also smooth and lethal."

During breakfast at the Bel-Air Hotel, Diller let Evans know in no uncertain terms exactly where he stood when Evans suggested he was eager to forge a good working partnership with Diller.

"Robert, let's get something straight. We're good friends, we're confidants, but we're not partners. You work for me. Is that clear?"

"No one can ever say you lack candor, Barry," Evans replied. "It hurts, but I respect it. It's your candy store. Now, can I go out and just make pictures, try to make a living?"

"Fine. I'll construct a producing deal that'll make you happy. I expect you to stay on for six months as head of the studio, at least to fill me in on who my enemies are."

Functioning as an independent producer, Evans brought Diller a gripping suspense novel called *The Marathon Man* that he wanted to adapt. "Fine," Diller said, "but we can't use Olivier as the old Nazi. He's uninsurable."

Unknown to the public at the time, Lawrence Olivier was riddled with a pervasive cancer that infected every major organ in his body. No insurance company would insure his life for the six weeks it would take to shoot the movie. Old and frail beyond his years, Olivier was broke, his acting career reduced to cameo appearances in movies such as *The Seven Percent Solution*.

Through the intervention of actor David Niven, Paramount convinced Lloyd's of London to take the gamble on Olivier's life for a hefty premium, making it possible to cast him in the film. Olivier and Dustin Hoffman, playing opposite each other, were a study in contrasts that worked to perfection. Olivier was from the old school; he studied a role, figured out the best way to portray the character, and got on with the job. Hoffman was a method actor from a later generation. He agonized for days, trying to become the character he was playing before going live before the camera.

"For God's sake, dear boy," Olivier said after Hoffman kept them waiting while deciding whether to play a scene with his shirt on or off. "Why don't you just *act*?"

On another occasion, Hoffman nearly drowned himself holding his head under water in a bathtub to prepare for a scene where hired killers were trying to drown him. For his part, Olivier exuded the precise aura of cold-blooded evil in his role as a Nazi sadist after observing a gardener tending roses.

"The delicacy of his touch," Olivier said. "That's how I shall torture Dustin. The character doesn't look upon his torture as wrong. Nor shall I."

The result was two virtuoso performances that won rave reviews from the critics, if not great revenues at the box office. Olivier miraculously defied the odds as his cancer slipped into remission, allowing him to prolong his acting career for another thirteen years.

Diller settled into his role as chairman quickly. He had negotiated a contract with Bluhdorn that gave him a measure of independence his predecessor never enjoyed, as long as he turned a profit for Paramount. Diller produced mixed results during his first few years at the helm. The film that nearly got him fired was *Black Sunday*, another project from Evans.

"*Black Sunday* will outgross *Jaws*," Evans told Diller.

"It's too big a gamble," said Diller. "So far you've been a lucky Jew. Don't be a dumb one."

Against his better judgment, Diller let Evans talk him into making the movie for Paramount. The story was based on the attack on the Super Bowl game in Miami by an Arab terrorist group. The controversy over the subject matter was bad enough to begin with. Complicating matters beyond redemption, however, Evans chose for some unfathomable reason to tell the story from each side's point of view in an effort to appear objective. The movie's main antagonist joined the Black September terrorist movement out of ideological conviction. It was tantamount to stating that Satan's role in the world was as valid as God's, that Nazism was a viable alternative to Judaism, that the struggle between evil and good was a question of which lifestyle one preferred.

The headlines that greeted the movie could not have been any worse. "HITLERITE!" was one of the kinder adjectives used to describe it. *Black Sunday* succeeded in alienating just about everyone, except possibly some renegade society on the dark side of the moon. Jewish organizations throughout the world called for a boycott of the movie. The Red Army of Japan threatened to blow up every theater that showed the movie on the grounds that it was an insult to the Arabs. Barry Diller pulled out the little hair that was left on his head when he saw the fiasco Evans had foisted on Paramount. Bluhdorn's reaction was more succinct. "I want to vomit," he said.

CHAPTER 10

ADDING BALLAST
TO WARREN BEATTY'S *COJONES*

FORTUNATELY, DILLER'S SUCCESSES more than made up for disasters such as *Black Sunday*. Paramount quickly bounced back to life under Diller's guidance, setting a new industry record for domestic film rentals, primarily from the box office receipts of *Grease*, *Saturday Night Fever*, and *Heaven Can Wait*.

Diller and actor Warren Beatty cemented a friendship during the filming of *Heaven Can Wait* that would survive the next two decades. The Paramount executive recognized a quintessential Hollywood movie star in Beatty, one of the last of a breed. Beatty, Jack Nicholson, Sean Connery, and a handful of others emanated a personal magnetism that was impossible to acquire; it was an innate quality they were born with. A room could be filled with other so-called stars and celebrities, but when Beatty entered it, all conversation stopped, all eyes turned to him. It had nothing to do with looks or height. It had everything to do with presence, the ability to dominate a room and command everyone's attention.

When filming was completed on *Heaven Can Wait*, Paramount cranked up the publicity mill to hype the movie before its release. The publicists produced a life-size cardboard cutout of the star dressed in a sweatshirt, sweatpants, sneakers, a halo over his head, and angel wings growing out of his back. Beatty invited a few friends into his office on the Paramount lot to view the poster, including Barry Diller, Robert Evans, and industrialist Norton Simon, who was married to actress Jennifer Jones.

"What do you think?" Beatty asked, a skeptical look on his face, according to Evans.

Diller, Evans, and Simon looked at one another, trying to figure out what was bothering Beatty.

"Well?"

"It's okay," Evans said first.

"Okay?"

"Yeah, it's okay."

"Fuck you!" Beatty yelled. Diller shot Evans a nasty look for opening up a can of worms. Everyone present knew Beatty's Achilles' heel, the chink in his armor, the hot button that set him off faster than anything else.

"Where are your balls?" Evans taunted him. "There's no crease in your sweat pants. It looks like you've got a pussy instead of a dick."

Diller said later that if he had a gun that day, he would have shot Evans in cold blood. Beatty's reaction was predictable and, therefore, avoidable. He went ballistic. The artwork was already finished and ready to be shipped. Beatty cared nothing about the bottom line, about the cost to the studio. He demanded that every poster and print ad based on it be destroyed immediately.

Paramount had little choice but to acquiesce to the star's demands. The result was the most expensive crotch retouch in film history, upwards of $500,000 before Beatty signed off on it. More than half a million dollars to add some ballast to Warren Beatty's *cojones*, thanks to Evans. Diller's list of grievances against his erratic producer was growing longer by the minute.

John Travolta was another rising Paramount star, thanks to the success of *Grease*, his first major movie role, and *Saturday Night Fever*. Diller wanted to cast him as the lead in *Urban Cowboy*, another story for which the studio had great expectations. Filming was scheduled to begin in June 1979 at Gilley's, the famous roadhouse (now defunct) owned by country and western singer Mickey Gilley, located in Pasadena, just outside of Houston, Texas. A major problem developed when Travolta showed up on the set wearing a thick black beard that all but obliterated his boyish good looks.

"Travolta refuses to shave off his beard because of a scratch above his lip where a cat bit it," Evans told Barry Diller and Michael Eisner when they arrived on location. "His cleft, his smile is what made him a star. He looks like a fuckin' Italian butcher."

"What does Jim think?" asked Eisner, referring to James Bridges, the director.

"He likes it. So does Travolta's whole coterie. He's got a bigger entourage than the president."

"How many scenes have you shot with Travolta?" asked Diller.

"About six. We're coming up to the part where Travolta applies for a job at a factory."

Diller came up with the solution. "That's the perfect place to write in a line where the boss says, 'We don't hire guys with beards.' Tell Travolta to shave it off for me."

After some hesitation, Paramount's star of the moment agreed to shave his face, once again unveiling his famous dimple for the viewing public.

Gilley's was Redneck Heaven, Texas style. The bar was crammed with cowboys, cowboy wannabes, and some of the toughest women west of the Mississippi River, all decked out in their best Saturday night jeans. Lone Star beer in long-neck bottles was the most heavily consumed beverage on the premises. Any male ordering anything fancier than beer and shots was likely to be hauled outside and stomped into the dust. The more beer that went down, the longer the line of guys looking to tame the mechanical bulls grew. Throughout the course of an evening, dozens of cowboys and cowgirls could be seen slipping out into the evening for a quickie in the nearest trailer.

Diller wanted a fresh young actress to play the tough female lead opposite Travolta—a part that would guarantee instant stardom. After thousands of interviews and hundreds of tests, Diller and director James Bridges boiled the selection down to two unknowns: a simmering blonde beauty named Michelle Pfeiffer and a sultry brunette named Debra Winger. It was a toss-up as to which one was better in the part. Diller cast the deciding vote in favor of the brunette, and Pfeiffer had to wait a few years longer for the role in *The Witches of Eastwick* that would make her a bona fide star.

And then there was *Popeye*, the movie that drove the final nail in Robert Evans's coffin. "I want to do it, Barry," he said to Diller.

"Fine. You want to do it that badly, it's your baby."

Diller gave Evans enough rope to make the movie his way, and Evans proceeded to hang himself with it. Evans's choice to play Popeye was Dustin Hoffman, who was also eager to take on the role. The producer set up a meeting between Hoffman and Jules Feiffer, the well-known cartoonist who was writing the script. Their initial encounter was nothing less than disastrous.

"I've had the worst day of my life," Feiffer told Evans over the phone. "Dustin threw me out of his apartment."

"What are you talking about?"

"He kept me waiting two whole days. By the time the little fuck gave me an audience, I was drunk."

Evans flew to New York to see if he could repair the damage, but Hoffman was adamant and refused to work on any film that Feiffer was part of. Unable to change Hoffman's mind, Evans approached Barry Diller and Michael Eisner about replacing Hoffman with Robin Williams.

"He's great on *Mork and Mindy*," Eisner said. "What do you think, Barry?"

According to Evans, Diller hesitated a moment and then replied: "Maybe he can pull it off. Hoffman might try to turn Popeye into too much of a Jew anyway."

Next, Evans wanted to use the eccentric, hard-to-get-along-with Robert Altman to direct the film. Diller hesitated about Altman, knowing the director had a history of slowing down production and running up production costs, as well as producing quirky films.

"He'll find a way to make *Popeye* look like a story about an ax murderer," Diller said. Finally he agreed. "It's your baby," he told Evans again. "Go ahead and use him if you think he's right."

Privately, Diller maintained his doubts about Evans's latest venture and decided to protect his franchise in his own way. Bluhdorn had picked Diller for good reason. Unconvinced that *Popeye* would work on the screen, he sold half of the movie to Disney. The two studios would share the cost of production as well as any profits. Paramount would distribute the movie in the United States, and Disney throughout the rest of the world.

The movie was set to shoot in Malta in October 1979, and Altman showed up with a group of hangers-on and sycophants that looked more like a traveling commune than a personal entourage. Greeting them on the Mediterranean island was a ragtag assemblage of local dignitaries that resembled a circus troupe. The locals included Miss Malta of 1979, a less-than-wholesome-looking, not-so-svelte beauty who could easily have played the earthy Serafina portrayed by Anna Magnani in Tennesse Williams's *The Rose Tattoo*.

Both Altman and Evans wanted Shelley Duvall to play Olive Oyl opposite Robin Williams's Popeye, but Diller was holding out for comedienne Gilda Radner of *Saturday Night Live* fame. Evans made his case for Duvall, telling Diller she was born to play the role. "Hell, she doesn't just *look like* Olive Oyl. She *is* Olive Oyl," he told Diller. "Radner's good, but her Olive Oyl would be strictly kosher." Again, Diller gave his nod of approval, letting the rope out a bit more.

What followed from that point on was a black tragicomedy of errors that destroyed what was left of Evans's tenuous relationship with Diller and Paramount. Malta's Marxist-Leninist dictator Dominic Mintoff was a major player in the side drama that was taking place while the movie was being filmed. Like most communist states, Malta had draconian rules against drug consumption that made the West's attempts to control mind-altering substances look feeble by comparison. At the time, Evans was an admitted snorter of cocaine, and his suitcase containing the contraband item was intercepted at the airport. In a panic, by his own admisstion, Evans duped his friend, former Secretary of State Henry Kissinger, into writing a letter to Mintoff asking him to extend a hand of friendship to Evans.

The deception succeeded in buying Evans a bit more time. Unfortunately, instead of using the time to extricate himself from what was at best a tenuous and compromising position, Evans only succeeded in digging his grave deeper. On the Memorial Day weekend of 1980, while Evans was in Malta overseeing the filming of *Popeye*, he received a phone call from his lawyer saying that the drug incident was far from dead. The prosecutor wanted to throw the book at him, charging him with fifteen drug-related counts ranging from using a contraband substance to attempts to distribute it.

"The entire charge has no validity," the lawyer told him. This particular batch of cocaine belonged to Robert's brother Charles, who represented half of the Evan-Picone fashion company.

"The validity is ink," Evans replied, meaning that the prosecutor was eager to make his name in a case against a well-known Hollywood producer that was sure to capture headlines. Robert Evans panicked, afraid that Mintoff would try to embarrass the United States by releasing Kissinger's letter to the media, dragging the former secretary of state into the mess.

In a desperation move, Evans asked Senator Jacob Javits to intervene on his behalf. "Absolutely not," Javits replied sharply. "Your deportment is shameful. Call Henry immediately. Warn him."

Evans was too afraid to call Kissinger and warn him about the trap he had inadvertently laid for him. Against the advice of his closest friends and associates, including Barry Diller and Charles Bluhdorn, Evans pleaded guilty to the charges in an effort to shield his brother. The media had a field day with the story, giving it international prominence, and sticking Evans with the moniker "Robert 'Cocaine' Evans."

During an emergency meeting at Paramount, Bluhdorn and Diller devised a strategy to keep the studio from being tarnished by the sordid publicity. They issued a press release stating succinctly: "Evans is not an employee of Paramount and has not been an employee of Paramount for four years. He is an independent contractor producing pictures for us."

Popeye ended up turning a significant, if not record-breaking, profit for Paramount in the face of lukewarm-to-hostile reviews. *Urban Cowboy* fared substantially better, benefiting from rave reviews and wider box office appeal. Paramount survived the crisis, its coffers further fattened by the success of the two movies, even while the fate of their producer faded into oblivion during the next ten years.

Barry Diller was everything Bluhdorn hoped he would be when the older man tapped him to be the chief executive officer of Paramount in 1974. He was tough, loyal, and shrewd—traits held in the highest esteem by the equally shrewd but excitable Bluhdorn. Diller was a workaholic, logging twelve- and fourteen-hour days in his office, six, sometimes seven days a week.

There was only one thing Bluhdorn could not figure out: Diller was well into his thirties by then. How could it be that a young man with all his talent, all his success and prominence in the most glamorous business in the world, was still unmarried? How could it be that a nice Jewish girl, a smart girl, a looker with a real brain in her head, would not have succeeded in landing him for a husband by now?

Barry had to get married and give up his crazy social life. You can burn the candle at both ends when you're twenty-five, even thirty years old. But sooner or later it takes its toll on you. Bluhdorn could not afford to have his star, his chief executive officer, burn himself out. Barry needed a wife, and Bluhdorn was determined to find him one if it was the last thing he did.

CHAPTER 11

PARTYING AT STUDIO 54

MARRIAGE WAS THE last thing on Barry Diller's mind. Bluhdorn's attempts to fix him up with a suitable Jewish girl were an annoyance to Diller, an intrusion into a liberated social life that would have sent the conservative Bluhdorn into a snit had he been aware of the all the details. However, to keep peace with his blustery but well-meaning boss, Diller dated a couple of women Bluhdorn lined up for him. He resigned himself to Bluhdorn's periodic interrogations about where the relationships were leading.

Barry developed a friendship with Diane von Furstenberg that would blossom into marriage—some said a marriage of convenience for both of them—many years later. Diller and von Furstenberg began to appear frequently together in public, which got Bluhdorn off Diller's back for the time being at least. There is little question that their friendship was genuine, but those who knew them well had little doubt that their relationship was based more on a platonic kinship than on romance and passion. Still, she provided good cover for Diller while Bluhdorn was trying to capture his fancy with other women.

Diller kept his real passions as discreet as possible during the time he ruled Paramount under Bluhdorn's sufferance. At the time, no gay entertainment industry executives had the temerity to confess their sexual preferences to the world. In the mid-1970s, Hollywood was still a socially conservative town run by tyrannical heterosexual men who valued traditional family values second only to wealth and power. Over the years, even superstars like Anthony Perkins, Montgomery Clift, and Rock Hudson had hidden their gay lifestyles from the public. The odds still favored discretion over honesty, and Barry Diller had not gotten as far as he had so far by bucking the odds.

The playground of choice for swinging singles in New York City throughout much of the 1970s was a den of iniquity on West 54th Street that took its name, Studio 54, from its location. Nothing was considered off limits and everything was possible at Studio 54. Straight sex, gay sex, interracial sex, drugs, and sights and scenes not viewed in public since the days of the Roman Saturnalia were on full display there. Vodka, quaaludes, and cocaine were passed around openly, and sexual adventurers could find any sex object they desired, from beautiful young women to muscular young boys—one or the other or both at the same time.

Studio 54 was the brainchild of Steve Rubell, a shy, skinny, star-struck, drug abuser from Brooklyn who had long dreamed of owning a club where he could indulge his wildest fantasies. On any given night, the crowd on the street outside Studio 54 clamoring to get inside might include male and female cross-dressers, West Point cadets with their freshly scrubbed dates, mobsters wearing fedoras and pinstriped suits, well-tailored fashion models, bikini-clad hustlers of both sexes parading back and forth on roller skates, and the so-called bridge and tunnel crowd consisting of middle-class kids from the outer boroughs of New York City and the suburbs of New Jersey hoping to rub shoulders with celebrities.

It was this last group in particular—one Rubell originally belonged to himself—that he took extraordinary measures to keep from getting inside his club. It was as though Rubell did not want anybody around him who reminded him of his provincial working-class roots. Hulking thugs with nasty dispositions guarded Studio 54's entrance, nodding unsmilingly and opening the door to those who struck Rubell's fancy, and scowling menacingly at those who sought entry without the little man's permission.

No one was more star-struck than Steve Rubell himself. Celebrity of any kind, whether earned through talent and achievement or through some nefarious activity, guaranteed access to Studio 54. Beyond that, it strictly depended on Rubell's whims and momentary moods. One night he might admit only the young and beautiful, the following night a preponderance of half-naked freaks, the next a mix of outrageous eccentrics and bankers in three-piece suits.

Barry Diller and his circle of powerful entertainment industry executives were among those ushered into this palace of hedonism with open arms. Rubell was only too happy to welcome his wealthy, fun-seeking guests to his version of a Roman Saturnalia. The scene inside was a combination of New Year's Eve, Mardi Gras, and *Animal House* magnified one hundred times. Studio 54 occupied the premises of a converted opera house and television studio, electrified with piercing strobe lights and thundering music. A man in the moon snorting cocaine decorated the ceiling, and well-muscled, bare-chested male bartenders in tight jeans presided over a huge circular bar.

The coed bathrooms strategically located throughout the upper floors were used only incidentally for nature calls. Couples comprising every conceivable combination of gender and race filled the stalls and engaged in myriad varieties of oral sex, copulation, and sodomy. The inner sanctum in the basement, otherwise known as the Playground because it was furnished with swing sets, monkey bars, and Astroturf carpeting, was reserved for Steve Rubell's "special guests"—certified celebrities and powerful media executives like Barry Diller, David Geffen, Calvin Klein, Ryan O'Neal, Diana Ross, Robin Williams, Mick Jagger, Truman Capote, Andy Warhol, and other well-known names.

During the twenty months that it survived before being summarily put out of business by the IRS, which charged Rubell with tax evasion, Studio 54 was an addiction for Diller, Geffen, Calvin Klein, and their tight circle of friends. On any given night, they might be treated to the spectacle of a troupe of Hell's Angels riding their Harley Davidsons around and around the dance floor, naked men on horseback celebrating someone's birthday, or a family of dwarfs performing a tumbling routine across the circular bar. On New Year's Eve 1978, the entire downstairs area was covered by a foot of gold and silver confetti. In May 1978, five months later, so many people tried to crash Studio 54's first anniversary party that they overwhelmed the bouncers and almost broke down the front door, terrifying the guests inside.

Sexual liberation was definitely "in" during the late-1970s, not only in New York City but in other areas of the country as well. Swinging parties, where couples swapped partners and had sex in front of others, were fairly commonplace. Swingers clubs like Plato's Retreat and the St. Mark's Baths attracted married couples who did not mind sharing their mates, and homosexual bathhouses operated at full capacity. Permissiveness prevailed in every area of human social activity. The pool at Plato's Retreat appeared to be one part water, one part sperm, and one part chlorine to suppress the threat of sexually transmitted diseases. AIDS, although it had begun to make its presence felt on the social scene, was not yet recognized outside of certain medical circles. But crabs, genital warts, and herpes were making the rounds with increasing frequency. Everything was possible in 1978, and nothing was off limits.

Barry Diller and his entourage were not enjoying any pleasures at Studio 54 that the rest of society was not also indulging in; they were just rubbing shoulders—and other body parts—with a more glamorous crowd. Calvin Klein joined Diller's group when David Geffen brought him around the year Studio 54 opened. Gay attorney Roy Cohn arrived one evening with a group of lawyers and judges in a fleet of limousines. The prominent jurists were ushered in quietly through the back door, only to practically trip over Klein and one of his sex partners locked together in a moment of passion. It was at this time that someone stuck Diller and his friends with the label "The Velvet Mafia," a term that most of the group found offensive and denied applied to them.

"It's nonsense," said David Geffen. "I have no idea why the label is used nor do I care. It's just something people like to call famous gay people."

One of Geffen's friends, publicist Howard Bragman, said, "The term 'Velvet Mafia' reminds me of the anti-Semitic stuff that was said in the past about Jews controlling the industry. The implication is that there's a gay casting couch for plum roles. It's insidious."

Hollywood agent Sandy Gallin claimed, "It started at Studio 54 in the late seventies. Somebody pointed to a group of people and said, 'Oh, there's the Velvet Mafia.' Some of them could have been straight because Bianca Jagger and Diane von Furstenberg are supposed to be part of it."

Whatever the case, the appellation stuck. Whenever Barry Diller, Sandy Gallin, David Geffen, Calvin Klein and even Diane von Furstenberg— were mentioned—the phrase automatically came to mind.

That so many gays had ascended to positions of power in the entertainment industry should have been a source of pride, as it is when any minority group advances in society. Instead, others were cast as leaders of a vicious cabal that ruled the entertainment industry according to their personal sexual preferences. The irony here was that heterosexual casting couches had existed in the business for decades, with no one but a few ardent feminists complaining about the practice. Suddenly, because a few homosexual men had risen to prominence in the industry, gay-bashing pundits became exercised about it.

The so-called Velvet Mafia was composed of men who were businessmen first and foremost. The idea that Barry Diller, even if he were gay, would let a well-padded crotch affect the bottom line of any company he ran was absurd on the face of it. Profit was his middle name, the only shrine he worshiped at. Everything else was chopped liver.

When Jews and Italians first began to rise above their immigrant roots, concerns about "kikes" and "wops" taking over various businesses escalated alarmingly. Similarly, by the late-1970s, the notion of "fags" running Hollywood or the fashion industry had become a homophobic slur that survived into the 1990s. In more recent years, journalists working for sensationalist rags have written stories purporting to "peek over the lavender walls of Tinseltown," only to find vicious old queens engaged in salacious conspiracies to fill our living rooms and movie theaters with degenerate sleaze. One reporter referred to a "Pink Curtain," behind which was "a power so far-reaching it's mind-boggling."

No doubt, envy was behind some of the comments about Hollywood's Velvet Mafia. As the years progressed, Diller's ability to deal with the slurs improved with maturity, but in 1978 he was only thirty-six years old, a relatively young man in a highly responsible position and still grappling with the insecurities of youth. He was uncomfortable enough with his alleged sexuality, coping with the struggle of being different with a determination to be the best at what he did.

Geffen, about the same age as Diller, was a record business entrepreneur and a Hollywood and theatrical producer who was the first among his peers to become a billionaire. Sandy Gallin was the architect behind the careers of Dolly Parton, Cher, and Michael Jackson when he was only thirty years old. If they all felt like chartering a plane to fly to a party at Calvin Klein's house in Key West, they had the means to do it. They could call one another up to discuss their common personal problems, and also to seek one another's business advice. To many on the outside, Diller's world seemed remote and glamorous, but to him and his cohorts it was more often insular and claustrophobic because of society's strictures on their social activities.

More often than not, many members of the Velvet Mafia met together for Sunday brunches followed by a walk in Central Park, weather permitting. They enjoyed going to the muscle-man contests at the Felt Forum sponsored by *Blueboy* magazine. One or the other might rent a vacation home in St. Bart's, where they would show up with their respective dates—male models and others whom they picked up at Studio 54. They often passed their more attractive companions down the food line, so to speak, and met later to compare notes on their experiences, similar to the way many heterosexual men talked up their female conquests with their friends in the locker room.

"We all liked to get laid a lot," Geffen said, "and Studio 54 was the perfect place to do it."

By his own reckoning, Barry Diller was a veritable Brillo pad with a rough, steely surface when it came to business, and his buddy David Geffen was considered an atomic weapon. Legendary agent Swifty Lazar once said that "you're lucky if you're not in [Geffen's] sights." Geffen was already powerful enough by 1978 to have toppled Walter Yetnikoff from his perch as president of CBS Records. Supposedly, word got back to Geffen that Yetnikoff told his girlfriend she should get lessons from Geffen on "sucking cock."

Calvin Klein's beach house in the Pines on Fire Island, one of the barrier island's two gay communities, was another popular hangout for the group. Built of cedar shakes with a wide wrap-around deck overlooking the beach, the five-bedroom house was the place for gay young men to be on warm summer weekends. Where else could they get a chance to share a bed with the most powerful movers and shakers in the entertainment and fashion worlds? One of the guest bedrooms was outfitted with a large bed set into a semicircular alcove with floor-to-ceiling mirrors. It was a far more tastefully done version of some of the hotels located near New York's JFK Airport, where you paid for a mirrored room by the hour.

All good things come to an end sooner or later, and the end for Studio 54 occurred twenty months after it first opened its doors, in May 1977. The primary cause of the shutdown was Steve Rubell himself. The wealthier and more powerful he grew, the more obnoxious and egotistical he became. Most nights he could be found at the bar of his club, stoned or drunk, bragging loudly about all the famous people he knew.

The public came to resent his policy of barring people based on his personal whims and the roughhouse manner in which his bouncers dealt with unwanted patrons. One was kicked so hard by a bouncer that his testicles were crushed. Rubell hobnobbed openly with mobsters and other underworld figures. The final straw was when Rubell bragged publicly about how he was screwing the IRS.

"What the IRS doesn't know won't hurt it," he said on television one night. "It's a cash business, and you don't have to worry about the IRS," he told another reporter.

At that time, the IRS—arguably the most hated and bloated bureaucracy in the country—was lean and mean, operating at the peak of its power. It dispatched armed goons, who were empowered to operate outside the law, into middle-class homes to terrorize ordinary citizens over disputed tax bills. They seized bank accounts, automobiles, and locked people out of their homes without due process. The IRS's TCMP audits were widely regarded as the audits from hell. Agents literally moved into taxpayers' homes and treated them like criminals until they accounted for every single deposit they had made and were able to prove they had reported every cent of income. If you were hiding anything from the IRS in the late-1970s, the last outfit you wanted to hear about it was the IRS.

In this atmosphere of unrestrained terror, Steve Rubell bragged about his cash business, brazenly and stupidly taunting the most powerful tax-collecting thugs in modern history. He might as well have challenged a battalion of 800-pound gorillas to a fight. The result was predictable. Dozens of armed agents raided his premises with search warrants one night, seizing everything in sight, including Rubell and his partner Ian Shrager. The agents hauled off two enormous garbage bags stuffed with cash, keys to a safety deposit box containing nearly another $900,000 in cash, pounds and pounds of cocaine, and other goodies.

The agents also carried away with them a list kept by Rubell containing the names of his customers—hundreds of the biggest names in show business and the fashion industry. When Barry Diller first heard about Rubell's list, he froze with terror. "What's on the list?" he screamed at David Geffen. As it turned out, Diller did not have to worry. The names composed a list of Rubell's drug customers, but nothing about their sexual escapades. Diller breathed a sigh of relief. He was a health nut, a fitness buff. One thing he did not do was drugs.

AIDS REARS ITS UGLY HEAD

PERHAPS MORE THAN anyone else in his circle of friends and confidants, Barry Diller was a study in contrasts. A political liberal, he was also a tough, hard-nosed businessman. Cultured and sophisticated, he was an avid motorcyclist. Almost paranoid about his health, Diller was a skiing enthusiast willing to risk life and limb on the most challenging slopes. He watched his company's bottom line like a hawk, but he also enjoyed high-stakes poker games with other celebrity gamblers like Johnny Carson and Warren Beatty. One moment he could be the most charming man in the business, the next a killer lashing out at an adversary's jugular vein. Because of his contradictions and unpredictability, Diller could be a fascinating man to spend time with but a terrifying boss to work for.

Business was war to Barry Diller, and in his world there was no point to being a businessman unless you were determined to win. His obsession with coming out on top, being the best at what he did, prompted his critics to describe him as a lion on the prowl for new victims. His aggres-siveness landed him in trouble with the Justice Department in 1980, when Paramount—along with Twentieth Century-Fox, Columbia Picture Industries, MCA, and Getty—was charged with employing "guerrilla warfare" to gain control of the rapidly growing pay-television business.

In papers filed in federal court in New York City, the Justice Depart-ment attempted to block the creation of Premiere, a joint venture planned by the defendants. The government contended that Diller and his confed-erates were trying to control the pay-TV distribution system for their own benefit, while the defendants countered that they were merely interested in fostering competition. Justice Department attorneys cited memos writ-ten to Diller by a Paramount executive, stating that the studio's ultimate goal was "substantially eliminating or severely altering HBO." Home Box Office, which was owned by Time, served more than 65 percent of homes subscribing to cable TV services.

A second Paramount memo stated that several other companies, including Times-Mirror and Cox Broadcasting, could soon establish their own pay-TV networks. While Paramount welcomed such competition for HBO, the studio was also concerned that it could be left out in the cold if it failed to establish its own beachhead. "Control of distribution" should be "established early on through a joint venture," the memo to Diller advised. The type of venture envisioned "would have the ability to force marginal movies into the pay-TV distribution channel."

This language was enough to convince the government that Diller and his joint venture partners conspired illegally to fix prices. The Justice Department claimed they were guilty of *per se* antitrust violations. That meant "any proffered justifications for Premiere are irrelevant as a matter of law," according to the government. HBO president Peter Gross used the opportunity to claim that "the philosophy behind Premiere is to grab control of pay television rather than encourage competition."

Considering that HBO already had a quasi-monopolistic market share of pay TV, Gross's statement was more than a trifle self-serving. Nevertheless, the Justice Department prevailed, and the joint venture was scrapped. The type of tactics employed by Diller and his partners is routine in virtually every industry. Jockeying for market share among competitors is standard operating procedure. In the end, the language contained in Paramount's internal memos was what caused the venture to fail. Had Diller's lieutenants phrased their strategy more diplomatically, their case would have been stronger. Diller learned an invaluable lesson from the experience. Like many Federal Reserve chairmen who use the most obscure language possible to make economic forecasts, Barry Diller learned to develop his own verbal subterfuge when discussing his plans for the future.

Diller applied his mania for cost-cutting to Paramount's bottom line with a vengeance in an effort to increase profit margins. In 1972, feature films issued by major studios cost an average of $2.5 million to produce. By 1980 that figure had risen to $9.5 million.

"That's just suicidal," Diller said. "Films cost too much."

Paramount's movie *Reds*, a creation of Warren Beatty set against the backdrop of the Russian Revolution, took three years to produce at a total cost of $33 million, $11 million over budget. Warren Beatty was a good friend of Diller, but $11 million has the ability to strain even the most solid friendships.

"We have simply told everyone upfront that we're going to treat them well, but there aren't going to be any more huge, expensive trailers used as dressing rooms," Diller said afterward. "We aren't going to pay a leading lady's makeup man five times scale. And we aren't going to take on a director's favorite camera crew for an extra seventeen thousand dollars a week."

Diller devised a deal allowing Paramount to pay stars reduced salaries in return for a larger percentage of the gross. The results for Paramount were encouraging. In 1981 the company had filmed seven pictures with budgets ranging from $2.5 million to $9 million, with an average cost of $6 million. However, it was not all sevens and elevens for Diller. He had his share of snake eyes as well. While *Raiders of the Lost Ark* and *Terms of Endearment* were enormous successes, *Dragonslayer*, an $18 million sword-and-sorcery tale, bombed at the box office and had to be written off at net realizable value.

Diller was well rewarded for his executive abilities. In 1983 he was the highest-paid executive in the country, with a total compensation of $2,120,000 compared with a median of $419,000, which was 15 percent higher than the year before. Only forty-seven other U.S. executives earned more than $1 million that year. How times have changed, when $1 million today is regarded as chump change in top executive circles, and Diller's compensation soared to more than 100 times his 1983 earnings.

Life for Diller was humming along smoothly when he was suddenly shaken by an event that almost knocked him off his feet. Two years earlier, the acronym AIDS was barely visible on the social horizon. By 1983 it was capturing headlines around the world. The controversy over the subject struck close to home for Diller, when a rumor circulated that his friend Calvin Klein had fallen deathly ill with the disease. The very mention of the illness sent shockwaves through the gay community. At the time, AIDS was regarded as a disease that afflicted gay men and intravenous drug users only—a notion fostered by fundamentalist preachers who self-righteously proclaimed it to be God's wrath on their idea of decadence. It was as though some malevolent force had taken hold, slowly draining lives in a long, torturous sequence of events that culminated in a horrifying death.

The rumor about Calvin turned out to be unfounded; he had actually been felled by viral meningitis, serious enough in itself, but an ailment that could be cured. Nevertheless, the rumor had the effect of reminding all who traveled in his circle that they were especially vulnerable to a modern plague that no one understood. As far as most heterosexuals of the period were concerned, AIDS was a marginal ailment that had no relevance to their own sexual behavior. Virtually everyone had been participating in the libertine mores of the era for fifteen years or longer at that point, but only the gay community appeared to be vulnerable to the disease.

Klein gave a semi-hysterical interview to *Playboy*, during which he held nothing back, as though the act of unburdening himself in a candid mea culpa could undo the harmful effects of his years of excess. "I've fooled around a lot. I stopped at nothing," he said. "I would do anything. I stayed up all night, carried on, lived out fantasies, anything . . . Anything I wanted to do, I did . . . Quite frankly, my best sex has been with people who didn't know who I was."

When Diller, Geffen, and the others in their clique read that, they panicked, according to several of their associates at the time. Hadn't they *all* done pretty much everything they felt like, slept with strangers, taken their chances as if their actions had no consequences? Were they any different than their friend Calvin? If it was his turn to pay the piper, might it not be their turn soon?

Heterosexuals had also been sleeping around with multiple partners since the late 1960s, but all they had to show for it so far was warts, crabs, herpes, bouts with syphilis or gonorrhea perhaps—bad enough in themselves, but tame in comparison to AIDS. Nothing compared with AIDS. It slowly ate people alive. Later on, of course, the world discovered that no one was immune, but in 1983 it appeared to be a preternatural curse that exclusively affected the gay community.

Although the rumor about Klein turned out to be false, it instilled the fear of God in Diller and his tight circle of friends. It stunned them all. It was as though a chill had settled over the group and the industries they represented, then spread through the rest of society and brought the age of sexual excess to a thundering halt. When Steve Rubell was released from jail and tried to reopen Studio 54, his attempt at a comeback fell flat on its face. The crowds had simply evaporated, and not even an abundant supply of cocaine could bring them back.

In the midst of this seemingly instantaneous change in the country's sexual mores, Calvin Klein shocked the world with a totally unexpected announcement: he was getting married to a member of the *opposite* sex. Suddenly he was seen in public with Kelly Rector, a young beauty who worked for him. Klein had been married once before to a middle-class girl from his Bronx neighborhood. The marriage lasted ten years and produced one child, a daughter whom Calvin loved and doted on. But the ill-fated marriage was destined to fail, a victim of Klein's many affairs with young men and women. He never felt comfortable defining himself as a homosexual, but rather said that he was in love with beauty no matter who possessed it. However, his friends knew better.

"But Calvin likes boys!" exclaimed Georgio Sant'Angelo, one of Klein's confidants, when he heard about Kelly.

"I thought it was just a phase he was going through," was Barry Diller's assessment of the situation. He understood the urge to try to be straight in a predominantly straight society.

It may have been their mutual friend Warren Beatty who made up Calvin's mind to propose to Kelly. Geffen, Diller, Klein, and most of their friends were half in love with the womanizing actor, as were most of the leading ladies he worked with in Hollywood. Kelly Rector accompanied Calvin on a business trip to the West Coast and met Beatty at an A-list party in Beverly Hills. Calvin was infatuated with Beatty, but the actor only had eyes for Calvin's employee, and she for him. After Calvin returned to New York, Beatty called Kelly at her hotel and invited her to his house. When Kelly flew back to New York several days later, all she could talk about at the office was the time she spent with Warren Beatty on the coast. She was clearly smitten, literally star-struck and star-*fucked* at the same time.

Calvin Klein was livid with jealousy. One of his friends remarked that going to bed with Kelly was the closest Calvin would ever come to sleeping with Warren Beatty—though vicariously, via sexual osmosis as it were. If Kelly was good enough for Beatty, she was good enough for him. It was shortly afterward that he seriously wooed Kelly and determined to marry her.

For Diller, however, the AIDS issue was far more important than whether or not one of his friends had suddenly developed a preference for women. AIDS was killing off many of his friends and associates with frightening regularity. The latest to be afflicted was Chester Weinberg, an early activist in the gay rights movement. At one time Chester had designed clothing for wealthy society matrons under his own label, but when his business failed Calvin Klein offered him a job as a designer in his blue jeans division.

Weinberg was *especially* promiscuous in the largely promiscuous world he traveled in, dragging along stray pickups he barely knew to weekends in Fire Island and frequenting the seedier gay clubs in Greenwich Village. Barry Diller, David Geffen, and others in their circle were frequently shocked by Weinberg's behavior, cautioning him to show more discretion in his sexual proclivities.

By this time, it was too late for the warnings to have any effect. Weinberg's energy began to flag, he slept late and took frequent naps, his weight declined alarmingly, he was always cold, and he took on the aspect of a shriveled old man. In October 1984, doctors at New York University Hospital diagnosed his ailment as toxoplasmosis, a brain disease that is a primary symptom of full-blown AIDS. Six months later he was dead.

Diller was horrified by what was happening, and he joined with others in a united effort to combat this insidious assault on their community. Almost overnight, it seemed, an army of organizations designed to fight AIDS sprung up, including the Gay Men's Health Crisis, God's Love We Deliver/Equity Cares, and The American Foundation for AIDS Research. Diller, along with other wealthy executives primarily in the entertainment and fashion industries, gave his name, support, and money to their efforts. Elizabeth Taylor, Michael Jackson, Marvin Traub, Peter Allen, David Geffen, Jeffrey Banks, Brooke Shields, Claudette Colbert, and Gloria Steinem were among other prominent sponsors.

The war against AIDS had become one of the most important missions in Barry Diller's life, but not the most important. The pursuit of money and power still took priority over everything else. His reputation as a tight-fisted, cost-cutting executive had long since taken root. His relationship with junk bond king Michael Milken and the investment bankers at Drexel Burnham Lambert had grown stronger and more integral to his business dealings. In 1983 Diller was still only forty-one years old and already at the top of his profession.

And then something did. Out of the blue, as it were, his boss and mentor Charlie Bluhdorn died unexpectedly while on a business trip, at the age of fifty-six.

CHAPTER 13

DAVIS PLUS DAVIS EQUALS AYN RAND IN A BAD MOOD

ONE REPORT OF Bluhdorn's death stated that the effusive entrepreneur was stricken by a massive heart attack at the age of fifty-six while on a jet flight from one of his company's properties in the Dominican Republic; another was that the ailment that killed him was leukemia. Other reports were more intriguing, ranging the gamut from foul play to undue sexual exertion in mid-flight. Several less titillating variations covered the landscape in between.

The problem for Barry Diller was Bluhdorn's successor at Gulf + Western, Martin S. Davis. To say their reaction to each other was akin to hatred at first sight might be overstating the case a bit, but not by much. Publicly at least, the relationship between the two men was as cordial as humanly possible for two people who clearly did not get along. Diller was brilliant, tough, opinionated, and determined to run the entertainment arena of Gulf + Western's empire his way. Davis was shrewd, tough, and equally determined to take

control after years of working for the domineering Bluhdorn. The result
was two stubborn men at loggerheads.

At the time of Bluhdorn's demise in February 1983, Barry Diller
occupied the apex of a Paramount triumvirate, with his friend Michael
Eisner serving under him as president and Frank Mancuso next in line as
president of the motion picture division. The three were widely regarded
as a highly effective team with a joint gift for spotting trends early and
marketing films successfully. Under Diller's leadership, Paramount was
regarded as the most successful television and film production company
in the industry, with such major hits as *Terms of Endearment, Trading
Places*, and *An Officer and a Gentleman* to its credit.

Diller and Eisner, in particular, complemented each other perfectly.
Those who were close to them professionally described them as opposite
sides of the same coin. Barry Diller tended to be somewhat quiet and
introspective and surrounded himself with the best possible people for
their jobs. Eisner was manic and voluble, spewing out dozens of ideas
each day as they popped into his head. Diller and Eisner often clashed but
respected each other enormously and, more often than not, found a way
to resolve their differences.

Michael Eisner was not on the best of terms with Martin Davis either.
Davis was not particularly fond of Eisner or his tactics and said as much
to company executives on several occasions.

"While Marty may respect some of Eisner's creative abilities, they just
don't like each other," said a company spokesman close to both of them.

Davis was especially incensed about Diller and Eisner reaping most of
the credit for Paramount's successes, with little or none of the praise filter-
ing back to him or other Paramount executives. For example, he thought
Jeffrey Katzenberg's role in selecting some of the successful scripts
Paramount acquired for production had been little appreciated. Diller
invited Davis out to Paramount's offices in Los Angeles in an attempt to
resolve their disagreements.

On a Friday night in September 1984, Diller hosted a dinner at his Beverly

Hills home for Davis and twenty-four other executives. What Davis did not know prior to the meeting was that Barry Diller was just as unhappy with Davis as Davis was with him. Like the accomplished poker player he was, Diller played his cards close to his vest; he had an ace in the hole he was not about to show Davis until he was ready. For months past, he had been conducting intense negotiations with Twentieth Century–Fox to leave Paramount and take over as chairman of the rival studio.

Several months before the dinner, an eccentric Texas oil billionaire named Marvin Davis (no relation to Martin) called Fred Silverman, president of ABC. "What's the story on Barry Diller?" he wanted to know. He was considering asking Diller to run Twentieth Century–Fox, which he gained control of early in 1984.

"Barry's an outstanding executive in every way," Silverman told Davis. "He'd be a fine choice to run Fox."

Fox had been under pressure for some time. Its chairman, Alan Hirschfeld, the third in less than two years, had resigned in September 1984 following a lackluster performance at the helm. Fox had made no headway in either the television or feature film markets and had earned an unenviable reputation as a distributor of films made outside the studio.

"Fox has been in a morass for some time," industry analyst Alan Cole-Ford of Paul Kagan Associates said at the time. "Fox has been more of a picture picker than a picture maker. There has been no real management continuity and no consistent product flow."

Fox's most recent box office bombs included *Silkwood*, starring an ill-cast Meryl Streep, and the laughable *Rhinestone*, starring Sylvester Stallone and Dolly Parton—casting that was almost frighteningly inept.

Marvin Davis offered Barry a substantial package, including a $3 million base salary plus an advance on a 25 percent share of profits over the next five years, to come over and run Fox. It was an offer that Diller had to take very seriously.

Diller announced his resignation from Paramount on September 11, 1984—as did Michael Eisner—and two days later Martin Davis responded by announcing a shakeup at Paramount. Diller was replaced by Frank Mancuso as chairman and Michael Eisner by Arthur Barron as president. Diller also joined the Board of Directors at Fox, along with Marvin Davis's thirty-year-old son John, Marvin himself, Gerald Gray, and well-known attorney Edward Bennett Williams.

Marvin Davis issued a statement, stating that Diller's appointment represented Fox's "commitment to develop quality entertainment product in motion pictures, television, and other media. We intend to support his efforts with whatever resources are necessary to make his role here a successful one."

Davis was particularly impressed by Diller's track record over the years, his contacts in the industry, and his reputation as a ruthless and tough negotiator, which he observed first-hand during their compensation discussions. Diller had originally asked Davis to sell him half of Fox, which Davis refused to do. But Diller did end up with a 25 percent equity share, a hefty bonus arrangement, stock options, and a $1.5 million interest-free loan—an extraordinary package for a man who was ostensibly only an employee.

The loss of both Diller and Eisner, who left to run Disney, was a tough one for Paramount to swallow. Diller's replacement, Frank Mancuso, was regarded as an able executive but one whose strengths lay more in the marketing and distribution areas than in the creative sphere. He was a New Yorker both geographically and temperamentally and lacked the Hollywood contacts deemed necessary to run a studio effectively. According to one producer with close ties to Paramount, a lot depended "on whether the East Coast managers can get the feel of what these highly paid creative executives do to make movies. Handing the studio over to the marketing types will change the structure of Paramount to a by-the-numbers company."

Paramount's loss was Fox's gain, notwithstanding the high price tag Diller commanded. Founded by Hungarian-born William Fox, the studio started out as a nickelodeon on Broadway at the beginning of the twentieth century. Fox later ventured into the movie and newsreel business, its fortunes rising and falling with the undulating tides of the entertainment industry itself. By 1980, with the stock market still in the doldrums prior to the incredible bull market that began two years later, Fox's book value (the net worth of its assets minus its liabilities) far exceeded the market value of its shares. A publicly traded company in such a position is a ripe candidate for a leveraged buyout.

At this point, the loud and somewhat larger-than-life Texas oil man Marvin Davis entered the breach. Davis was a killer shark in a predatory world of buyout kings and junk bond specialists. It was a world where those who thought they were tough and shrewd were gobbled up by others who really knew how to play the game—people with names like Michael Milken, Carl Icahn, and Marvin Davis. Davis had made his money in the oil patch of east Texas, and he particularly benefited from the OPEC oil crunch of the 1970s, which propelled his already vast fortune further into the stratosphere.

Boisterous, tough as nails, and jovial when necessary, Marvin Davis was a study in contrasts, as many highly successful people are. He was as rich as Midas but also painfully crude and unsophisticated. He believed *The Sound of Music* was one of the greatest movies ever made, and he was fond of practical jokes and took a childlike pleasure in having fun.

Davis acquired Fox for about $700 million in April 1981. His partner in the venture was a soon-to-be notorious oil and gas broker named Marc Rich. When the Justice Department investigated Rich for both tax evasion and selling oil illegally to Iran after the 1979 hostage crisis, Rich fled to Switzerland. In retaliation, the government seized his assets, including his half-interest in Fox. (Rich and his wife became heavy contributors to Bill Clinton throughout the 1990s, and one of Clinton's last acts in office was pardoning Rich for his transgressions.) Davis spent the next couple of years restructuring the debt he had assumed to buy Fox, and by 1984 he was able to take out all of the money he had originally put into the deal.

It did not take Barry Diller long to find out that he was going to have his hands full with Marvin Davis. The two were so different in every possible way that people in the industry referred to their relationship as the "Hitler–Stalin Pact."

"I couldn't believe the man," Diller said. "One of the first things he asked me to do was make a sequel to *The Sound of Music*."

Diller's biggest problem after assuming the reins at Fox was finding enough money to make any movies at all. With interest rates at record high levels, the cost of servicing Fox's $430 million debt came to $70 million a year. When Diller asked Davis to pump more money into Fox so they could make some pictures, the fun-loving oil man refused. "Go talk to Mike Milken at Drexel Burnham," Davis replied. "He'll figure out a way to get money."

This was standard operating procedure for Davis. The only way to buy anything, in his book, was with OPM—financial industry shorthand for Other People's Money. He now owned half of Fox for zero dollars out of pocket, thanks to refinancing the debt and extracting his initial investment, and he was not about to put a nickel of real money (*his* money) back into the company.

Milken offered to raise $250 million for Diller through the sale of junk bonds, but Diller turned him down when Davis once again refused to sell him a real equity stake in Fox. Early in 1985, less than six months after Diller joined the company, Davis astounded everyone again by acquiring Marc Rich's half share of Fox from the U.S. government for a mere $116 million—about one-third of Rich's cost. This was a classic example of the government's penchant for wasting taxpayers' money. Federal bureaucrats specialized in selling assets for thirty cents on the dollar after acquiring them for triple their value.

Davis could barely contain his glee, according to people who worked for him. Knowing he could resell Rich's half share of Fox for much more than he paid for it, he put the word out that 50 percent of Fox was up for sale. He found a willing buyer in Rupert Murdoch, the calculating Aussie, who was happy to pay him $250 million for a half interest in Fox. Davis more than doubled his investment virtually overnight, and Murdoch reckoned he would still be getting a bargain buying into a rejuvenated Fox with Barry Diller running the show.

As far as Diller was concerned, he found himself in an unlikely position. He had allowed himself to be manipulated between a rock and a hard place by two master wheeler-dealers. On one side stood a crafty oil magnate from Texas with the cultural tastes of a barbarian, and on the other was a resolute Australian with a mind like a computer and the political inclinations of Ayn Rand in a bad mood.

Davis was the devil that Barry Diller knew and felt he could deal with, but he did not know what to make of Rupert Murdoch. Diller had cut his deal with Davis before Murdoch had entered the picture. Murdoch's reputation was even more fearsome than Diller's. Murdoch was widely hated on both sides of the Atlantic by the liberal press and political establishments. He was known to be a brilliant, some said ruthless, businessman with a talent for acquiring properties at somewhat bloated prices and somehow turning them into profit centers over time. How would Diller get along with such a man given his own political and social leanings and his need to run things his way? He had no way of knowing.

To protect himself and his interests, Diller told Davis that he wanted the right to terminate his contract with Fox within the first year of Murdoch's ownership if things did not work out. Davis panicked at first, but Murdoch told him not to worry about it.

"I knew how Diller felt about Davis and did not mind gambling that I could get along with Diller better than Davis did," Murdoch said later. While they might not see eye to eye on political issues, Murdoch had enormous respect for Diller's ability and figured he could win his confidence. Murdoch granted Diller the exit rights he asked for and inked the deal with Davis.

Barry Diller was fond of saying that, under his leadership, things tended to get worse before they started to get better. His tenure at Fox was no exception.

His first disaster was the science fiction movie *Enemy Mine*, which went into production about a year before Diller joined Fox. The film was originally budgeted at $17 million but came in between $40 million and $50 million, which meant it needed to gross more than $100 million to break even. The rule of thumb was that marketing and distribution costs run about two-and-a-half times a movie's production costs.

The movie bombed. One Fox executive stated off the record that it did not matter how much the movie had to bring in at the box office to break even, because it would not make anything near that amount. The movie developed problems right from the start. Since *Enemy Mine* was filmed mostly in Iceland and Budapest under the direction of Richard Longcraine, costs quickly escalated beyond control. In addition, the script had weaknesses that were never resolved.

"What was coming back just wasn't what we expected," said Stephen Friedman, whose company had developed the script. "There were serious problems with the look of the picture."

Production head Joe Wizan made the decision to halt production on the movie after Fox had already spent $9 million on it, but when Diller took over he reversed Wizan's call and replaced him with Larry Gordon. Together they hired Wolfgang Petersen, who had directed *Das Boot*, to replace Longcraine as director. Diller's reasoning was that the $9 million would be lost forever if they failed to make the film. Instead of cutting his losses, Diller opted to charge full speed ahead.

Unfortunately, *Enemy Mine* needed more than a new director and some script doctoring to save it from extinction. The *New York Times*'s influential movie critic Janet Maslin said it was "a costly, awful-looking science fiction epic with one of the weirdest story lines ever to hit the screen." Others called it "bewildering," "overblown," and "overextended." Surprisingly, popular critic Gene Siskel praised it, but his endorsement failed to save it from sinking under the frigid Arctic waters where much of it was filmed.

Diller compounded his mistake by backing *Enemy Mine* with an expensive advertising campaign. He ran full-page ads in forty-three leading newspapers around the country and thirty-second television commercials simultaneously on all three networks—a "network roadblock" in the parlance of the industry. All the money spent turned out to be good money thrown after bad. It further drained Fox of valuable operating revenue at a time the studio could least afford it.

Barry Diller was not off to the best of starts in his new job, and his life grew even more complicated when another larger-than-life figure, a man named John Werner Kluge, arrived on the scene with some television stations he wanted to sell.

"The price he's asking is absurd," Diller said to Murdoch.

"Don't worry about it," Murdoch shot back.

Diller could only stare at Murdoch in awe, wondering what in the world his unfathomable new boss had in mind.

CHAPTER 14

SOMETIMES WHOLESALE COSTS
MORE THAN RETAIL

THE STORY OF John Werner Kluge was the stuff of legend. He emigrated to the United States from Germany in 1922 when he was eight years old, attended Columbia University, and then went on to become one of the richest men on earth.

Kluge started off as a food broker before venturing into radio. In the 1950s, he expanded into television and bought a controlling interest in the Metropolitan Broadcasting Corporation, which he renamed Metromedia. Within five years, he was sitting on top of a media empire comprising dozens of radio and television stations in major markets throughout the country. By 1978, Kluge had turned Metromedia into the largest independent broadcasting company in the United States. In 1985 he decided to retire from the media business, and he found an interested buyer for his properties in Rupert Murdoch.

Kluge and Murdoch were much alike in many ways. Both had come to the United States from foreign shores, both were nonpareil entrepreneurs with a penchant for taking inordinate risks, both assumed mountains of debt to whet their appetites for acquiring assets. Like Murdoch, Kluge combed through weekly profit and loss statements for each division of his empire, checking every number himself, searching for areas where he could trim costs further. Both men were divorced and remarried, Kluge for the third time to a beautiful Anglo-Iraqi Catholic. Kluge converted to Catholicism so he could marry the former model in New York City's St. Patrick's Cathedral, with Murdoch's wife Anna as matron of honor (Murdoch has since divorced Anna and remarried again). The third Mrs. Kluge received an estimated settlement of $80 million a year when the two were divorced in 1990.

By the time Kluge and Murdoch began serious negotiations for Kluge's media properties, Metromedia was saddled with $1.3 billion in junk bond debt that had been created by Michael Milken. Nevertheless, Kluge was asking a lot for his radio and television empire—and not the entire empire at that. He wanted to keep his station in New York and had already pledged his Boston outlet to the Hearst Corporation. Kluge's asking price was over $1 billion for his stations in Chicago, Los Angeles, Dallas–Fort Worth, Houston, and Washington, D.C. The price tag amounted to almost 50 percent more than was the norm at the time.

At a meeting attended by Kluge, Murdoch, Michael Milken, Barry Diller, and a host of lawyers, Murdoch agreed to pay the price if Kluge threw in New York as well. The older man first refused but eventually accepted Murdoch's demand. Even at that, Diller told Murdoch the price was absurd. Murdoch told him again not to worry about it.

"We're paying a premium for them all coming together," Murdoch said. "It's the one time in life when wholesale is more expensive than retail."

Murdoch viewed the situation as a once-in-a-lifetime opportunity to become a global force in communications, with the U.S. properties forming the core of his empire. He would have killed to get his hands on them. Paying a higher price than usual for assets, which he reckoned would return his investment many times over during the years to come, would prove to be shrewd in retrospect and the linchpin of Murdoch's *modus operandi*.

For Diller, watching Murdoch in operation was a lesson he would never forget. For all of his adult life, Diller had been a high-paid employee, a top notch executive in his industry but an employee nonetheless. Murdoch and Kluge were true risk takers and empire builders. They gambled everything on a roll of the dice. They represented everything that Barry Diller aspired to become. Murdoch was piling tons of high-priced debt on top of debt to get what he wanted and telling everyone else not to worry about anything. The only sticking point in the entire deal was Marvin Davis, who failed to share Murdoch's media ambitions and was reluctant to part with any more money for expansion.

"Name your price," Murdoch told him, "and I'll buy you out."

As he had originally anticipated, Murdoch won Diller over to his side in his struggle with Davis. Every time Murdoch agreed to Davis's price, the oil man kept raising it. "You can't rely on anything he says," he complained to Diller. As different as they were, Murdoch and Diller respected each other as men of integrity. Their word was their bond, and they believed in living up to their commitments once an agreement was reached. But Davis operated in an entirely different fashion.

According to Murdoch, Davis finally agreed on a price and suggested to Murdoch that they flip a coin to see which man would buy the other out. Again Davis reneged on the arrangement. They argued loudly and continuously through the summer of 1985 until Murdoch could no longer stand it. Davis also began to feel the pressure of having Murdoch and Diller lined up against him.

In the end, Murdoch agreed to pay Davis $325 million for his share of Fox, a price that included the $85 million Murdoch had already loaned the studio. Davis accepted on the condition that he would be allowed to keep part of Fox's lot in Hollywood, the company's Aspen Skiing Company, and the Pebble Beach resort in Carmel, California, which he eventually sold for another huge profit. To both Murdoch and Diller, it was a cheap enough price to pay to finally be rid of the infuriating, foot-dragging, deal-breaking Texan.

* * *

Despite his political differences with Murdoch, Barry Diller got along far better than he had anticipated with his new boss. Overbearing and sensitive at the same time, Diller could be charming when it suited his purposes and abrasive when he failed to get his way. Now in his early forties, Diller still had a penchant for fast cars and motorcycles, and he continued to play high-stakes poker with his buddies Johnny Carson, Warren Beatty, and other Hollywood high-rollers. Murdoch was quick to acknowledge that Fox's success as a studio rested largely on Diller's shoulders.

"Barry is one of those rare people who has a combination of great creative talent and a very sharp business head," said Murdoch. He was happy to find such honesty in an entertainment industry executive, and he sweetened Diller's compensation package with $60 million worth of News Corporation stock to make sure Diller would stick around. If he knew anything about Diller's personal life, or even cared about it, Murdoch did not let it interfere with business, despite his own conservatism.

Diller quickly developed a reputation around Fox as "a sly leprechaun," a "killer," a well-manicured and meticulously dressed take-charge executive with a whip for a tongue. "Don't just nod your head!" he screamed at timid underlings who were reluctant to stick their necks out on a project. "Go bananas if you like something! Don't take no for an answer! Do you love it? How much do you love it? Enough to lie down on barbed wire for it?" What he hated above all was indecisiveness, and he had no tolerance whatsoever for people around him who were afraid to risk their jobs for something they believed in.

Barry Diller and Rupert Murdoch shared the same goal for Fox: to turn the studio's hodgepodge collection of independent television stations into the country's fourth major network. ABC, NBC, and CBS were all in serious trouble in 1985. Diller, ever on the alert for blood in the water, saw an opportunity to break up the stranglehold the networks had on American television. Their share of the viewing audience had been slipping steadily for years, from 93 percent in 1977 to less than 70 percent in

1984, an erosion that was largely due to aggressive competition from the independent stations, cable, and satellite TV.

The odds against Diller succeeding in his mission to launch Fox as a major contender in the race for market share were enormous. The three major networks were an ensconced shared monopoly, thanks to a favorable regulatory environment created by their cronies in Washington, D.C. Federal bureaucrats, in their unflagging effort to protect the American public from unsavory programming, had enthroned the majors as the "official" channels through which a steady diet of inoffensive pabulum could be spoon fed to a lobotomized captive audience. Hacking away at all the red tape that safeguarded the networks from unwanted competition would be difficult enough. An even greater challenge for Diller was creating the kind of programming that was capable of stealing market share away from both the networks and the rest of the competition.

However, Barry Diller had a few more tricks left in his hand. He succeeded at ABC by targeting his programming to the young. The formula that worked at ABC—shows featuring attractive young men and women in active roles—could work again, Diller reasoned, as long as he updated it for the times. American culture had changed considerably since Diller's days with ABC. An element of cynicism had taken hold in an atmosphere of rising divorce rates, a near epidemic of sexually transmitted diseases thanks to rampant experimentation in the 1970s, and four years of "malaise" under the hapless Carter administration. If Diller could find a way of tapping into the mother lode of satire that American life had become, he just might pull it off.

Unfortunately, Diller's first television foray turned out to be a bomb that detonated in his face. The bomb's name was Joan Rivers, a friend of Diller; he had seen her subbing for Johnny Carson on *The Tonight Show* and believed, mistakenly, that she could compete successfully against Carson with her own show for Fox.

Diller had last seen Joan Rivers perform live in a show at Carnegie Hall in 1983. At the time, Rivers was at the crest of her career. Her irreverent wisecracks about sex and marriage were just right for the time. She was a raunchy woman, down to earth, crude, brassy, with a good sense of timing. Young women, in particular, responded enthusiastically to her brand of humor. She told the kinds of jokes only male comedians had delivered before. She was outrageous, funny, and offensive, but politically and socially conservative at the same time. Diller thought her act contained the right combination of ingredients that might appeal to the audience he wanted to reach at Fox.

Diller ran into Rivers again at a party Steve Rubell threw for her at Studio 54, which in 1983 was a pale imitation of its original incarnation. The celebrity crowd turned out that night in force, Diller noticed, as he roamed through his old hunting grounds, shaking hands with Truman Capote, David Geffen, Calvin Klein, Andy Warhol, Bianca Jagger, Halston, and dozens of other old friends and acquaintances. Joan Rivers was hot enough to attract people to her party who were currently in vogue with the nation's youth.

Rivers was already on Diller's mind when she approached him in the summer of 1985, through her lawyer Peter Dekom, about doing a show for Fox. Dekom arranged a lunch with both Diller and Rupert Murdoch and reported back to her later that they were receptive to the idea. One difficulty for Diller was that he was a close friend of Johnny Carson, with whom Rivers had a contract at NBC. Not wanting to jeopardize his relationship with Carson, Diller made it clear to Rivers that it was up to her to sever her ties to *The Tonight Show* without involving him. If she was willing and able to pull it off, Diller said, he would be interested in developing a pilot show for Fox.

Rivers agonized for weeks over which road to take. On one hand she had a measure of security as Carson's backup host, but she was still merely an understudy to the great star. On the other hand, by going off on her own she had an opportunity to inherit Carson's mantle as the dean of late-night television after he retired. Should she take the familiar path and play it safe or choose the riskier path that offered a potentially greater reward? To some degree, she would be competing not only against Carson—a formidable challenge in itself—but against a thirty-year-old NBC tradition that began with Steve Allen in 1953 and continued with Jack Paar a few years later.

"If Jesus came back on another network, the public would still turn first to channel 4," her husband cautioned her.

Terrified of the risk, yet wanting to be a star in her own right, Rivers asked for a guaranteed three-year contract with Fox to cover her butt if the show failed. Diller replied that he could offer her only two years, and he refused to budge on the issue. With neither side willing to give in to the other, the contract negotiations remained on hold until the spring of 1986.

In late March, Diller visited Rivers at her home in Los Angeles. Anxious to lock up a deal, Diller was at his charming best, entertaining everyone present with show biz gossip about movie stars he had grown up with in Beverly Hills. Finally, Diller turned to the main issue at hand.

"I know Johnny well," he said, referring to Johnny Carson. "He's starting to get tired of doing the show. I promise you he'll be gone in one or two years."

What Diller did not tell her was that he knew that Rivers had not been able to secure a promise from NBC that she would be Carson's permanent replacement after he left. Without a contract with NBC to fall back on, Rivers had little choice but to strike out on her own—if not right away, then a year or more later after Carson retired. Her act was popular at the moment, but the viewing public had fickle tastes; there was no telling how long her popularity would last. Knowing this, Diller closed in for the kill.

"I want you now while you're hot. I may not need you next year. But I want you to know that if we can't work out a deal tonight, we can still keep the door open and stay friends."

Diller had a gift for sizing people up and zeroing in on their weaknesses. Rivers had a big ego, he felt, but he also thought it was fragile. She was basically insecure, delighted with her success so far but unsure about her ability to sustain it. Security was key to winning her over; it meant more to her than money.

"I won't give up everything for a two-year contract," Rivers insisted.

"Fine. I'm willing to give you three," Diller said. But he cut her price almost in half. There was no way he was going to pay her anywhere near what Carson made.

The most skillful negotiators know that the best way to clinch a deal is to give the other party what he or she wants the most, but to make sure you set the terms yourself. The terms drive the deal. The price itself is secondary as long as the terms are in your favor. The devil is in the details, and the details are everything.

The parties met again for lunch a few days later at Diller's luxurious spread in Coldwater Canyon. Once again, Diller was at his charming best and introduced Rivers to Jamie Kellner, the president of Fox Broadcasting. Diller and Kellner promised to let her run the show any way she wanted.

"It'll be totally up to you. We will give you the show," was the way they put it.

Kellner amazed her by pulling out a spreadsheet showing Carson's rating numbers, including the nights she filled in for him. Together, Diller and Kellner schmoozed her like a couple of pros, empathizing with her lament that NBC was not treating her properly, not fully acknowledging her contribution to the program. At Fox, it would be different, they told her. At Fox she would be the *star*. The word was like an aphrodisiac to Rivers. *Star! Queen! Maharani!* They hit her hot button over and over, feeding her ego until it was bloated. Rivers could not get enough of hearing about herself. They massaged her to the point of inducing a psychic orgasm.

On March 24, 1986, Diller invited Rivers back to his house for a drink before the Academy Awards ceremony. There she met Rupert Murdoch and his wife Anna, who was a talented novelist with a gift for telling a good story about interesting characters that were generally set in Australia.

At a party at Swifty Lazar's house after the ceremony, Rivers received an eye-opening lesson about playing hardball in the major leagues with the big boys. Sitting at a table when she arrived were Barry Diller, Rupert Murdoch, and Johnny Carson, the three of them laughing and chatting together like long-lost buddies. This was the same Johnny Carson whom Diller had accused of not treating Rivers fairly at NBC. With the ink now dry on her contract with Fox, Rivers observed the powerful three-some joking together as though she didn't exist. She had signed for three years at $5 million a year. Carson was reputed to be making $8 million a year plus a share of the profits. She had no equity participation, and she was locked in at the same salary for the term of her contract, no matter how well the show did. Suddenly, her three-year guarantee did not seem like such a good deal after all. No wonder Diller and Murdoch were laughing.

Rivers finally understood why those who knew Diller told her he was one of the smartest men they had ever met. While she had known him only socially before signing with Fox, she was aware of his reputation as a forceful but inscrutable manager. Those who thought they knew Diller well found out later that he was not really knowable at all. He was said to be sociable when it suited him, yet he also made a practice of buying the seat next to him on a commercial airliner so he would not have to make conversation with strangers. He was a philanthropist and a compassionate champion of social causes who was capable of sizing up people's weaknesses and destroying those who got in his way. Trying to fathom Barry Diller was like trying to peel an onion: you kept stripping away layers only to find dozens more lurking beneath the surface.

Diller saw the handwriting on the wall even before Rivers went on the air. Feeling as though she had been trumped by Diller at the negotiating table, Rivers attempted to sweeten her deal by making annoying demands, usually through her lawyers or via her unemployed husband Edgar. Diller regarded Edgar with contempt, viewing him as a nebbish, a nobody, a backstage "mother" hen with nothing else to do except get in the way of his wife's career by making a pest of himself.

Edgar demanded more office space for his wife and more of the trimmings that went along with the star status only Johnny Carson could command. When Diller told Jamie Kellner what was going on, Kellner snapped, "If she's no good, she'll be out in nine months."

Diller recognized Edgar's weak spot instinctively. He viewed him as an insecure man of no accomplishment, whose only claim to fame was his wife's celebrity. At a meeting attended by Diller, Kellner, and lawyers for both sides, Diller waited for his opportunity to humiliate Joan Rivers's husband publicly. As soon as Edgar opened his mouth, Diller glowered at him and said with ice-cold precision, "Shut up!" A hush fell over the room as the outgunned Edgar slunk further into his chair. Pressing his advantage, Diller told him to "Fuck off!" a few weeks later when Edgar attempted to rehabilitate what was left of his tattered self-respect. More than anything, Diller resented Rivers for not keeping her family problems out of her business dealings with Fox, according to Diller's associates.

Through it all, however, Barry Diller and all the other top honchos at Fox were pulling for Joan Rivers to succeed. Five million a year was far less than Carson was making, but it was a lot of money for a struggling studio to invest in a single show. Diller saw Rivers's late-night talk show as the linchpin that would hold Fox's independent stations together in an effort to create a fourth major network. Rivers was his first major gamble, and he could not afford to stumble, particularly with a demanding boss like Rupert Murdoch staring over his shoulder. If only Joan would shut up and do her job, let the show rise or fall on its own merits instead of making him crazy with a lot of picayune demands.

CHAPTER 15

MURDOCH'S MURDOCH COULD
MAKE IT HAPPEN

"CAN'T YOU PRODUCE the show without all these people, without all this space?" Barry Diller screamed at Bruce McKay, the producer of Joan Rivers's talk show.

"Well, I guess I could do it with less," McKay stammered, totally intimidated by Diller's overbearing manner, according to several observers.

Next, Rivers wanted to hire Mark Hudson as her orchestra leader, but Diller balked at his asking price. "He wants too much money," Diller said.

Rivers countered with a demand for an orchestra as large as Johnny Carson's.

"Too many musicians!" Diller thundered.

Every time Joan Rivers thrust, Barry Diller parried. Her show had not even been tested yet, and all she cared about was shoring up her delicate ego. Johnny Carson was the benchmark against which she measured herself. If Carson had a huge orchestra, she had to have one as well. If Carson had writers on his staff who commanded $2,000 a week, how could

Joan Rivers make do with writers who earned only $800? Saving face was everything to her. Never mind that Carson presided over the most successful late-night show in the history of television, while Joan Rivers appeared night after night in the same forum and was still an unknown quantity. And, if she was not difficult enough, her meddlesome husband was impossible to deal with.

"You're the only one who can keep Edgar away," Diller told Rivers. "You've got to do it. He's destroying the show by causing major problems."

Every day was a new battle. Rivers found herself trapped in the middle, refusing to intervene, wanting peace with Diller and Fox on one hand and yearning for the same kind of refinements Johnny Carson commanded with a snap of his fingers on the other. In frustration, she had her lawyer Peter Dekom write a letter to Diller that only succeeded in infuriating the exasperated executive even more. "Joan being prepared to start the show in October is, of course, predicated on having all the requisite elements in place to her satisfaction sufficiently in advance . . ."

Diller hit the roof when he read it. In response, he demanded a face-to-face meeting with Rivers at her house. This time around, he was not his charming self. For this meeting, he sharpened his fangs and displayed them in all their bloody glory. He did not appreciate the adversarial letters he was receiving from her lawyer, Diller said. When Edgar tried to defend them, Diller glared at him and said simply, "Fuck you!"

The outcome of the meeting was inconclusive in that it failed to put an end to their differences. A week later, Rivers decided that the security guards Fox assigned to protect her were little more than Keystone Kops, and she demanded the equivalent of ninja warriors instead.

"This is my lot, and you are my guests," Diller told her.

"I don't feel safe without my private guards," Rivers replied, "so I cannot be your guest on the Fox lot."

"So don't be my guest." Diller rarely changed his mind once he made a decision. In the end, Rivers gave in on this issue, but the atmosphere between her and Diller turned even more toxic. At this point, he decided he could not deal with her any longer. From that moment onward, Barry

Diller made himself unavailable to the would-be maharani of late-night television. When she wanted to talk to him, Joan Rivers had to reach Barry Diller through one of his intermediaries.

The outcome of this long encounter with Diller was more than a trifle ironic. At NBC Rivers never enjoyed access to Johnny Carson, the man she stood in for on occasion. When she wanted to deliver a message to him, it was through one of his flunkies. Now she had maneuvered herself into the same position with Diller at Fox.

The Late Show Starring Joan Rivers finally made its debut on October 9, 1986, and the response from the viewing public was underwhelming. Rivers panicked when she got word that Carson threatened to ban anyone from his show who appeared as a guest on hers. She sent word about her plight to Diller, who said he would make a personal appeal to all his friends as well as to the stars who were currently under contract to Fox. Thanks to Barry Diller's clout with the stars and to his friendship with Carson, Rivers was able to play hostess to Jack Nicholson, Barbra Streisand, Jane Fonda, Michael Douglas, Cher, Elton John, and other major celebrities, but even they failed to turn the tide in Rivers's favor.

The problem was the forum; it was just not right for Joan. She was a standup comic, good for twenty minutes to half an hour of belly laughs, but her particular brand of humor did not translate well to the role of interviewer. Carson also delivered a funny five-minute monologue, but his true genius was bringing out the best in his guests. He had a talent for pushing the right buttons and letting his guests perform. That role required self-assurance, an ability to sit back and let your guests take center stage for a while. Rivers needed to be the star *all* the time; she had to be funnier, wittier, cleverer, and more popular than everyone else on the show. Her innate insecurity did her in. It was too much for anyone to command center stage for hours on end, night after night. As a result, she fell flat on her face.

The show played itself out for seven months of excruciating pain for everyone involved with it. Nothing anyone could do was sufficient to boost her ratings numbers. The reviews were almost universally negative, some needlessly cruel. "No need, Johnny, to lose sleep over the new challenger," one headline trumpeted. Her audience comprised morons and airheads, said another. Tom Shales of the *Washington Post* took the nastiest swipe of all, writing "Maybe Rivers should spend less time at the beauty parlor and more time with her writers. The beauty parlor would appear to be a lost cause for her anyway."

Buried under an avalanche of poor ratings and hostile press clippings, Rivers begged Diller for more time to hit her stride and find a way to make the show work. But as far as Diller, Murdoch, and the other powers at Fox were concerned, the program was beyond redemption. "It was just not funny," Diller said later. Diller was not going to throw good money after bad again. When you've got a loser, he now realized, the best solution was to cut your losses early and get out. Try something else. There was no percentage in trying to resuscitate a corpse. Diller shared his thoughts with Rupert Murdoch who agreed with Diller's assessment.

"Buy her contract out," Murdoch told him. "If we're going down, let's cut our losses and try something else."

Rivers believed that Fox owed her $15 million—$5 million a year for three years—but Fox's lawyers managed to convince her otherwise. In the end, she settled for somewhere between $2.5 million and $5 million. Once again she had been outfoxed by Fox's master negotiators. Diller alone was formidable enough. Diller and Murdoch *together* packed a devastating wallop. People in the industry who saw them in action said they formed a brutal combination that should have been ruled illegal on humanitarian grounds alone.

Barry Diller was not a man who believed in looking back and brooding over past mistakes. It was time to move on. The key to Diller's success at ABC was appealing to the young, and that was precisely the formula he intended to put to work at Fox. Unfortunately, he had yet to come up with a way to put his theory in operation.

Fox's losses in 1987 alone totaled $96 million. A series starring George

C. Scott entitled *Mr. President* was one more disaster adding to the studio's problems. So far Rupert Murdoch had invested more than $125 million in product development with nothing but red ink to show for it.

"We were grafting an alien thing, and it just didn't take," Diller said.

Fortunately, the company that Fox had been folded into, Rupert Murdoch's News Corporation Ltd., had deep enough pockets to withstand the losses. By 1987, Murdoch had built his communications kingdom into one of the largest in the world, encompassing 250 separate subsidiaries. News Corporation comprised book publishing, newspaper, movie, television, and other media companies, as well as interests in bauxite mines, an airline company, wool production, and gambling enterprises. Profits generated by the sprawling, worldwide empire had risen 83 percent during the second half of 1986.

A looming problem for Murdoch, which had financial analysts in London, New York, and Sydney, Australia tingling with alarm, was the staggering debt the Australian-born magnate had taken on to expand his reach. In the rarified world inhabited by financial risk takers with nerves of steel, Murdoch stood among the boldest. He used leverage like a weapon, financing and refinancing his way to greater wealth with a nonchalance that left mere mortals shaking their heads, wondering when his tottering conglomerate would come crashing down around him.

It never did, although there were times when even Murdoch himself feared it might. In 1987, News Corporation owed assorted banks around the world a total of about $3 billion, an amount that approached the company's annual gross revenues. Only Murdoch's vision for the future, his belief in his own judgment about the ability of his far-flung enterprises to eventually pay off, allowed him to sleep the four or five hours he required each day.

As far as Fox was concerned, Murdoch never entertained the slightest doubt that his selection of Barry Diller to run the show would produce positive results over time. Murdoch believed in Diller more than Diller believed in himself. Barry Diller was Murdoch's Murdoch at Fox, even though Diller did not see this at the time. Diller, too, half expected News Corporation's fragile structure to crumble at any time, and when it did he was prepared to salvage Fox from among the ruins by buying it from Murdoch.

He never got the chance.

Falling interest rates in the mid-1980s allowed Murdoch to refinance once again and lower the cost of his debt from 13 percent to 7 percent, cutting his interest payments almost in half. Richard MacDonald, a media analyst with First Boston, crunched the new numbers and discovered that cash flow from Fox's seven television stations finally exceeded the financing costs. Murdoch had turned the corner, notwithstanding the continuing red ink at Fox, and reckoned it was only a question of time before Fox's earnings would be in the black.

Barry Diller, whose innate caution was both an asset and a liability, started to become a believer himself. Diller's conservative approach to business saved him from major disasters but would also keep him from seizing opportunity when it was available some years later. He understood that the great empire builders—Murdoch, Bluhdorn, Ted Turner, the Hunts of Texas—were willing to risk everything on a roll of the dice, but so far he had not been able to take the big plunge himself, even though he aspired to their ranks. He was still young, however, and he had always been quick to learn from others. Working for Murdoch was an emboldening and enlightening experience for Diller, a great leap forward in his ongoing education.

"Anyone looking for an edge will try to offer what isn't being offered," Diller said, expounding on his favorite theme of counter-programming. To Diller, counter-programming was the golden key to Fox's future. In an age of fossilized sitcoms and stale game shows, finding programs that appealed to the nation's youth became Diller's mantra, his religion, his mission for Fox.

He found some measure of success with such shows as *Small Wonder* and *9 to 5*, both of which Fox produced for its affiliates and sold into syndication, and also with reruns of the popular program *M *A *S *H*. The last show alone accounted for nearly $30 million of News Corporation's cash flow. But, together, they failed to provide the alchemy needed to turn losses into profits at Fox.

Suddenly, out of the blue, Fox received a godsend in the form of the 1988 screenwriters' strike in Hollywood. The strike created a logjam in the stream of new program development for the major networks, forcing them to air reruns. Fox, however, had recently introduced a new lineup of shows that were beginning to catch on. One of Fox's more popular offerings was *The Tracey Ullman Show*, an offbeat and slightly wacky comedy series that began to attract a youthful audience since it first aired in April of the previous year. While the networks ran rerun after stale rerun, Fox's share of the viewing public started to rise slightly.

Fox's film division was the first to generate bona fide profits. "We cratered the old company," Diller said. "It was so bad. We got rid of every senior executive except one and then really juiced it up and got it back into profits."

The movie *Big*, starring Tom Hanks in the role of a grown-up little boy, grossed more than $100 million in 1988. *Working Girl* with Melanie Griffith and *Die Hard* with Bruce Willis helped push the film studio's earnings up 35 percent to nearly $36 million in the second half of the year. This performance was a major turnaround from the nearly $300 million Fox's film division had lost in recent years.

Television loomed as the major challenge for Diller, and it was one he was determined to surmount. "We had to do shows that demanded your attention, that yanked you by the throat to get you to change the channel," Diller said. One way or another, Murdoch's Murdoch at Fox was going to find a way to make it happen.

CHAPTER 16

GUIDING THE LITTLE SKIFF
THROUGH THE WATER

THINGS STARTED TO come together for Barry Diller with the advent of *The Simpsons*. Bart Simpson and his benighted family were the brainchildren of Matt Groening, an irreverent cartoonist who was perfectly attuned to the youth subculture of the late 1980s. Groening's satire on the values that characterized American family life during the period was precisely on target. It struck a receptive chord with high school and college kids throughout the country, who raced home from wherever they were to catch the show out of fear of missing an episode. By the fall of 1990, nearly 50 percent of Fox's audience was from twelve to thirty-four years old, compared with between 25 percent and 37 percent of the same age group for the major networks. Diller's strategy of targeting the young was beginning to strike pay dirt.

The success of *The Simpsons* boosted Fox's advertising revenues 75 percent in one year to $550 million in 1990. Advertisers across the land had been lusting for a way to reach this age group, and virtually overnight Fox emerged as the most effective means of doing it. Bart Simpson was their pipeline to the youth of America. Singlehandedly, the brash youngster with the porcupine hair launched Fox as a credible, if fledgling, new network.

The success of *The Simpsons* further strengthened the partnership between Barry Diller and Rupert Murdoch. Murdoch could not sing Diller's praises high enough, indirectly endorsing his own good sense in giving him so much power at Fox. And Diller was clearly in awe of Murdoch's financial acumen and single-minded commitment to his goals. Their greatest differences were in the area of politics, which for the time being remained a buffer zone where each of them declined to tread.

With Bart Simpson and his family capturing the youth market for Fox, Diller launched a second offensive with the introduction of *Married . . . with Children*. The depiction of the hilariously despicable Bundy family was another assault on the prevailing myths about American family life. No American father was more sexist or boorish than Al Bundy, no mother more fatuous than his wife Peg, no daughter more alarmingly seductive than Kelly, no son more inept with the opposite sex than Bud, and no dog more unlikable than Buck. The Bundys represented the worst extremes of American family life writ large, and they were an instant hit with the same target audience that would never think of missing an episode of *The Simpsons*.

Married . . . with Children was so effective in attracting the nation's youth to Fox that it prompted an irate housewife from Michigan to launch a one-woman campaign against the program. If pissing off uptight adults who lacked both a sense of humor and a sense of irony was a measure of success, Fox won the gold medal. The major networks trailed so far behind in this time slot that they were off the radar screen.

"We're the little skiff slicing through the water," Diller gloated, "as the big ocean liners are throwing off furniture and bodies to stay afloat."

Fox was able to pull off its coup with a staff of approximately 200 employees, compared with the thousands who worked at each of the networks. Turnover was ruthless at Fox as Diller kept paring the ranks of unproductive creative people and filling their slots with others attuned to the network's irreverent mindset. The re-engineering of the company started to pay off handsomely as Fox's red ink disappeared and losses metamorphosed into profits.

It was only a question of time, however, before Diller's political differences with Murdoch bubbled to the surface. The major problem was that neither man was reticent about his views. Both were political animals to whom differences over social, fiscal, and monetary issues were matters of life or death. Diller was a gut-level liberal who devoted both time and money to AIDS research and moderate-to-liberal politicians of both major parties, while Murdoch was an ardent and outspoken conservative who contributed heavily to the Republican Party in the United States and the Conservative Party in Great Britain.

"He is more able to make fun of our differences than I am," Diller complained. "I can't make fun of conservatives. I just get crazy, tied up."

It bothered Diller more and more that he was working for a man who was vilified by the liberal press throughout the English-speaking world. British left-wingers could barely utter Murdoch's name without frothing at the mouth. It was more than merely his disagreements with Murdoch that tormented Diller; it was Murdoch's stature as the preeminent conservative power in media circles that drove Diller to distraction. In effect, Rupert Murdoch was the symbol of everything Barry Diller loathed in the political arena. Murdoch's newspapers, in particular, reflected his political bent in the way they covered and editorialized the news—not because he intervened personally in their editorial makeup, but rather because of the writers and editors he hired to staff them.

However, the umbilical cord of profits that linked Diller and Murdoch proved to be more formidable than the yawning political rift that separated them. The cord was strengthened further in 1987 with Fox's introduction of *A Current Affair* starring Maury Povich. The *New York Times* gave the program a glowing review, encouraging Diller to move it to a primetime slot earlier in the evening.

According to Diller, "It had been a nice, populist, sweet little tabloid, not mean-spirited but fun. Then Maury put it right over the line and the show really took off." Profits from Povich's show alone hit $25 million by the end of 1989.

Diller followed this success with a couple of gritty crime shows, *America's Most Wanted* and *Cops*, both of which were big hits with the public. The first show led to the arrest of real-life criminals and became the second most popular Fox program after *Married . . . with Children*. Each episode featured a different crime and ended with an appeal for viewers to respond with any information they might have about the perpetrators. The second program showed real cops under fire busting the scum of American society without pulling any punches.

By 1990, advertising revenues at Fox soared to more than $500 million largely because of Diller's programming genius. Civil libertarians and the left-wing press in general raised a clarion call against this new genre of crime show, claiming it violated the rights of unconvicted criminals. If Diller felt any misgivings about being on the politically incorrect side of this issue, he was notably mute about it. Rather, he thumbed his nose at his political brethren by coining a new word and maintaining that his crime shows were actually "prosocial." Diller may have been a left-leaning political animal, but he was a businessman first and foremost. The bottom line was his personal demarcation line between political consciousness and financial stupidity.

Barry Diller's schizophrenic relationship with Rupert Murdoch continued along its bumpy path until a new development threatened to derail it once again. The problem centered on the conflicting roles played by Murdoch's print and electronic media divisions.

On one hand, Diller was breaking new ground at Fox with his revolutionary, countercultural, antiestablishment programming ventures. On the other hand, the newspapers Murdoch owned under the umbrella of his News Corporation flagship company were stridently conservative, bashing the very antifamily values social agenda that made Fox so successful. All this was going on with Murdoch's blessing. Everything was

fine with Rupert as long as his far-flung properties were generating profits. However, the tension was beginning to cause a rift between the television and film crowd on one side and the print people on the other.

"I couldn't stand it anymore," Diller said. "We were being attacked by
Rupert's pit bulls at the newspapers for doing things that put more and
more money into Rupert's pocket. It was crazy, hypocritical. It just didn't
make any sense."

Murdoch decided to defuse the issue by holding a company powwow
in Aspen, Colorado, right after China's massacre of antigovernment dis-
sidents in Tiananmen Square in June 1989. The timing of the meeting,
considering the problems it was called to address, could not have been
more ironic. Communism was under attack everywhere, thanks largely
to the beefed-up military spending by a Republican president, Ronald
Reagan. Against this historic backdrop, Communist China, which along
with Cuba were the most beloved dictatorships on earth in some circles,
had slaughtered its own unarmed citizens who had been clamoring for
democratic reforms. The entire heinous, stomach-churning event had
been filmed by CNN for the entire world to see.

Murdoch was simultaneously incensed at the bloodshed and intrigued by
the possibilities for Fox. "Watching the events in China on CNN was the most
amazing experience," he said. "It was an extraordinary moment in history, to
know that what was happening in China was really happening because we
were all watching it." The idea of launching an all-news station to compete
with CNN took root in Murdoch's brain at that precise moment.

Diller and other Hollywood notables who tilted to the left, including
Jane Fonda and Shirley MacLaine, had at one time been apologists for
the Chinese regime, and Diller was uncharacteristically struck dumb by
the grisly spectacle. However, Diller did not allow China's fall from grace
with the left to deflect him from his mission at Aspen—to resolve once
and for all his grievances against Murdoch's so-called Australian Mafia—
the clique of mostly conservative political writers Murdoch had imported
from Down Under.

Rupert Murdoch had tried to set a broad agenda for the Aspen conference, but the print versus television/film brouhaha quickly erupted to the surface, eclipsing all other concerns. Barry Diller despised most of the print journalists who staffed Murdoch's newspapers, and he particularly loathed Murdoch's favorite Aussie right-winger, Steve Dunleavy.

Dunleavy was a legend among his peers, an archetypically boisterous, hard-drinking old-school reporter who was capable of sinking to the lowest depths to find a story. Dunleavy was deliberately outrageous. His idea of an interview was an intimidating confrontation with his subject pushed to the point of a barroom brawl. And if it actually came to that, Dunleavy was always ready for a fight. Big, beefy, in-your-face, openly hostile to everyone to the left of Margaret Thatcher and Ronald Reagan, Dunleavy was not beyond picking a fight with anyone who crossed him just to be able to write about it later. If he had a fictional counterpart, it was Sebastian Dangerfield, J. P. Donleavy's hard-living protagonist in *The Ginger Man*.

Steve Dunleavy personified everything Barry Diller hated about Murdoch-style tabloid print journalism. The mere sight of Dunleavy at the Aspen confab sent Diller into a paroxysm of rage. Unable to control himself, Diller attacked Dunleavy indirectly by stating loudly that he was tired of working for one part of the Murdoch empire while being abused by another.

Dunleavy responded in his inimitable style. He turned to someone next to him and remarked, "What a silly little gap-tooth faggot he is." Diller imploded, vibrating like a tuning fork. He was in good shape, not beyond a punch-out himself if the situation called for it. Clenching his fists, he appeared ready to leap upon the burly Aussie who was six inches taller and fifty pounds heavier than he was. One of Diller's cohorts grabbed him by the arms and led him away, while a Dunleavy confidant adroitly steered his man in the opposite direction. Thanks to the quick intervention of their respective handlers, a physical confrontation was averted.

Once Diller was able to collect himself, he got down to specifics. Stories carried in Murdoch's *News of the World* or *Premiere* magazine, for example, were counterproductive. Diller cited a story in the first tabloid, accusing Arnold Schwartzenegger's father of having Nazi connections at the same time Fox was trying to sign a contract with the film star. The latter publication published an unflattering portrait of Fox's Danny De Vito in one of its cover stories. Editorials in various Murdoch newspapers and magazines constantly attacked the kind of trash-TV shows and irreverent family satires that had put Fox in the black. All this internecine warfare had to stop.

Murdoch sympathized with both sides, but his management style was just as laissez-faire as his politics: he believed in letting his lieutenants fight their battles among themselves until the strongest emerged victorious. Meanwhile, he expected all those who worked for him to contribute to his empire's profitability regardless of their complaints about the others. He was a latter-day Roman emperor, somewhat bemused by the turf battles between his provincial governors as long as they did not allow their differences to get in the way of their respective duties.

Frustrated at his inability to resolve his grievances against Dunleavy and his cohorts satisfactorily, Diller left the meeting abruptly, hopped on his motorcycle, and roared off into the majestic mountains outside of Aspen. An hour later, he came hobbling back to the conference center in pain, nursing the ankle he had broken when he hit a rock and was thrown from his bike. All conversation came to a halt as the high-powered participants turned in unison toward the injured chairman of Fox. Finally, Murdoch broke the silence.

"I hope none of you were responsible for this," he said, staring at Dunleavy and his entourage with a smile on his face. Even Diller had to laugh as, for the moment at least, the tension of the meeting was defused.

There was no question, however, that Murdoch's first love was the kind of muckraking, right-wing, tabloid journalism practiced by his print minions. Print was where Rupert had cut his teeth, following in his father's footsteps. The elder Murdoch had earned a reputation as one of Australia's leading newspapermen. Despite all the new technology that powered his empire, his satellites in the sky that delivered news and entertainment to the masses, the electronic media that pumped out television series and feature films that titillated the youth of America, Rupert Murdoch was an old-fashioned ink-stained wretch in his heart and soul. There was no way he would seriously entertain any suggestion that he clean up his tabloids, make them politically less partisan, or elevate the content to appeal to a more upscale audience. It was strictly out of the question.

"There are two kinds of newspapers," Murdoch said in his final address at Aspen. "There are broadsheets and there are tabloids. Or, as some people say, there are the unpopular and the popular newspapers."

Murdoch's word was final. For Diller the handwriting, as it were, was on the wall. The only question remaining was how long he could continue to work for a man whose entire value system was diametrically opposed to his own.

CHAPTER 17

JOBLESS AT FIFTY

BY JUNE 1990, Barry Diller had more to worry about than whether or not he could coexist peacefully with Murdoch and his rowdy boys in the print area. While Fox's finances were in solid shape, thanks to Diller and his programming strategy, the same could not be said for the studio's parent company, News Corporation. Murdoch's flagship firm was staggering beneath the massive debt the entrepreneur had assumed to extend the boundaries of his empire. News Corporation's annual report for the fiscal year ending June 30, 1990, revealed a company in seemingly hopeless crisis. Even the normally ebullient and optimistic Murdoch began to question whether he had finally taken on more debt than he could handle. As he recalled, "I was so busy making acquisitions that I forgot to pay attention to some important details."

The annual report showed that Murdoch had rewarded Diller handsomely for his contribution to Fox with a base salary of more than Australian $12 million. At the time, the Aussie currency was worth a bit more than the U.S. dollar. In comparison, Murdoch's own annual salary was less than $3 million, so the dice-rolling, Australian-born empire-builder could hardly be accused of raiding his own company at the expense of the shareholders.

Murdoch needed to sell off assets in order to survive. His chain of travel magazines fetched almost three times the amount Murdoch paid for them a few years earlier. The upscale *Elle* brought in $160 million, thirty times its startup costs. Murdoch's weekly tabloid the *Star*, which had successfully captured market share from the competing *National Enquirer*, sold for $400 million. With Murdoch holding a garage sale to raise badly needed cash, Barry Diller saw an opportunity to escape from Murdoch's clutches and, finally, to become his own boss.

"I'm interested in buying Fox," he told Murdoch. "I won't have any trouble lining up the financing."

"We'll see," Murdoch said curtly. He did not shut the door entirely, but deep inside he knew there was no way he would let Fox go unless the proverbial wolf was ready to bite off his head. Fox was becoming a cash cow, and it gave Murdoch the television presence he needed to achieve his long-term goals. The opportunities to influence the public presented by America's fourth major network were boundless. Fox was the last property Murdoch would ever consider selling.

Murdoch's asset sales bought him some respite from the banks, which had been snapping at his heels for months. However, Murdoch was not completely out of the woods. He still needed to raise cash and bring down News Corporation's staggering debt ratio.

In December 1991, Murdoch and Diller flew in separate planes to a secret meeting in Hartford, Connecticut. "I'm off to humiliate myself again," Murdoch said as he left his apartment in midtown Manhattan before dawn. His bankers insisted that he forge a deal that would loosen some of his family's control over his company. Silently, his driver took him through the still-dark streets of Manhattan, beneath the Hudson River via the Holland Tunnel to New Jersey's Teterboro Airport, where his private Gulfstream III aircraft awaited his arrival with its engines running.

As reported by several sources, Murdoch's plane landed at a private airport in Hartford just after 8 A.M., from which he was whisked away in another limousine to a breakfast meeting with media analysts. The breakfast was attended by a dozen representatives of some of the leading financial institutions in the country, analysts whose respective opinions had the power to either attract investors to News Corporation's shares or to turn them away, further depressing share prices. Murdoch put on a creditable dog-and-pony show for the numbers crunchers, extolling the virtues of his long-term plan to Americanize global media.

At about nine o'clock, Barry Diller landed in Hartford after a brief flight from Washington, D.C., and headed directly to the offices of George Weiss Associates, a small asset management firm with substantial clout in investment circles. Diller was pacing nervously in the anteroom when Murdoch rushed in following his breakfast.

"I've bad news," George Weiss said when he emerged from his inner sanctum to greet his visitors. "I won't be able to meet with you today."

"Did something happen?" Murdoch asked in shock.

"No, just the usual. I'm jammed up with appointments I can't possibly break."

Weiss apologized awkwardly and disappeared into the cold morning air. Murdoch and Diller stared at each other in disbelief. Here they were, two of the most powerful men in the media industry, being stood up by a fund manager in Podunk, Connecticut, who was too busy to see them.

"This is outrageous," Murdoch fumed. "My entire net worth is tied up in this company, I'm being forced to dilute my shares, and this has all been just a bloody waste of time."

Diller was well aware of Murdoch's plight, and he also knew why Rupert had invited him along this morning for his aborted interview with Weiss. News Corporation was reeling, but Fox was healthier than ever. Murdoch wanted Diller along to help him mesmerize the investment crowd with some upbeat, razzle-dazzle talk about the future delivered in Diller's hyperbolic style. Diller was annoyed that he had allowed Murdoch to use him this way. Never again! He was growing more tired

than ever of shilling for Murdoch. One way or another, he was determined to go off by himself and run his own show. All he needed was the
right opportunity.

"If you're ever interested in selling Fox," Diller said once again, "you
know where to find me." Murdoch was too furious to even reply. Without
saying goodbye, he stormed off to his limo and directed the driver to take
him back to the airport.

The relative financial states of News Corporation and Fox were
reflected in their respective airplanes. Murdoch did not believe in spending money on frills. His tastes were plain and simple, and the appointments in his Gulfstream III mirrored them. Diller, on the other hand,
was forever a true product of Beverly Hills and the culture that spawned
him. His plane was decked out with tan leather seats and lavish furnish-
ings, and his hand-picked go-fer served him coffee in fine china cups. It
was enough for Murdoch to know that he was master of his realm; Diller
needed to act out his role in life and enjoy the trappings of his wealth.

Diller settled back into his soft leather chair and fumed during his flight
to New York City. The more he thought about his experience in Hartford
that morning, the more furious he became. His life had been a whirlwind
during the past week. It was not so much the activity he minded; Diller
was used to setting a frenzied pace for himself. It was jumping through
hoops for someone else that bothered him. Living in *his* whirlwind was
fine, but more and more lately he had been caught up in a whirlwind
of Murdoch's creation, darting from place to place at Murdoch's insis-
tence, helping his demanding boss shore up the crumbling structure of his
empire instead of devoting his efforts to creating one of his own.

"On Sunday night I went to Minneapolis," Diller complained to associates in his rapid-fire style. "Almost burned down my hotel room overnight, slept four or five hours, went to Chicago, went to a black-tie dinner
in New York Monday night, went to the wrong building, did meetings all
day yesterday, flew to Washington to make a speech, and then got up at 6
A.M. today to come to Hartford."

Diller thought the time he spent on the road could have been used more productively. For example, he believed that Murdoch could have sold far more shares teleconferencing instead of traipsing all over the place for face-to-face meetings. He did not blame Murdoch for that so much as the investment bankers and analysts who liked to have their asses kissed in person before they deigned to raise capital for them. Even so, it was Murdoch's problem, not Diller's. Fox was doing just fine, thank you, and all because of him. If Rupert wanted to keep rolling the dice to expand his empire, putting them all in jeopardy, that was his doing. Diller got along fine with Murdoch despite their palpable differences, but his patience was running out. It was clear that he would not be able to put up with it much longer.

Diller was a busy man who did not have much time for reflection, but he was in a pensive mood on the flight back from Hartford. Pretty soon he would be fifty years old. One can imagine the thought processes raking his brain. No longer was he the boy wonder of the business, the *enfant terrible* of the entertainment world. If he was going to make his mark as a world-class player, it had to be soon. He felt like a tennis player who had been challenging the top-ranked stars throughout his career but had so far failed to win the final at Wimbledon or the U.S. Open. Already incredibly rich, he was no longer motivated by megabucks alone. His ego had to be assuaged. Barry Diller had to become his own man.

Fifty is a pivotal age. It brings with it vivid intimations of one's own mortality. Before fifty, death and debilitating illness are events that affected other people. After fifty, you start to realize that personal disaster could strike at any time. You begin to understand that everyone is living on borrowed time. Things you used to take for granted, including a good bowel movement, could no longer be counted on with assurance.

Diller felt as though he were approaching the end of an era. A few years earlier he had attended the funeral of Abe Lastfogel, the oldest member of the William Morris agency that had given Diller his start in the business more than thirty years before. Lastfogel had long been a legend in

Hollywood, and his death from a heart attack at the age of eighty-six jolted everyone who had known him.

During the funeral at Hillside Memorial Park in Culver City, California, Diller ran into an army of friends and acquaintances that spanned the generations, from old-timers like Danny Thomas, Sammy Weisbord, and Lew Wasserman to relative youngsters like himself, Warren Beatty, and Stan Kamen. After Lastfogel was laid to rest beside his wife Frances, who had died eight years earlier, the mourners trooped back to Beverly Hills for a farewell party at Danny Thomas's house. Listening to everyone reminisce about the good old days at William Morris only reminded Diller that time was passing and he had yet to achieve his primary goals.

The presidential campaign of 1988 was another event that left Diller in despair. He had hosted a reception at his home in Coldwater Canyon for the hopelessly inept Democratic candidate, Michael Dukakis. Everyone who counted in Hollywood had attended, including power agent Swifty Lazar; Deborah Kerr and her screenwriter husband Peter Viertel; Jack Nicholson and Anjelica Houston, Nicholson's lady love at the time; Walter and Carol Matthau; Jack and Felicia Lemmon; Ray and Fran Stark; Robert Evans; and a cast of hundreds, all of whom had brought their checkbooks to help bolster Dukakis's flagging campaign.

All those with an ounce of political sense knew they were backing a loser in Dukakis, but in their collective anxiety to defeat George Bush and put a Democrat back in the White House, they managed to blind themselves to their candidate's shortcomings. Dukakis's own campaign manager said she knew the election was over the minute the diminutive Dukakis climbed aboard a tank and put on a combat helmet that covered his ears, making him look like a twelve-year-old boy playing war. Everyone there had seen the front-page photo of Dukakis, all but buried beneath his combat gear, splashed on newspapers across the country.

The pall cast over the funereal gathering by the humorless Dukakis was tragic enough in itself for Diller. It seemed that things could hardly get any worse, when suddenly Diller discovered he was being overly optimistic. Robert Evans, the man Diller replaced at Paramount and the only

Republican in the room, got hopelessly drunk and resumed a long-standing feud with Peter Viertel. Diller's guests cleared out before the rivalry became physical, bringing the party to an abrupt but apt conclusion.

As his plane landed at New York's LaGuardia Airport, Diller brought the discomfiting events of the past few months to closure. He resolved that one way or another, his life was going to change. He could no longer continue with the status quo. "I wanted to be a principal, not an employee," Diller admitted to the author. It was time to make a break with the past.

Another problem troubling Diller was the gnawing feeling that he was becoming increasingly expendable in Murdoch's eyes. Murdoch, he believed, was notorious for hiring people who served his interests at the time, then ignoring or discarding them later, once they were no longer valuable to him. Diller had already made a significant contribution to Fox. What more could he offer Murdoch than he had already given? What better shows could he possibly come up with? True, Murdoch rewarded him handsomely for his effort, but how much longer would the demanding and calculating media mogul be willing to shower him with his kingly compensation?

For Barry Diller, the course he had to follow was crystal clear to him. As eager as he was to go off on his own, he wanted to do it in his own time, under his own terms, rather than be cast adrift by a man who no longer valued him as highly as he once had. By his own estimation, Diller had more than achieved his goals in creating a major network out of Fox's string of independent stations. But this success had come at the expense of the film studio, which he had not had time to focus on sufficiently.

"I just Band-Aided it but never really fixed it," Diller said about his neglect of Fox's movie company. "You have to build a company from within. I never did it."

Diller's selection of Joe Roth to run the film studio had become a major point of contention between Diller and Murdoch. Roth's tenure had been less than successful, resulting in a string of box office disasters that ate away at Murdoch's profit margin. Diller knew he had to do something about Roth but kept putting it off, hoping Roth would be able to turn the studio around on his own. His gamble did not pay off.

By February 1992, a mere three months after his ill-fated flight to Hartford, Diller felt he had hit an impasse. He knew that if he did not leave Fox on his own soon, Murdoch would make their relationship even more unpleasant than it already was, thereby forcing him out. Some reports said Murdoch fired Diller, others said Diller quit. The truth is, both men knew they could not continue the status quo. Like a marriage of convenience that was troubled from the start, it was simply time to call it quits. The miracle was that it had lasted as long as it did and that it produced such fruitful results.

Both Diller and Murdoch put on happy faces during their joint announcement that Diller was leaving Fox. Diller said he had decided to go because he had just turned fifty and figured it was time to control his own destiny. He praised Murdoch as "the best" at what he does. "I would say that if you're going to work for somebody, work for him." In Barry Diller's book, Rupert Murdoch was "straight, supportive, honest, and clear."

Murdoch reiterated what he had said publicly about Diller in the past. Barry Diller was the best executive in the industry, a rare combination of creative genius and solid financial judgment. Murdoch's farewell gift to Diller was a gold, platinum, and diamond-studded severance parachute worth approximately $34 million. The generosity of the package lent credence to the rumor that Murdoch wanted Diller out of his hair as much as Diller wanted to slip out from beneath Murdoch's expansive wings.

As Diller pointed out to the press, he celebrated his fiftieth birthday the same month he retired from Fox. At the half-century mark, he was fabulously wealthy but strangely dissatisfied at the same time. For the first time since he was a young boy in Beverly Hills, Barry Diller had no place to go and nothing to do the following morning. For the first time in more than three decades, Barry Diller was out of a job.

CHAPTER 18

BARGAIN BASEMENT SHOPPING
WITH BARRACUDAS

ALTHOUGH DILLER SUDDENLY found himself jobless in February 1992, he was not totally inactive. His greatest concern outside of his professional life was the AIDS onslaught that was devastating the lives of more and more of his friends in the entertainment industry. Until this time, AIDS was still regarded as a disease that struck homosexuals and intravenous drug users primarily. However, the AIDS-related death of heterosexual actor Brad Davis in 1991 had shattered the complacency of those who thought they were immune to the pernicious ailment.

That same year, Diller and MCA president Sid Sheinberg pledged $125,000 to create Hollywood Supports, an organization dedicated to combating the twin problems of homophobia and the AIDS epidemic. In 1992, thanks largely to Diller's influence over Sheinberg, MCA/Universal became the first studio to extend health insurance benefits to the partners of gay employees.

"It was just the right thing to do," Sheinberg said. Diller had been unsuccessful in convincing Murdoch to do the same at Fox.

Diller also gave his support to Commitment to Life, an annual benefit established by Elizabeth Taylor to raise money for AIDS research. The first benefit was held at the Bonaventure Hotel in Los Angeles in 1985 and raised more than $1 million for the cause. Barry Diller co-chaired the event in 1991. In 1992, Diller's long-time friend David Geffen officially came out of the closet by announcing he was gay to an audience that included Barbra Streisand, L.A. mayor Tom Bradley, Billy Joel, Eddie Van Halen, Natalie Cole, and hundreds of others.

For years Geffen had maintained that he was bisexual, and he merely wanted to set the record straight. Others said Geffen had little choice but to admit openly what the press had been insinuating for some time, before the media succeeded in driving him out of the closet. Calvin Klein, who was perhaps closer to Geffen than even Diller was, claimed that Geffen's baring of his soul was an epiphany for him.

"He just seemed so relieved," Klein said afterward. "He felt he could be a role model. Gay men are not necessarily thought of as the shrewdest businessmen in the world. He felt he should do this publicly as well as for himself, and he's really much happier."

Diller was present at the inauguration of Calvin and Kelly Klein's East Hampton beach front home in the late summer of 1991, along with Diana Ross, Sandy Gallin, Billy Joel and his wife at the time Christie Brinkley, *Rolling Stone* publisher Jan Wenner and his wife (whom he subsequently left for a male lover), and other guests. Barbecued ribs and chicken, roasted potatoes, and Caesar salad were served buffet style around a huge dining room table.

The night was cool, and tall white candles flickered in the breeze that wafted through the open windows. Rock 'n' roll played on the stereo until late in the evening, when Billy Joel stepped up to the black grand piano in the living room and treated everyone to an impromptu performance.

Diana Ross joined him for a song before the night was over. All in all, it was a memorable occasion for Diller, as he commented to the author, one that reminded him how fortunate he was despite the frustrations in his professional life.

Diller's immediate circle of friends included Calvin and Kelly Klein, David Geffen, Sandy Gallin, Diane Von Furstenberg, and author Fran Liebowitz, who had recently joined the group. But there was tension in their midst, largely because of the resentfulness of Kelly, who was uneasy with Calvin's friends from his days as an active homosexual. Diller remembered a Thanksgiving dinner at the Kleins' house, during which Kelly fumed visibly and refused to engage in the repartee that swirled noisily around the table. Diller had liked her initially, but once she was married to Calvin, it seemed that her major goal was to isolate him from his old friends.

However, hosting AIDS fund-raising events and attending dinner parties with friends were not enough to keep Barry Diller fully engaged. Not one to remain idle for long, it was inevitable that Diller would cast about for new worlds to conquer. Since he was no longer willing to be a mere employee, his next move had to be big and dramatic, one that would propel him along the path he felt he was destined to travel. As all eyes in the media world began to focus on him, Diller felt the pressure. Half the people he knew were rooting for him to succeed; the other half secretly hoped he would stumble. He could not afford to make a wrong move. It was one thing to fail at a job working for someone else, and quite another order of magnitude to take the plunge on your own and find out you were in over your head.

Whatever course Diller chose was going to require the support of outside investors. He needed to court people with deep pockets who believed in him and his vision. The most obvious ones that came to mind were Diller's friend David Geffen, investment banker Herbert Allen, who had a history of brokering billion-dollar deals for other media titans, and cable king John C. Malone, with whom Diller had developed a solid working relationship. Any one of them could arrange the sizable financing Diller would need to buy a major media property.

"I wonder how many people are saying they're talking to Barry about becoming investors when they are really not," said an executive who had worked for Diller at Fox. "Only players talk to Barry, and nobody around here wants to be thought of as not being a player."

The rumors about what Diller might be up to next started to fly before the ink was dry on his departure contract with Murdoch. In March 1992, the analysts began to speculate that Diller would attempt to buy a major network. Maybe it would be NBC; then, perhaps, it might be CBS. And then there was Paramount. Everybody knew how Diller felt about his old nemesis Martin Davis and thought it was inevitable that Diller would try to buy the company he used to work for and kick Davis out in the street.

Asked to comment about the rumors, Diller said they were not worth commenting on. He claimed that the plans he was formulating were infinitely more interesting than that. What might they be? Diller's answer was his now-familiar gap-tooth grin and a cryptic shrug of his shoulders. Diller himself did not yet know what he would do next. He was more frightened about his future, he admitted to associates, than he had ever been before.

The potential investors were virtually tripping over themselves to be first in line to throw money at Diller. "I could find one hundred million tomorrow, no strings attached," said one Wall Street investment banker anxious to be part of a Diller deal. "There are a dozen institutional investors ready to go."

Every time Diller was seen in public with one player or another—lunch with Ronald Perelman in Beverly Hills, drinks with Herby Allen in Sun Valley, dinner in Los Angeles with Disney's Jeffrey Katzenberg—media analysts claimed to have an inside track on Diller's next move. Diller found himself both amused at and annoyed by the incessant speculation. It was flattering to be the focus of so much high-powered attention, but also a bit unnerving since he himself did not know when or where he was going to strike next. Diller knew he was going to take a gamble, but if he were going to gamble and fail it would be better to do it beyond the constant glare of publicity.

Of all the names being bandied about as a possible partner in Diller's next deal, the one that made the most sense and caused the most excitement was John C. Malone, the high technology–oriented CEO of Denver-based Tele-Communications Incorporated. TCI was the nation's largest cable operator, controlling 23 percent of all cable households in 1992. TCI's attraction for Diller was the enormous cable channel space it could offer throughout its cable TV systems.

Diller had gotten to know Malone well at Fox, where the two collaborated on a number of joint ventures. TCI had granted Fox affiliates favorable positions on local cable channels; in return, TCI benefited from its hookup with a national broadcast network.

If Barry Diller was a shark in the medium in which he operated, John C. Malone was a barracuda ever in search of prey. Diller and Malone circled each other warily, each not quite trusting the other but always regarding him with enormous respect. Diller knew he could work with Malone after coming to the conclusion that it is far better to cooperate with a formidable potential adversary than to unnecessarily engage him in combat. Diller and Malone were more alike than different, and each had something the other wanted. The synergy between the two men was dynamic.

Diller's primary concern as he put together a strategy for his next move was finding a multibillion-dollar backer who was also willing to grant him the autonomy he wanted. After all, he did leave Fox in order to become, finally, his own boss. But finding someone to support him financially without wanting a measure of control would not be easy.

As a Wall Street analyst put it, "Anyone who would give Diller the billions needed to buy something like Paramount, for example, isn't going to just give it to him. There will be strings attached. So he may have to refocus his sights."

Diller's first move after his retirement was to raise some cash of his own. In August 1992, he petitioned the SEC for permission to sell about $33 million worth of notes that he had acquired during his tenure with Fox. According to Diller's filing statement, he had paid cash for the notes with the understanding that he could sell all or any portion of them at any time. The notes were zero coupons, meaning they did not make ongoing interest payments. Diller bought them at a discount from face value, and they accrued interest at an annual 7.75 percent rate until the year 2002, when they could be redeemed for $66 million.

The securities were also convertible into the common stock of News Corporation, which pushed their potential value above $66 million if the common stock were to rise in price. However, Diller had already trimmed his 2,000,000-share position in News Corporation to under 900,000 shares by August 1992. He had little faith in Murdoch's ability to elevate the common share price (mistakenly, as it turned out; Murdoch not only survived his financial dilemma but went on to put News Corporation in the black). Diller was primarily interested in raising cash wherever he could for a purpose only he was privy to at the time. In a separate transaction, Diller sold back to Murdoch his 25-percent stake in seven Fox television stations.

Amusingly enough, Diller did hang on to one toy he acquired during his time at Fox. Unemployed though he was, he found it almost impossible to part with his elegantly outfitted corporate jet. Whatever he did next, he would still have to commute. A man of Diller's stature could hardly be expected to hop aboard the Metro-liner when he had to travel to a meeting.

Diller's purpose in raising cash became clearer as the summer of 1992 gave way to fall, and fall to early winter. In December he made a move that was stunning, not because of its grandiosity, but rather because of its puniness. Everyone had expected him to make the big play—a $1 billion-plus assault on Paramount or one of the networks. Instead, he announced that he was casting his lot with QVC Network, the nation's largest home shopping network—but only a home shopping network, nonetheless.

Home shopping? And Barry Diller?

It was so déclassé, so trashy, so mundane. Here was Diller the Beverly Hills brat, Diller the sophisticate, Diller the world-striding icon who rubbed shoulders and broke bread with international style- and trend-setters, buying into an enterprise that appealed mostly to the bridge-and-tunnel crowd inhabiting the boroughs and states surrounding Manhattan, and their counterparts across the country. What the hell was going on? No one could figure it out. Hollywood was agog. Wall Street was amazed. And Diller was mum about his intentions.

He announced that he was investing a paltry $25 million to acquire a 3 percent sliver of QVC's common stock. His long-term plan became slightly clearer a few days later, however, when Liberty Media, controlled by none other than John C. Malone, and Comcast, presided over by Malone's buddy Brian Roberts, declared that they were giving Diller voting rights over their joint 35 percent ownership position in QVC. Suddenly, Diller's deal, which appeared puny at first glance, took on more panache with Malone and Roberts entering the mix. Malone did not make trivial deals. Malone was a player, a mover and shaker, a big league operator who occupied the same playing field as Ted Turner, Rupert Murdoch, and other titans of industry. Diller's deal looked more and more like a single move on the chess board that was an integral part of a grand strategy.

At the time QVC, based in West Chester, Pennsylvania, was one of the fastest-growing companies in the United States. It was founded in 1986 by Philadelphia businessman Joseph M. Segal, who enlarged the company into a billion-dollar enterprise with a fat profit margin in just six years. Now Segal was slated to retire, and Barry Diller would replace him as chairman and CEO early in 1993. Thanks to Malone's large block of voting shares, Diller was receiving options on 6,000,000 shares of common stock exercisable at $30 per share, plus 160,000 shares of restricted stock. Diller's total compensation package had the potential to put upwards of $100 million in his pocket over time.

Barry Diller was no longer jobless. "I made a twenty-five-million-dollar bet, and I've placed it on cable," Diller said with a grin. "The significant developments in the future are going to be in that arena."

The arena he was talking about comprised a brave new world of signal compression, interactive media, and video on demand. To Diller, QVC was a springboard into a multichannel, interactive program environment that analysts were touting as the next generation in high technology. Malone, Diller's de facto partner in the deal, presided over a string of cable networks that included the Discovery Channel, Black Entertainment Television, the Family Channel, and others.

The synergy among Comcast, Malone's TCI, and QVC had the potential to provide cable viewers with more than 500 different channels offering pay-per-view programs, home shopping, banking, investment, game playing, and various interactive activities. The joke making the rounds in 1992 was that Diller had become a convert to this new high-tech religion after receiving his first laptop computer. Sources close to Diller said that their previously computer-illiterate boss had been mesmerized by his new toy and spent hours in his office exploring its many capabilities, as well as its application to cable television.

Skeptics wondered just how great the demand was likely to be for 500 channels pouring into living rooms when viewers already had trouble deciding what to watch on the existing thirty or forty channels. For example, pay-per-view movies would have to be priced pretty low to compete with $2 rentals at the corner video store. Home shopping could also be accomplished merely by picking up the telephone. Diller and Malone, however, were convinced the demand would materialize if viewers were offered a menu of creative programming choices instead of the mindless drivel to which they were constantly subjected.

More astute observers recognized a greater plan in the works behind Diller's investment in QVC. They viewed it as the first step in the eventual merger of QVC with its major rival, the Home Shopping Network. Their view was confirmed a few weeks later when John Malone's Liberty Media offered $150 million in cash and stock for HSN.

"It sort of signals a blueprint of what's going to happen," said Donaldson, Lufkin & Jenrette analyst Dennis H. Leibowitz. "They merge the two companies, QVC survives, and Diller draws up product to fill the 500-channel environment."

Suddenly, Diller's bargain basement shopping spree took on the aspects of something much bigger and bolder.

CHAPTER 19

SHARPENING HIS KNIVES
FOR COMBAT

IN APRIL 1993, Barry Diller sat down at a conference table with three other high-octane media titans to explain how the world was going to work during the next few years. Joining Diller at a multimedia conference at the San Jose Convention Center in California were Bill Gates, chairman of Microsoft; John Sculley, who then headed Apple Computers; and John C. Malone, Diller's ally at TCI. Whether these four men worked together or went their separate ways, many observers were convinced that they were going to have an inordinate influence on the information revolution that promised to transform the way most mere mortals lived, worked, and entertained themselves.

Malone talked about the coming convergence of computers, entertainment, telecommunications, and publishing. Homes, he said, were going to be wired with high-capacity communications links and computers that would be able to sift through an endless variety of audio, video, and text information stored on central network computers or servers. Anyone wishing to watch a movie, go shopping, read a newspaper, talk to friends and relatives, buy stocks or mutual funds, play a game, check out the weather a thousand miles away, or deposit money in her checking account had only to click a button on the remote control.

None of this was going to be quick, easy, or cheap according to Malone. The revolution, if it was going to succeed, would require a sophisticated new lineup of products, programs, and services that were still only in the development stage. He described these cross-industry alliances as "seven octopuses, all with their hands in one another's pockets." Some octopuses had deeper pockets than the others. Each one had "eight arms, which meant there might not be enough pockets to go around."

The analogy was colorful and apt, and Malone had no doubt that his octopus would get its fair share, and then some, of the profits. "The cable industry is the locomotive for these technologies," he said, "because we're the guys with immediate applications and the revenue to drive this thing."

His prescience was nothing short of amazing considering what has transpired during the ensuing decade and a half. The Internet—the so-called Worldwide Web—was not even a glimmer in the public's eye at that time. Most companies, let alone households, were not yet hooked up to it. E-mail was nonexistent, and even voicemail was a rarity in some corporations, where secretaries answered the telephone before they were called administrative assistants. The technological explosion that has occurred since Malone uttered those prophecies has propelled humanity leap years beyond where we were fifteen years ago.

Barry Diller concurred with his friend and financial partner. QVC was an integral part of his and Malone's grand strategy, as much for QVC's delivery potential as for its home shopping venue. Diller would be a direct beneficiary of Malone's $2 billion plan to wire nearly all of his ten million cable customers with fiber optics, the most ambitious installation of cable in the world.

The other octopuses at the conference, Sculley and Gates, also planned to find enough pockets in which to insert their own tentacles. They intended to develop and build the set-top cable box that was required for much of what Malone and Diller discussed. They also wanted to provide the software for the servers that would store and distribute the information and entertainment.

"The network will be preferable for most things," Gates said at the conference. This was a startling admission coming from a man who had extolled the virtues of CD-ROM only a short time before. Invented as recently as 1984, CD-ROM had been promoted as the primary vehicle for delivering a panoply of interactive multimedia software designed to enhance text-based computers. Now, turning on a dime as it were, Gates was sounding the death knell for this hugely successful technology and its replacement by the Internet and the Worldwide Web.

The next step in Diller's long-range plan occurred a month later when QVC granted him stock options worth nearly $140 million, a windfall he was expected to reap within the next year and a half. With QVC trading at about $56 a share in May 1993, Diller's options allowed him to buy $340 million worth of stock for about $200 million. The options put the icing on an enviable compensation package for QVC's new chairman, who threatened to revolutionize retail shopping with the combined marketing clout of QVC and HSN.

"I think we will end up with a competitive powerhouse in the broader retailing industry," Diller said.

In his view, home shopping was going to become a giant industry, stealing market share away from the giant department stores that anchored urban and suburban shopping malls. Diller viewed home shopping as an important part of the interactive technology that he, Malone, Gates, and Sculley were forecasting as the wave of the future. Home shopping was a cash cow, a great generator of immediate profits that could finance some of the more visionary projects, which would take longer to pay their own way.

To many, the concept seemed bizarre. Zircon rings and crude costume jewelry sold on television were going to constitute the cutting edge of technology? However, Diller was not nearly as enamored with the idea of selling low-class junk as he was with the potential for other venues. Over time, the electronic emporium was destined to challenge stores and shops as a more effective supplier of the merchandise craved by consumers. Efficiency and information were the twin pillars of Diller's plan. Consumers wanted more information because they wanted to spend less time shopping.

Diller had some numbers to back him up. In 1993 shoppers spent an average of seventy-two minutes on a shopping trip compared with ninety minutes a decade earlier. Moreover, while actual shopping trips had become shorter, the amount spent each time had grown larger.

With time pressures increasing throughout society, all the activities people engaged in had to be more efficient. The average person no longer had time to dawdle. People wanted their news NOW! Their sports and weather NOW! Stock reports, financial transactions, vital information NOW! And when they needed to shop, they did not want to fight traffic jams and waste an hour or two driving back and forth to a store just to buy a pair of shoes. Everyone was looking for instant gratification. Everyone was more impatient than ever before. This was the need that Diller hoped to fill at QVC/HSN. Efficiency driven by impatience driven by pressures on people's time leading to the brave new world of tomorrow presided over by Diller, Malone, and a handful of fellow visionaries. Or so he hoped.

"Shopping is not entertainment," Diller said (he would later change his mind). "It's a quest for information, that's what it's all about. People shop for information about prices, colors, features, fashions, trends. Then they make a decision and move on to the next piece of business."

Without doubt, Diller had invested his money in a growing enterprise. Both QVC and HSN had been in business less than a decade and had combined sales of more than $2 billion a year, enjoying an annual growth rate of nearly 20 percent. Shopping center sales generated $800 billion a year in total revenue, indicating that Diller still had a long way to go before he put a significant dent in that market. Many were not convinced that he would ever do it.

"It will be a supplement to going to the store, not a substitute," said retail analyst Monroe Greenstein of Lazard Frères.

The line of apparel that Diller sold on television appealed primarily to hefty older women who, presumably, did not look forward to the humiliation of going out in person to try on tent-like clothing. Greenstein and others maintained that physically fit people of all ages actually enjoyed trying on clothing made for them to get an idea of their fit and feel. Perhaps the new technology would divide the nation into two broad camps: fatties ordering their muumuus via home shopping, and the fit and slender checking themselves out in mirrors at the mall. QVC and HSN had developed their markets by asking viewers to describe any bodily peculiarities, such as bulging waists and sagging derrieres. That way, everyone could be fit to size without leaving the sofa and the bag of chips beside it. It was a formula that had worked well so far.

In September 1993, Diller made the move that everyone had expected him to make after he cut his ties to Fox. He changed direction abruptly and indicated that he was about to go after his old employer Paramount. Wall Street lowered its proverbial eyeshade and got ready for the war it had been anticipating for a year or more. No one loved a good fight more than financial traders did, and the ensuing battle between Barry Diller and Martin S. Davis, who still headed Paramount, promised to be a classic struggle. It would pit titan against titan, ego against ego. The bad blood between the two men was out in the open, and Barry Diller was a creature driven by strong passions and lusts. In this instance, he lusted after revenge.

The first foray against Paramount was actually launched by the unpredictable Sumner Redstone, chairman of Viacom. With Paramount officially in play, Barry Diller could hardly sit on the sidelines and allow somebody else to snatch his prize away from him. But Diller could not do the deal alone. He needed the help of John Malone. First he needed to convince Malone that the synergy was precisely right for their joint enterprise, and more important, he had to convince Malone that his interest in Paramount was more than a personal vendetta.

The numbers made sense. Paramount was the last of the great old studios to go on the auction block. It was a ripe plum ready to be plucked. Paramount's film library could serve as a major source of programming for Malone's TCI, as well as the combined delivery capacity of QVC and HSN. Programming was the major weapon Malone lacked in his fierce rivalry with Time Warner. If he continued to show weakness in that key area, he would eventually be subsumed by the huge conglomerate.

Barry Diller understood only too well the clout of Paramount's movie and television business, having developed it himself over a decade. Acquiring Paramount would put Diller and Malone a giant step closer to their goal of establishing a fifth television network. So, while the appearance of revenge entered the picture (although both Diller and Davis vehemently denied that it was so), Malone could see for himself that the deal made sense for everyone concerned.

In order to succeed, Diller and Malone needed the right stock market conditions and a forgiving regulatory environment. Malone had battled in the past with politicians who viewed him as a symbol of an arrogant and greedy cable mogul running roughshod over consumers with rate increases and lousy service. Recent court decisions had gone Malone's way, however, bolstering his position. In early September 1993, a U.S. District Court in Washington, D.C., ruled that the government had no right to limit the number of subscribers a cable operator could serve.

Since Viacom's bid for Paramount was primarily a stock swap, a decline in Viacom's share price would turn off Paramount shareholders, who would be receiving nonvoting shares of Viacom. Wall Street arbitragers were buying shares of Paramount, driving up their value, and selling short Viacom stock in an effort to depress its price. In essence, the traders were hoping to encourage a rival bid for Paramount to fatten their own wallets. Wall Street cowboys love nothing better than a bidding war that drives stock prices either into orbit or into the toilet, since they hope to profit by being on the right side of each position. As Viacom's stock fell closer and closer to $50 a share, one trader could barely contain his excitement.

"The party's over," he said, meaning another bid was sure to emerge.

Sumner Redstone gritted his teeth in fury when he saw what was happening. He was a risk-taking businessman who once crawled out of a window onto a ledge to avoid a fire in Boston's Copley Hotel and subsequently underwent thirty hours of intensive surgery. He snapped at the others, "This deal is not going to be torn apart by anybody. Period!" He looked over his shoulder where Barry Diller and John Malone were salivating a few paces behind him.

Complicating the issue further was Diller's close relationship with investment banker Allen & Company, which had supported Redstone in his 1987 takeover of Viacom. Diller could offer a stock deal of his own, using QVC stock as collateral since its price had doubled during the short time Diller had taken control of the company. Making Paramount an even more enticing target was its debt-free financial structure. This meant its considerable assets could be leveraged to raise much of the money needed to buy the company.

Diller, Redstone, and Malone were not alone in their interest in Paramount. Standing in the wings waiting to pounce was Atlanta buckneer Ted Turner, who also lusted after Paramount's extensive film library. Turner had confided in friends that he was "hellbent on lassoing" Paramount into his media empire. Martin S. Davis wanted Ted Turner even less than he welcomed a bid from Barry Diller. Diller was the devil Davis knew and despised, but at least he had worked with him before. Turner was a brash outsider with a loud voice and a mountain-sized ego. Davis would rather break bread with Genghis Khan than do a deal with Ted Turner.

"By God," Turner boasted exuberantly to a friend, "we're gonna get it."

Turner, who was known alternately as Ted the Terrible, the Mouth of the South, and Captain Outrageous, was in a good position to offer a stock deal for Paramount since he controlled 51 percent of the Turner Broadcasting System. His financial advisers included the top honchos at Merrill Lynch and Apollo Capital, who had the expertise to slice and dice a lucrative deal in ways most financial wizards had not even heard of.

Diller and Malone struck first with a $9.5 billion bid, mostly stock, for Paramount. Turner was viewed as the dark horse in the takeover derby because he was already saddled with far more debt than either Diller/Malone or Redstone, which hampered his ability to take on additional debt to finance a more attractive offer. He approached Diller about making a combined offer, but Diller shot him down in short order. Diller liked Turner even less than Martin Davis did, which was no secret to anyone who knew them, and though he viewed the brash Atlantan as a brilliant visionary, he regarded Turner as essentially undisciplined, unpredictable, and impossible to work with. Even on a personal level, Diller did not care for Turner much at all.

To his own consternation, Turner had also been involved in tender offers for New Line Cinema and Castle Rock Entertainment when Paramount was put in play. Paramount represented bigger spoils, but Turner had no way to back out of the other bids quickly or gracefully. One Turner associate compared his boss to a spoiled child who grabbed for a lesser toy because he could not afford the one he wanted, only to discover afterward that he could actually have afforded his dream toy had he waited a little longer.

"Paramount is one of the last great entertainment companies," said another source close to Turner. "If it happens to be in play, you have to think twice before letting it go. It's a valuable prize. Every entertainment company would have to be taking a hard look at it."

Prior to Barry Diller's bid for Paramount, Martin Davis had grown so paranoid about the lineup of suitors for his company that he did the unthinkable: he swallowed his pride, picked up the telephone, and invited Barry Diller to lunch at Paramount's headquarters in New York City.

The two men met on a hot, humid day in late July and shook hands stiffly for the first time in a decade. Davis wasted little time with formalities. No sooner had the two men sat down at a table in Davis's private dining room than Davis broached the subject directly.

"What about these rumors that you want to make a bid for my company?"

Diller sat back and remained noncommittal, refusing to tip his hand about his intentions. Davis fumed visibly. Lunch was served, and both men picked at their food, paying little or no attention to what they were eating. Davis did most of the talking, questioning Diller nonstop about the rumors. Diller shook his head back and forth, neither affirming nor denying Davis's assertions. He was sorry he had accepted the luncheon invitation. There was absolutely nothing to be gained from it. Davis was as impossible to deal with as ever. The trip to New York had been a waste of time.

Without warning, Davis pushed his chair back and stood up, looking down at Diller. His face was purple, the veins in his neck appeared ready to burst. Davis pointed his finger at Diller and screamed, "I know you're coming after me! Don't deny it! I know you're coming!"

Davis turned and stormed away, almost knocking the waiter down as he raced from the room.

CHAPTER 20

REAL PREDATORS EAT TOUGH
GUYS FOR BREAKFAST

BARRY DILLER WAS in a pensive mood in September 1993, as reported by several sources, pacing back and forth in the living room of his sumptuous apartment in the Waldorf-Astoria Towers, high above Manhattan. The struggle for Paramount was his first taste of battle in a takeover war, and Diller was worried about being outmaneuvered and routed by Sumner Redstone, the veteran chairman of competing bidder Viacom. Diller did not yet know it, but Redstone was already in the process of filing an antitrust suit against Diller and his financial backers.

All week long, Diller had been meeting with investment bankers and Wall Street analysts, trying to convince them he was a serious player in a league with Redstone, Ted Turner, and Rupert Murdoch. Noted for his abrupt, some said rude, ten-second telephone conversations, Diller found himself in the uncharacteristic role of having to be pleasant toward people he would rather not even talk to. Diller's ego was huge, but the egos of Wall Street financiers were humongous. Before they agreed to raise the huge sum required for takeovers of this magnitude (notwithstanding the millions they earned for their efforts), they insisted on having their asses kissed first.

Diller had little choice but to go along with the unpleasant charade, unappealing though it was. Diller strode to and fro nervously as he expounded on his reasons for wanting to acquire Paramount. "I'm not a great believer in the mostly meaningless usage of 'synergy,' but for us," he said, speaking also for his partner John C. Malone, "investing in interactivity is part of our lifeblood. We really are doing it because we have to."

Barry Diller was sensitive to suggestions that he was pursuing a personal vendetta against Martin Davis. He had been going out of his way lately to be less solitary and tense, to be seen in public more than he had been in the past, and to lay to rest the reputation he had earned as a late-night devotee of notorious watering holes such as the old Studio 54. Two nights earlier, on September 22, Diller was all smiles as he sailed through a crowd of 1,000 cable industry executives at the New York Hilton, with Jane Fonda on one side and her husband Ted Turner on the other. Anyone might have thought that Barry Diller was running for public office instead of engaging in combat with some of the leading financial warriors of the modern era.

One criticism in particular that ruffled Diller's feathers was that he sometimes created bottlenecks at the companies he worked for because of his penchant for micromanagement. Some viewed him as a corporate version of former President Jimmy Carter, who was compelled to get intimately involved in every decision that affected his benighted administration, no matter how trivial it was.

"Not true," said Diller. "I've matured. I'm fifty-one, and I've grown beyond micro. I demonstrated it at Fox, and I think I'm demonstrating it at QVC. I intend to demonstrate it in the future."

Diller needed to come up with $3.5 billion in cash according to the terms of his bid for Paramount. Two billion were already accounted for; half of it would come from Malone and the other half from Paramount's own cash reserves. (In leveraged buyouts, the target company's cash reserves could be used for a down payment.) That left $1.5 billion that Diller had to raise on his own.

"Is there anybody in the world who doesn't think I can borrow one billion, one and a half billion?" Diller asked rhetorically, a line he had used over and over again to convince Wall Street that he had the "juice," as Diller liked to call it, to do the deal.

Diller already had detailed plans drawn up for Paramount once he captured the prize. First, he would sell its television stations to comply with federal guidelines prohibiting ownership of cable systems and TV stations in the same market. While QVC did not own any television stations, its acquisition partners, Liberty Media and Comcast, did. Next, Diller planned to spin off Paramount's theme parks, which were only marginally profitable, and beef up the studio's publishing enterprise.

As far as top management was concerned, Diller refused to tip his hand. Obviously, there was not enough room at Paramount (or in the western hemisphere) for both Barry Diller and Martin Davis. Davis would have to go. Anyone who knew Diller had little doubt that the peppery executive would execute a complete makeover in the management ranks, weeding out deadwood and installing his own people in key areas.

By the middle of October, Diller had raised the extra $1.5 billion he needed to complete his deal. The seed money was pledged by a consortium comprising banks, Cox Enterprises, and Advance Publications. The number of partners Diller now had on board made him look like a polygamist. Some critics wondered why Diller wanted to buy Paramount in the first place if it meant having so many anxious faces peering over his shoulder. How much control would he actually have in this type of relationship? Diller claimed he was not worried. He would not proceed without bona fide guarantees that he could run Paramount as he saw fit.

Diller's primary concern was that Sumner Redstone would up the ante, forcing Diller to match any new bid or fold his hand. "Diller's got more cash if he needs it," said a Diller associate, "but this is a pretty good start. He's not going to do anything more until he sees the reaction to all this."

Politics and war make for strange bedfellows, and financial wars are no exception. Diller's foray against Paramount forced Martin Davis to choose sides, and the shark he opted to swim with was Sumner Redstone. Davis's position was unenviable at best. His fiefdom was about to be sacked by two marauding armies, and his only viable option was to decide which one he would rather be pillaged by. To Davis, the rough-and-tumble Redstone, who held no personal animosity toward him, was preferable to the razor-fanged Diller, who was out to flay his hide.

Redstone was not without formidable partners of his own. In addition to his own substantial assets, Redstone's marauding army included Nynex, the regional telephone company that pledged more than $1 billion to his campaign, and Blockbuster, Wayne Huizenga's video empire, which made a $600 million commitment. The lineup of raiders and allies in the battle for Paramount had become so complicated that Merrill Lynch analyst Harold Vogel commented, "You need a road map to follow it all." Paramount, following an acquisition, could be called either Paramount QVC Comcast Liberty Cox Advance Publications, Inc., or the Paramount Viacom Nynex Blockbuster Corporation, depending on which side won the war.

Two years earlier, takeover deals in the industry had been more straightforward. Sony bought Columbia from Coke, Matsushita bought MCA from its shareholders, Time bought Warner. By 1993, however, borrowing demands and the scramble among various players to be part of the emerging new technology had significantly altered the landscape.

"Companies can gain advantages from strategic alliances and avoid all the commitment of capital," said media analyst Jeffrey Logsdon of The Seidler Company in Los Angeles, in an effort to explain the latest rules of engagement.

The war over Paramount was complicated further by crafty strategic maneuvering on the part of Martin Davis, who was anxious to hang on to his own job. Since Paramount's cash reserves could be used by an acquirer to finance a takeover, Davis attempted to get rid of the money by making a $500 million cash bid for Macmillan Publishing Company, a major book publishing concern. Macmillan was still owned by Maxwell Communications, which had filed for bankruptcy following the suicide of the company's flamboyant founder Robert Maxwell. But both Diller and Redstone laughed at the defensive movement, claiming they had sufficient reserves of their own to acquire Paramount with or without its cash hoard.

Barry Diller responded by going over Davis's head. He appealed directly to Paramount shareholders by increasing the cash portion of his offer to just under $5 billion. Shareholders of an acquisition target ordinarily prefer cash to a stock swap because cash does not fluctuate in value, whereas new stock shares offered in exchange for those shareholders own in the target company have a nasty habit of plunging after a deal is consummated.

Suddenly, the ball was in Redstone's court. Will he call Diller's hand by upping his own bid, or won't he? That was the question that titillated Wall Street traders. Any increased bid would serve to drive the price of Paramount shares higher. Wall Street earns a good portion of its living on the "Last Fool" theory. Keep buying stock all the way up into the stratosphere, until you finally sell it to the last fool. The last fool then tries to sell it to someone else, only to discover that all the buyers are gone and there's no one left to sell it to. It's like a game of musical chairs—the last schmuck left without a seat loses all the marbles. The big challenge is to make sure that someone else is the last fool.

In an effort to raise the stakes higher, analyst Gordon Crawford of Capital Research, which traded media stocks for its own account and owned 8 percent of Paramount, issued a statement saying, "The Paramount board has been extremely unresponsive to an offer that I think is clearly, demonstrably superior to the current Viacom proposal. I think it's tremendously beneficial to shareholders to have a tender offer in which they can, in effect, state their preferences for which offer is superior."

What all that high-blown pontificating translated into was that the shareholders wanted more money, and Crawford's outfit was one of Paramount's leading shareholders. Let the last fool come forward with a basket full of money so Capital Research was not left holding the bag, he seemed to be saying.

Diller's tender offer went into effect in late October. Paramount's board was required to respond with a recommendation to shareholders within ten days, along with its reasons for preferring one offer over the other.

Martin Davis adopted a new defensive strategy to protect his company against Diller by creating a so-called poison pill provision in the form of new stock. Target companies will often flood the market with new securities—diluting the value of their shares—in an effort to thwart unfriendly suitors. The net result of this strategic maneuvering is to preserve top management's high-paid jobs while screwing the average shareholder. Martin Davis would continue to collect his multimillion-dollar compensation package each year, but Paramount shareholders' proportional ownership of the company would shrivel in size. The poison pill was designed to be swallowed only in the event of a Diller victory—it did not apply to Redstone.

As expected, Redstone countered Diller's move with a sweetened offer of his own. Both bids amounted to about $10 billion, but Redstone increased the cash portion of his bid, making it more appealing to shareholders. Barry Diller flew to Los Angeles from New York on Saturday, November 6, 1993, to meet with John Malone and his other partners. The war of nerves grew hotter, and tempers flared as the pressure mounted. One prominent family was split down the middle, much like families caught up in a civil war who support opposite sides. Viacom's chief executive Frank Biondi was firmly in Redstone's camp, while his investment banker brother Mike advised BellSouth about contributing as much as $2 billion to Diller's cause.

As the number of allies, partners, potential partners, and assorted bedfellows grew, Barry Diller began to fret openly about losing control of his deal. He was visibly perplexed and voiced his concerns on several occasions to key confidants. Publicly he presented his tough guy face, maintaining that he had the juice to run Paramount as he saw fit once he got it. In private, however, he was agitated, less cocky, less self-assured. The more he had to rely on partners to help him succeed, the more autonomy he would have to cede to them. In addition, the amounts of money involved had begun to overwhelm him.

"It's clear Diller has to raise his cash bid to more than five billion dollars," said Lisbeth Baron, who followed media stocks at S.G. Warburg.

Suddenly, Barry Diller was feeling a whole different dimension of pressure from anything he had experienced before. He was learning first-hand the difference between being a highly compensated employee and an empire builder in his own right. This was his first attempt to compete in the big leagues with real predators, and he was feeling the heat. He felt as though he were losing control of a situation for the first time in his life. The people he was consorting with now demolished mere tough guys and left them bleeding on the side of the road. He began to doubt his own ferocity, his stomach for the fight. Never before had he doubted his own ability to come out on top.

The ball was now in Diller's court. The next move was his—his and his backers, who now included Home Shopping Network, TCI, Liberty, Comcast, Cox, Advance, and BellSouth. It was an unwieldy coalition that was starting to come unglued. How long could Diller hold it together? Every time he made a move, Sumner Redstone, who was now in his mid-seventies and still spoiling for a fight, turned up the pressure, testing his mettle, trying to see what Barry Diller was made of. What was Barry Diller made of? Diller, who had always had supreme confidence in his own abilities, would find out for himself before too long.

CHAPTER 21

THEY WON, WE LOST, NEXT

DESPITE HIS SELF-CONFIDENCE, that sinking feeling in the pit of Barry Diller's stomach had to unsettle his sense of equilibrium to a great extent. Could it be he was losing his juice, his love for the fight? Diller's shaky psyche was much in evidence in November 1993 during an auction for antique Asian art, which was one of his major passions outside of business. Ordinarily he plunged ahead, spending whatever it took to acquire a particular work he coveted. On this occasion he dropped out of the bidding, allowing a rare painting to elude his grasp after a competitor topped his bid by a few million dollars.

"Unless you can lose with grace, you're a fool," Diller said, tipping his hand about his campaign for Paramount more than anyone realized at the time.

As Diller's gamble to seize control of Paramount began to falter, he found himself playing the unlikely role of underdog to the tenacious Sumner Redstone, a man more than twenty years older than Diller with a cast-iron nervous system. Diller turned increasingly to friends and confidantes for advice, something he had done in the past only on rare occasions. Fran Lebowitz was one friend who sought to bolster his spirits. Privately, she did what she could to comfort him psychologically, and publicly she had nothing but praise for him.

"Barry's a daredevil," she said. "I've never seen him happier. I told him he's glowing. He looks like he just got back from three weeks on the beach."

If Barry Diller was glowing, it was because he was red with embarrassment about the prospect of dropping out of the race. This was his biggest test yet, an attempt to break out of the second tier of powerful studio executives into the front rank of real killers like Rupert Murdoch and Ted Turner.

During the process of trying to make the transition, Diller had begun to feel that maybe he was being outclassed. His stage until now had been the rough-and-tumble, somewhat brutish world of Hollywood-style negotiation through intimidation. The major players operated in a more sophisticated, buttoned-down realm of subtle financial homicide. They all had a genius for slipping a stiletto between your ribs as they dazzled you with humorless smiles and watched you die with stone-cold eyes.

Was Diller up to this level of combat? The only thing he was sure of was that the financial altitude was beginning to make him dizzy.

He found himself a star player in a takeover saga reminiscent of the wildest days of the 1980s. Diller and Redstone were the key combatants in a media industry civil war, complete with peripheral skirmishes and mega-million-dollar lawsuits involving other participants. As a new combatant on this turf, Diller suddenly became the most closely watched corporate executive in America. After spending most of his life in someone else's shadow, he was now encircled by the spotlight of publicity and felt uneasy in its glare.

Typically for him, Diller jetted back and forth from coast to coast at a frantic pace, from his Malibu beachfront bungalow to his suite at the Waldorf Towers. Most of the time Diller traveled alone in his private jet, crisscrossing the country a half dozen times in November alone, then commuting in his helicopter across the Hudson River from Manhattan to QVC headquarters in Pennsylvania. Still a physical fitness maniac at fifty-one, he worked out every day, bicycling down Park Avenue in a bomber jacket with "Barry" scrawled across the front and "The Simpsons" on the back.

Diller lived with a telephone glued to his ear. Associates complained of talking into dead air, thinking Diller was still on the phone after he called them, only to discover that he had hung up abruptly after bombarding them with instructions. Diller was notorious for calling aides and associates three, five, seven times a day, early in the morning and late at night, peppering them with rapid-fire questions and comments, then hanging up and dialing the next number on his list.

"He talks so much and so fast, sometimes he can't remember who he talked to last," said one QVC executive. "Then he withdraws into a shell for a long time. You can almost see the wheels turning, the devils churning inside him. It's as though something's alive inside, eating him up."

Meetings with bankers and lawyers involved in the takeover deal kept Diller up as late as 3 A.M. in New York City, only to find him at work at his desk in Pennsylvania four hours later. In the midst of this insanity, of this frenetic pace that would have landed less hardy souls in the hospital, Diller still maintained an active social life on both coasts.

One day he was at a New York Public Library reception for well-known photographer Richard Avedon, and the next day he flew to Santa Monica for the bar mitzvah of Hollywood agent Michael Ovitz's oldest son. Two days later he was back in New York, attending a party to celebrate Edmund White's biography of Jean Genet at the Tribeca home of artist Ross Bleckner, where he chatted incessantly about his pet beagles and his love of motorcycles, fast cars, skiing, and bicycling.

Some regarded this hectic schedule as his attempt to get away from some of the demons that tormented him. In the back of his mind, he knew even then that he was going to lose the battle for Paramount. "I never thought we had more than a fifty-fifty chance of getting Paramount," he said. "If we don't get it, there will be other opportunities." His comments seemed more designed to mitigate his own disappointment than anyone else's.

Through it all, there were many in the investment community who appeared to be more optimistic about his chances in acquiring Paramount than Diller was. Media investor Mario Gabelli, who ran a family of mutual funds under his own name, was convinced that Diller had what it takes to do the big deal. "Barry has demonstrated that he can put global resources together to acquire a major asset," said Gabelli.

Diller would not admit it to anyone, but the fear of losing control over Paramount should he get it had begun to weigh heavily on him. His two major partners, John Malone and Brian Roberts, president of Comcast, were not the problem. "John Malone and Brian Roberts deferred to Barry and treated him as an equal," said an executive close to all of them. "BellSouth is a different matter."

While BellSouth's top executives had a high regard for Diller and his ability to run Paramount, Diller's style rankled their sensibilities. To many of them, Diller was a cultural oddball, a Hollywood freak set loose in the staid world of investment banking. "He's very histrionic, very theatrical in the way he presents everything," said Charles "Buddy" Miller, vice president for strategic planning at BellSouth.

Diller frequently lost his temper at meetings with lawyers, bankers, and accountants. Many of them did not realize at the time, however, that his tantrums were often staged for effect at critical moments in lengthy discussions. Very often he would deliberately shock a roomful of high-octane professionals into a stunned silence to win negotiating concessions.

"I understand you don't want to give me everything!" he often screamed during a lull in negotiations. "But just tell me one thing you will give me, just one thing!" That ploy often lulled the opposition into thinking he was willing to settle for crumbs. In reality, Diller usually walked away from the table with an extra concession on top of many others he wanted. However, BellSouth's conservative culture troubled Diller as much as his flamboyance bothered the company, and Diller began to feel that BellSouth was using him to get its hands on Paramount, only to shunt him aside later.

Brian Roberts of Comcast was particularly impressed by Diller and learned a lot simply by observing him. Brian was the thirty-five-year-old son of Comcast's founder Ralph Roberts, and he was widely regarded as a worthy heir to his father's media empire. Those who dealt with him considered him to be shrewd, tough, competitive, and financially savvy.

Brian was primarily interested in elevating the cable business he inherited from his father to the next level, the rarified realm of a mega-media conglomerate. Comcast had gone on a buying binge in 1992, acquiring two cellular phone providers in the northeast, making it the fourth-largest cellular company in the United States. Cellular accounted for about 20 percent of Comcast's total revenues.

Since cable companies were also interested in entering the telephone business, the synergy among telephone, cable, digital wireless, and other technology companies was expanding exponentially. The area where Comcast was weak, however, was in programming, and that's where Barry Diller and QVC came in. Diller had the programming talent and ability to add extra voltage to Comcast's communications clout. Roberts was interested in drawing Diller more deeply into Comcast's orbit and then helping him develop a popular programming lineup to feed Comcast's cable pipeline. Diller needed the financial backing of Malone, Roberts, and the other players whose goals were in sync with Diller's, so the complicated relationship came full circle. The idea of letting Paramount slip away, along with the chance to even the score with Martin Davis, was like a knife twisting in Diller's stomach. Yet, as badly as he wanted the big prize, he was afraid it would elude him in the end.

As far as Davis was concerned, it was clear that he was headed for defeat no matter which side came out on top. If Viacom won, Davis would get to enjoy a psychic victory over Diller, but he would be forced out by Redstone sooner or later. There simply was not enough room for two monumental egos like Davis's and Redstone's at Paramount's helm. But while Davis favored Redstone for personal reasons, his board of directors was pulling him toward Diller. With stock prices where they were in January 1994, Diller's bid was worth nearly $10 billion, about $500 million more than Redstone's. Unless Redstone was willing to sweeten the pot, the directors had little choice but to recommend going with the highest bidder.

Davis put the best face he could on the situation, denying his strategy to forge a deal with Viacom would end in failure. "I don't think it's a failure in the long term," Davis said. "If you go back to what we started to do in 1983, we've been consistent in what we've done. We have built shareholder value. We built a superb company, as evidenced by the fact that we have an auction going on. Somebody wants it and is willing to pay a steep price."

Obfuscation rather than eloquence was Davis's strong suit. One of the players who wanted to buy Paramount was Barry Diller, whose advances Martin Davis welcomed with the same warmth he would have had for a warthog in heat chasing him. It was all Davis could do to keep from clenching his teeth whenever the subject of Diller was raised. "I have spent most of my professional career here," Davis said, "so I'm not prepared to just leave tomorrow. I will stay on as long as I can."

Davis was unapologetic about his attitude toward Diller. "I had a style," he said. "I make no apologies for it, and I could be very tough about it, and I would insist on certain things because I wanted this company to survive. Now, some of us had differences of opinion, and I dare say Barry Diller was not the only one who left. The only difference is that in the motion picture business in Hollywood, if somebody gets a scratch, right away it's cancer. If this was a machine tool company, nobody would give a shit about me and Barry Diller. If you put us in the ring in Madison Square Garden, twelve people would show up, all of them from the press."

As it turned out, Davis did not have to worry about Diller leaping for his throat as soon as he got his arms around Paramount. Redstone turned up the heat on Diller by spicing up his own offer, and Diller responded instinctively with a terse comment that summed up his psychological state of the past few weeks.

"They won, we lost, next."

Diller's bravado in the face of defeat was a gutsy public act, particularly since he was churning inside with the humiliation of losing his first major battle in the big leagues of takeover lottery. Diller stuck out his chin defiantly and stared down the press with his riveting blue eyes, but he was all aquiver after months of grueling combat. What he needed more than anything else was a private place to go off by himself and lick his wounds.

Redstone's victory was made possible by an esoteric financial product developed by Smith Barney, Redstone's main adviser, which pocketed a $30 million fee for cementing the deal. The product that Smith Barney unveiled on Redstone's behalf was a complex package of securities that protected investors against a decline in the issuer's stock price. The package comprised two call warrants, a debenture, and a contingent note structured in a way that also reduced the issuer's tax liability. In other words, what Smith Barney put together for Viacom was an ingenious basket of securities that allowed Viacom to cushion its own stock price and receive a tax write-off while doing it. So when Paramount's board rejected Redstone's bid in favor of Diller's higher offer, Redstone was able to counter in January 1994 with a kicker that boosted Viacom's stock, thereby raising the total value of Redstone's offer. It was nothing less than a stroke of financial genius for which Barry Diller had no answer.

CHAPTER 22

NOT A DIME
MORE THAN $10 BILLION

VIACOM'S VICTORY IN the battle for Paramount ended an epic five-month war that was one of the hardest-fought and longest-running takeover sagas in American corporate history. In the end, Sumner Redstone won more than 90 percent of Paramount voting shares in the proxy contest against Diller. Redstone took home some of the crown jewels of entertainment from the battlefield, including Paramount's film and television studios and a library of almost 900 pictures. It was a classic 1990s-style struggle that reflected the merger mania sweeping the media industry in the quest for programming to channel onto the electronic superhighway.

Time had all but run out for Sumner Redstone. Suddenly, on the afternoon of Sunday, January 16, 1994, Redstone sat down for a "skull session," as he called it, at a conference table on the forty-ninth floor of Smith Barney's offices in midtown Manhattan. Joining him were Robert Greenhill, Smith Barney's chairman; Michael Levitt, a thirty-five-year-old whiz kid who had a scheme, he said, that would "blow Diller out of the ballpark"; and other top-level executives of both firms.

Levitt presented his package of securities, which he referred to as a contingent value right, or collar, that would guarantee the value of Viacom's bid if its stock failed to reach a certain price within three years after a merger with Paramount. In a worst-case scenario, the collar would cost Redstone an additional $1 billion beyond his current bid if Viacom's stock languished. If the stock price rose above the fixed level, the collar would cost nothing.

"It's too risky," Redstone said.

Greenhill rose from his chair and began pacing around the room. He had anticipated Redstone's response and was prepared to deal with it. Thirty million dollars in potential fees were at stake, $30 million that would evaporate into thin air if Redstone allowed Diller to clinch the deal.

"Look!" Greenhill snapped. "Do you want to win this thing or not?"

Redstone conferred privately with Frank Biondi, Viacom's president and CEO, and both agreed that the collar was their only viable option if they were going to outflank Barry Diller. Redstone decided he wanted Paramount badly enough to adopt whatever measure was called for to snatch the prize away from Diller. On Thursday, January 20, four days after the meeting at Smith Barney, Redstone announced he was raising the cash portion of his bid by $3, to $107 a share, for just over 50 percent of Paramount, and then he added the collar as his trump card.

"We wondered what Barry would do," Redstone said. "Barry had said he would not raise his bid again, and I believed him."

As it turned out, Redstone had sized up his opponent correctly. Diller had already told confidants that his last offer was final; he would not go any higher. However, few outside Diller's inner circle believed he would fold his hand at this point in the game. As he approached the eve of his fifty-second birthday, Diller was within a hair's breadth of pulling off the deal of his lifetime—and settling old scores with Martin Davis while he was at it. Diller was too tenacious, too daring to give up now. It was now or never for Barry Diller, said those who claimed to know what made him tick.

Several weeks earlier, Diller had taken off for a Caribbean vacation on a rented yacht named *Midnight Saga*, with ten pounds of Paramount financial documents for company. While he cruised in the water off St. Bart's, according to several sources, he picked his way slowly through reams upon reams of financial data related to the company. At the end of his sojourn in paradise, Diller concluded that Paramount was not worth a dime more than $10 billion.

"When I came back on January third," Diller recalled, "I said we're not going to exceed our offer. The company is, with a real stretch and some real hard work, worth what I've offered, but I'm not going to offer any more. It would have been irresponsible, I thought, and I held to that belief."

Not all of Diller's allies agreed with his position. Top executives at BellSouth, which had put up $1.5 billion toward a Paramount acquisition, and Diller's chief financial adviser, Bruce Wasserstein, urged him to counter Redstone's latest offer with a collar of his own. Diller weighed their suggestions carefully, then rejected them in the end. "A collar just doesn't make sense," he insisted, arguing that a stock market collapse would only force QVC to dilute the value of its stock and hurt shareholders.

Putting the interests of shareholders before his own was an honorable position to take, but there were deeper currents rippling beneath the surface. Diller had enjoyed an insider's view of Rupert Murdoch's *modus operandi* at Fox, and he had witnessed close up how a massive debt load nearly bankrupted an otherwise healthy corporate enterprise. It was true that Murdoch had saved his empire in the end after his death-defying financial gambles almost destroyed it, but Diller was not willing to expose his own company to such a high level of risk.

Killer Diller, as it turned out, lacked the ruthlessness of the Rupert Murdochs, Ted Turners, and Sumner Redstones of the world. The war for Paramount simultaneously brought out both the best and worst aspects of Barry Diller's nature. He had been tough, shrewd, and evil-tempered at various times during the five-month-long battle, but his basic decency and integrity kept him from capturing the prize he coveted more than anything else in the world.

Sumner Redstone celebrated his triumph in late February 1994 with a victory dinner at New York's famous 21 Club. It felt good to unwind after "the cruel, abusive, and sometimes ridiculous battle for Paramount," Redstone said. Redstone, Frank Biondi, and two other Viacom executives raised their champagne glasses in a well-deserved toast.

"Here's to us. We won," Redstone said simply, relieved that the frustration, stress, and animosity of the past few months were finally behind them.

Redstone's victory was not without an ironic element. In winning the bid for Paramount, Redstone did to Viacom what Barry Diller refused to do to QVC; he saddled his company with $10 billion worth of debt that dealt a heavy blow to the company's shareholders and financial backers. Later, Redstone admitted that he paid $1.5 billion more for Paramount than he thought the company was worth when he began his campaign. Viacom's stock went into a tailspin after the merger, hammered down by institutional investors and financial analysts who reevaluated the terms of the deal in the sobering aftermath of the war, only to decide they did not like what they saw.

Redstone's bargaining position was shakier right up to his moment of victory than anyone, including Diller, knew at the time. Had Diller been aware of the financial maneuvering taking place behind the scenes in the enemy camp, he might have been able to strike a preemptive blow before Redstone finally topped his bid.

Just before Christmas 1993, Wayne Huizenga and Steve Berrard of Blockbuster, one of Redstone's key allies, had demanded a separate collar to protect Blockbuster shareholders in the event the deal turned sour. Blockbuster was slated to be acquired by Viacom as part of its takeover of Paramount in exchange for $8.4 billion in cash and a lot of Viacom stock. Huizenga and Berrard wanted their own insurance for the stock portion of the deal, but Greenhill of Smith Barney turned them down on the grounds it would put Viacom's acquisition of Paramount in jeopardy.

"No collar, no deal!" Berrard had insisted.

Without access to Blockbuster's healthy cash flow, Redstone would not be able to pay the interest on his Himalayan debt after he bought Paramount. Both sides played hardball over the next few days until the impasse was broken on Christmas Day. Michael Levitt, Greenhill's point man in the negotiations, reached Berrard on a golf course in Arizona from the car phone in his Jeep Cherokee in New Jersey.

"Steve, let's talk," Levitt said.

Levitt set up a conference call with Frank Biondi, who was vacationing in Scottsdale, Arizona, and two other Viacom executives at their respective homes in Houston, Texas, and the Hamptons on Long Island. "How can you guys not agree on this?" Levitt pleaded.

"What would you say if you were advising Blockbuster?" Berrard countered.

Levitt softened his position and offered Berrard a short-term collar for Blockbuster, protecting the company's shareholders against a decline in Viacom's stock price for one year following the acquisition. Berrard was noncommittal, stating that he would talk to Huizenga and a few other people at Blockbuster and get back to him.

"Viacom's stock sucks right now," said John Melk, a Blockbuster director, when Berrard explained the terms of the collar to him, "but this is a tremendous deal."

Together, Berrard and Melk recommended the collar to Huizenga, the real power and empire-builder at Blockbuster. Huizenga talked openly about creating his own fiefdom in Florida, a de facto separate country complete with its own laws and regulations covering everything from planning and zoning ordinances to codes of behavior. In an earlier age, Huizenga would have challenged Alexander the Great for world domination. He began his business career with a single garbage truck, created a billion-dollar company called Waste Management, which became the largest waste removal company in the U.S., and then parlayed that into his video rental empire. At fifty-six, Huizenga considered the septuagenarian Redstone and calculated that he would be running the entire Paramount/Viacom/Blockbuster kingdom by the time he was sixty, according to several analysts. "It's a go," Huizenga told Berrard and Melk. "Let's do it."

In one sense, Barry Diller succeeded in weakening Redstone and his allies as potential adversaries for years to come by forcing them to assume such heavy debt. Servicing the interest on the debt while simultaneously trying to manage their sprawling new empire would strain their combined talents and energy for the next three or four years. This would give Diller an opportunity to scout the playing field for new areas of conquest.

Within days of conceding defeat, Diller reorganized QVC, expanded its electronic retailing operation, and developed new interactive services including an online computer shopping enterprise. Diller did nothing to squelch persistent rumors that he would strike quickly at another target, perhaps Time Warner or Universal Studios, which was owned and badly managed by Matsushita.

"We're not going to talk, comment, or hint about any future issue," Diller said cryptically, fueling the speculation that swirled about him. "When we've got something to say definitely, we'll say it."

All Diller knew for certain at that moment was that Paramount and other American film studios were quintessential dream machines, and if he could not afford to buy one on his own terms, he was determined to build one himself.

When Diller failed to strike quickly following his photo-finish loss to Redstone, the media soon grew tired of speculating about his next move and turned elsewhere with their insatiable appetite for hot new stories. The truth was that Barry Diller was mentally and physically drained after the grueling battle for Paramount, and he needed time to let his batteries recharge. The incessant barrage of questions about what he was going to do next had become irritating, particularly since he was not quite sure himself. Diller kept a low profile during the spring of 1994 and finally surfaced on June 8 at a broadcasters' convention in New Orleans, where he delivered the keynote address to 4,000 delegates from the television industry.

Diller strode erectly to the podium, looking more tanned and rested than he had in months. He gripped the lectern with both hands, his bald head shining under the lights as he surveyed the audience through glinting blue eyes. In an earlier age, he might have been a Roman general declaiming his vision about the future of the empire to the packed halls of the Senate. In the late spring of 1994, dressed in an impeccably tailored suit, he conveyed the manner of a latter-day contender for the throne who had been scarred but not irreversibly defeated in corporate warfare.

"This languid, delicious city may move at a slower pace," Diller said, "but it is out of step with the wild run the world of media and communications is fast becoming, seeping through into almost every part of society, everyone running in place, busier and busier, life moving faster, getting more complicated and hectic. We work harder, longer, we travel further, faster. Decisions are based on tons more data, contradicting and conflicting with one another. Life is getting infinitely more complicated. Instead of illuminating and making our lives easier, modernization and technology are leaving us mostly confused."

The audience was quiet, almost hypnotized. It was clear this was not going to be an ordinary speech. It was more an incantation, a call to arms, and a philosophical treatise all in one. Four thousand industry delegates, who had hoped to glean some hint of what direction Diller would veer off in next, sat transfixed. The speaker had them in his grip.

"The average American is literally bombarded daily with facts and opinions, products and promotions. Each year the endless morass is a little less effective, each year it makes people a little more insecure about their effectiveness, their ability to influence events, to take action, to react to events. . . . What is really distressing is that while we are getting more and more information, we find it increasingly difficult to know what's going on."

It was hard to know where Diller was going with this, where he was leading the crowd. The audience was still, wondering if he was going to reveal any secrets about how they could all do their jobs more efficiently, how they could stay ahead of the competition nipping at their heels.

"We depend upon the news for factual balance—television, magazines, talk radio, all these reporters and pundits pumping up every story, tearing it apart and then dropping it. Remember the War on Drugs?

Does anyone know who the current Drug Czar is? Or if we even have one? Or what about the radon scare? Or global warming? The media are both contributors to and victims of this explosion. They are simply crying for attention. And the public, dazed and over-stimulated, only hears the loudest voices. Even our language is exploding. Since 1966 we've added more than 60,000 words to the English language. As consumers and as providers of information and entertainment, we need help!"

Yes, but they still didn't know what it all meant. The audience sat on the edge of its collective seat, wondering if Barry would wrap it all up for them. You could almost hear the brain synapses popping in the skulls of delegates throughout the convention hall.

"Remember the old days when we all sat down to watch one of three networks? We used to have a remote control with two buttons on it. It was called the clicker. Now it has seventy-six buttons. No person's finger is thin enough, and very few brains are fat enough to work these things. And what are you watching on TV? Thirty-six channels? Forty-seven? Ninety? Twenty years ago there may not have been a lot of diversity, but at least we sat down and watched. Now we do not have the slightest clue what is on unless we thumb through *TV Guide*, which is taking on the weight of the *Yellow Pages*. We don't even watch anymore, we surf. And why not? How are we supposed to categorize all these options and then choose?"

A wave of panic rippled through the audience. It was true, horribly true. But what was the industry supposed to do about it? It was all so confusing.

"When I left Fox two years ago and was wandering around the U.S., I was thinking about these things. Just what was going on in entertainment, communications, computers, and technology? And did they in fact have an interrelationship? When we find an easy, national way to send information back and forth that is powered by a smart computer, we will open up the world. We will not go from seventy channels to the 500 that scare you, but to one channel. This channel will access thousands of possibilities and opportunities. You will be able to edit your own information, watch the television shows you want to watch, and buy anything at any time at the best price. You will get back the clicker with just two or three buttons on it, and the machines will tailor all these available choices to your life, taste, location, and income."

Now the crowd was numb. "One channel," did he say? It sounded like One World Television, which sounded something like One World Government. How could you have thousands of choices to make by turning on one channel? It didn't seem to make any sense. Barry Diller had succeeded in giving everyone a Killer Diller–sized headache.

"This is not an elective, we have no option. Getting to this simplified future is not going to be easy. The jargon alone can kill you. Asynchronous transfer modes. Multi-user dungeons. How about moos or rasterbators? We've gone from megabytes to gigabytes to terabytes, from infobahns to infobondage, and from bauds to broadband to boredom."

For the first time since Diller started to speak, there was an uneasy stirring in the audience. Once rapt, the delegates shifted as one in their seats. The men pulled at their ties, and the women tugged at their skirts. A collective suspicion appeared to emerge that Diller, the crafty old con artist, was just fucking with their minds.

"What should be understood is that all this nonsense will sort itself out, but it will not be easy. There is, in front of us, a radical revolution coming in information, and how we process it will affect all of our lives forever. We are now at the most terrible time, the apex of confusion in this technological revolution. Also making this difficult to comprehend is the cacophony of noise coming from many of the players. Those who are supposed to be guiding us into the future are more often confusing us with pronunciations that make little sense."

They seemed to get it now: Barry was basically talking about himself. They were dreaming if they thought that Barry was going to clear up the confusion for them.

"So what are we going to do? Is there a principal idea strong enough, big enough, simple enough to pull this all together?"

Finally! The audience grew quiet once again. Was he actually going to give everyone some answers to the questions he raised?

"I think there may be. Look at the development of the personal computer for a hint: word processing and spread sheets. They each did one simple thing, but it was a very powerful simple thing, and you just could not do it anywhere else as easily. Now, think of frustrations with information, with television viewing, with shopping. What is the linkage? What are the possibilities?

"I think that they lead to one simple thing: smart agenting. Linking a computer and its power to search, find, and help us sort through this complicated world . . . that is what I call smart agenting. Using it to gather the data for only what we need or want to know. Using it in television entertainment and shopping by giving us choices based on our interests and needs. Smart agenting would do the homework for us in each of these areas, homework for which we are hopelessly ill-equipped today."

So that was it, the punch line. Smart agenting! Computers linked to the individual brain of every single human being on earth.

"It could be linked to an information system that culled and collated the things you wanted and needed to know, and it could also tell you that it had stored the program you would have missed otherwise. It would already know everything about you: what you like and what you do not like, what you can afford to pay and what will not kill you to eat. It will tell you where to go wherever you are. It will give you a clear map to get there in a millisecond."

This sounded uneasily like a Brave New World of the Supercomputer as God, the Supercomputer that knew everything there was to know about each one of us, a smart agent that told us what programs to watch based on our personal tastes, that told us which restaurants to go to based on our personal finances and gastrointestinal systems, that took us by the hand and led us through life like some disembodied Big Brother leading children through the wilderness.

Many in the audience stared at one another apprehensively. Was Barry Diller advocating a One World Collective, an Orwellian-Platonic Lobotomized Utopia, or was he warning everyone against it? Did Barry

Diller want to preside as Lord and Master of it all? Was he serious, or was he just pulling everyone's chain?

Diller peered out over his audience as the hall echoed with a hearty round of applause, his familiar gap-tooth smile firmly in place, his bald dome shining lustrously, and a slightly fiendish, somewhat diabolical glimmer illuminating his eyes. Those looking for a definitive answer about whether Diller was advocating, or warning us against, his vision of the future would have to figure it out for themselves.

Today, with the benefit of fifteen years' hindsight, the age of cookies in our computers, tracking devices on our automobiles, and electronic identity cards in our wallets sounds eerily like the Brave New World Diller talked about in 1994. Big Brother knows everything about us, everything we are doing. Diller and his friend John C. Malone had positioned themselves as the Nostradamuses of our time.

CHAPTER 23

RALPH AND BRIAN TAKE BARRY TO THE WOODSHED

IF BARRY DILLER really expected to rule over an Orwellian world of lobotomized programming one day, the next move he announced seemed to be nudging him in a different direction. In early July 1994, one month after his speech in New Orleans, he appeared at a press conference along-side Laurence Tisch, the Machiavellian chairman of CBS. Diller and Tisch could almost have passed for twins with their matching bald pates and wide, humorless smiles cemented in place. They had called their joint press conference to announce that CBS intended to acquire 53 percent of QVC in a so-called merger of equal partners. Tisch would be chairman of the combined entity, and Diller its president and CEO.

"Barry will be the boss," Tisch said through a humorless grin.

Those who knew Larry Tisch well could only shake their heads in disbelief at the notion that he would ever play second fiddle to anyone. It was apparent to everyone who knew him that Tisch had something else up his sleeve in agreeing to a partnership with Diller. CBS was in big trouble, mismanaged from the start by Tisch who first began accumulating stock in the network nine years earlier. Tisch's interest in luring Diller aboard his foundering enterprise was obvious: QVC's chairman brought credibility to CBS at a time when Tisch's lunch was being eaten by Rupert Murdoch, who had enticed eight CBS affiliate stations over to the Fox network. But some analysts suggested that Tisch had a grander scheme in mind than a partnership with Diller—namely, that he was really using Diller as bait to solicit a bid for CBS from someone else.

"CBS had to do something to break out of the doldrums," said Paine Webber media analyst Christopher Dixon. "With this move they enter the modern age, albeit laughing, kicking, struggling, and crying. They are now where they need to be to compete in the rapidly developing broadcast world of the nineties."

"CBS is clearly in play," said analyst Bruce Thorp of PNC Bank, meaning that Tisch had succeeded in using Diller as a lure. "This deal implies that it's open to all corners."

Tisch fumed at the notion that there was more than met the eye about his public embrace of Barry Diller. "This company will not be shopped," he said. "This deal will not be shopped. We are not selling. We are simply merging two companies, and it's a genuine merger." Adamant as Tisch appeared to be, Wall Street could only laugh at the idea that Tisch would not consider a better deal with a potential buyer.

At the same time, most observers refused to believe that the normally wary Diller would have allowed himself to be manipulated so transparently by Tisch. Hungry as he was to sit on top of a media empire of his own, Diller was simply too smart to be bamboozled by another wily septuagenarian hammered from the same mold as Sumner Redstone. As badly as Diller appeared to want the deal to succeed, it was a long road between the public announcement and the official closing.

"It's not as though the boards of directors are coming in tomorrow to ratify the merger," said an executive close to both Diller and Tisch. "They're not getting together for another ten days. You've got the July Fourth weekend in the middle. What do you think is going to happen over that time? A lot of meetings. You can name ten possible suitors for CBS, all the studios that can afford a five- or six-billion-dollar deal, plus telephone companies. How many is that right there?"

The best guestimates on Wall Street put the price tag on CBS at somewhere between $6 billion and $7 billion. There was little question that CBS, with all its missteps over the past seven or eight years, was an attractive target for such behemoths as Disney, the regional Bells, and even Diller's old nemesis Marvin Davis, who had already expressed interest in buying NBC.

CBS under Tisch had developed a lineup of popular shows, such as *60 Minutes*, *Murphy Brown*, and *David Letterman*, that initially boosted the network's ratings. However, CBS failed to follow these successes with a new generation of programs that could expand its popularity to a broader segment of the viewing public, particularly to the nation's youth. In addition to losing several of its key affiliates to the Fox Network, CBS also suffered a major blow when Fox acquired the rights to the NFL football games, which had been a CBS franchise since 1956. Then Larry Tisch blew a strategic opportunity to force the cable systems to accept a CBS cable channel in return for transmission rights to the network's programming.

As one industry observer said, "CBS could have gotten a cable channel for almost nothing. They would just have to have invested some start-up money. But to Tisch it didn't mean anything because he doesn't feel it in his gut like Murdoch or Diller does. He walked away from every deal he was presented. He has no vision about what the mass media business is going to be, no feeling for where the future is."

CBS's institutional investors were harsher in their assessment of Tisch's leadership, viewing him as a shopkeeper rather than an entertainment visionary. Rush Limbaugh joked that there were "three major networks—four if you count CBS."

By 1994 Larry Tisch's CBS had begun to look like an aging athlete who had passed his prime and lost his competitive edge. Its core programming was still solid, but the network had failed to meet the demands of a changing marketplace. It was an enterprise in need of resuscitation. Tisch had become disillusioned, drained by month after month of misadventure and declining ratings. He needed someone with vision who knew the business inside and out to step in and overhaul his network or, barring that, a buyer with deep pockets to come along and relieve him of his mounting burden at a considerable profit to himself.

Enter Barry Diller.

It was Larry Tisch's son Danny who first approached Diller through one of Diller's lawyers, Martin Lipton. Diller was talented and hungry and anxious to redeem himself after his defeat by Redstone. Diller took the bait, first offering to buy CBS for terms that were unacceptable to Larry Tisch. Then Tisch, a wily negotiator if not a media genius, countered with his own proposal for the merger. Diller's acquiescence in the deal gave Larry Tisch the boost he needed, thanks to Danny Tisch.

"Diller will create synergy," said Bichap Cheen, an analyst with Kagan Associates. "He'll wear three hats: the network hat, and there he's a Hall of Famer; the programming hat with good, cheap programming; and the merchandiser hat, which has never been worn at CBS with great authority. He'll merge two favorite American pastimes: shopping and watching TV."

Aside from pulling Barry Diller into his orbit, Tisch would also gain access to QVC's bulging cash reserves—assuming that Tisch's primary goal of inciting a bidding war for CBS failed to materialize. QVC's revenues rose 14 percent during Diller's first year at the helm. The company was largely regarded throughout the industry as a lucrative cash cow, even if a trifle déclassé standing on its own. Diller, of course, tried to change QVC's image of an electronic flea market with his quest for Paramount. With that failure behind him, CBS struck Diller as his next best means of elevating QVC into the realm of mainstream entertainment.

According to one of his executives, "When Barry went to QVC, he saw it as a platform for making a big, transforming acquisition."

In that regard, Diller needed Larry Tisch to help him move on to his next goal as much as the older man needed Diller to keep him from going under. The big question was which man stood to gain the most.

"Larry gets to walk out, not as a failure but as someone who took the company and turned it around," said Merrill Lynch analyst Harold Vogel. "Diller is Tisch's exit strategy."

If Diller was perplexed over the charge that he was being used by Tisch for Tisch's own purposes, he showed no signs of it. "This is a good fit for both of us," Diller said. "Sometimes who is using whom is strictly a matter of interpretation. Sometimes a deal is exactly what it appears to be, a good arrangement for both parties. Not every deal has a winner and a loser. In some instances, everybody wins. This is one of those times."

Perhaps, but more often than not in business, as in warfare, someone wins and someone loses. In his desire to close the deal, Barry Diller made a strategic blunder by failing to enlist the support of his financial backers, primarily John Malone and Ralph and Brian Roberts. Had he done so, Diller would have discovered that they had less enthusiasm for an alliance with Larry Tisch than Diller did.

On July 8, 1994, seventy-four-year-old Ralph Roberts and his thirty-five-year-old son Brian summoned their investment bankers from Lazard Frères, Steven Rattner and Felix Rohatyn, to Comcast's headquarters in Philadelphia. Comcast sent the company jet to fetch Rohatyn from his retreat in the Hamptons, and Rattner flew in from his house on Martha's Vineyard. When the two financial dynamos arrived in Philadelphia, Roberts senior and junior immediately told them of their concerns.

"We don't want this deal with CBS," said Ralph Roberts. "We need to stop it."

The only way to stop Diller, the bankers told them, was to buy Diller's company out from under him before the shareholders of QVC and CBS met to vote on the merger in two weeks. Once that deal was approved, Comcast's ownership of QVC would be sliced from 15 percent to less than 5 percent. The Roberts's influence over the combined entity would be diminished. In addition, federal regulations restricting cross ownership of TV stations would have further limited Comcast's participation. Malone had similar objections to the QVC/CBS merger.

Brian Roberts was troubled the most about doing anything to undermine Diller. "Are we doing this only because we're angry?" he kept asking.

"Brian was very taken with Barry," said an executive close to both of them, "because when Barry turns on the charm, he can be quite impressive and effective. You have this older guy and this younger kid, and what really must have hurt is when Barry did an about-face. If he had gone to the Robertses and made them feel a part of the CBS deal, this might not have happened."

"You have to give Comcast credit," agreed a consultant to the company. "When Barry was on the line for Paramount, Brian Roberts killed himself to support Barry. He worked the phones, he worked the press, he worked the investment community. He was an extremely loyal and effective ally in Barry's biggest battle. When a guy does that and the next thing he does is turn around and screw him, it's not easy."

Brian and his father placed a phone call to Diller at 2:00 P.M., according to one account, hoping to arrange a meeting with him at his apartment in the Waldorf. Diller's secretary informed them that Diller was en route to New York City from Los Angeles with CBS entertainment president Howard Stringer and other network executives. Diller's plane was scheduled to land at New Jersey's Teterboro Airport in about four hours. With Rohatyn's help, the Robertses drafted a letter to Diller notifying him of their desire to buy his company, and quickly left for Teterboro to meet Diller's plane.

Diller's private Gulfstream jet touched down on New Jersey soil just after 6:00 P.M. When he stepped onto the steaming tarmac, Diller froze at the sight of Ralph and Brian Roberts standing there waiting for him. As soon as Diller saw their expressionless faces, he knew something had gone awry. Brian looked down at the ground as his father handed Diller the letter. Diller read it slowly, digesting the terms of their offer to buy the remaining 85 percent of QVC that Comcast did not own for $44 a share, $8 more than QVC shareholders were to receive in a merger with CBS. Diller excused himself from his CBS entourage and followed the Robertses to a conference room in the terminal.

"It isn't a complete surprise," Diller said in resignation. "I'm surprised a bit at the lateness of it, but it doesn't come as a surprise. I don't consider it to be an evil act of any kind."

Once again, Diller had been blindsided by a strategic move he should have been able to foresee. Surprisingly, he accepted his fate calmly, almost reverently, admiring the deftness of the strike. Not so surprisingly, Larry Tisch was less sanguine about this new development when Diller called him from Teterboro to cancel their dinner engagement for later that evening.

"Hollywood couldn't have written a script like this," a spokesman for Tisch said the next day. "All these cable-cum-broadcasting people have three traits: they're phenomenally greedy, they're phenomenally jealous, and they're filled with a lot of hate for their competitors."

Tisch's reaction was understandable, considering that Comcast's preemptive bid for QVC dealt CBS a heavy blow. QVC had no other choice than to accept the highest bid for shareholders, and Tisch had to move immediately to keep CBS's stock price from plummeting into the abyss. Tisch announced a $1 billion-plus buyback of CBS shares to shore up the price and formed a strategic alliance with Westinghouse days later in order to acquire additional TV stations in major markets such as Boston, Philadelphia, and Baltimore. All in all, Tisch commanded the field like a true general, responding brilliantly to an assault that could have devastated his forces. He did not know much about running an entertainment empire, but he did know a lot about survival.

And Diller? Diller climbed into a limousine with Ralph and Brian and rode solemnly back to Manhattan with them to negotiate the terms of his surrender.

CHAPTER 24

FRIENDSHIP IS OFTEN BETTER THAN SEX

BARRY DILLER DID not walk off the battlefield empty-handed. The severance package he negotiated with the Robertses fattened his bank account by more than $100 million in profits on his original investment in QVC stock, a handsome consolation settlement by anyone's standards. But increasing his wealth was not his primary purpose in life, particularly at this advanced stage.

"Barry's not a pig," said his good friend Diane Von Furstenberg, who knew him better than most. "The money is a consequence but not his first goal. Barry has always fulfilled his dreams." Diane could be forgiven for defending her buddy, but the truth was Barry Diller had yet to fulfill his biggest dream of all: ruling his own media kingdom. Until now, he had always managed someone else's. At fifty-two years of age, with two failed campaigns for a major property now behind him, Barry Diller fought off the deepest depression of his life.

Wall Street analysts who had once touted Diller as the new Media

Messiah were perhaps the most disappointed of all. Hell hath no fury like an analyst whose forecast is derailed because he hopped aboard the wrong train. "Diller has done very little to impact the core business of QVC," griped UBS Securities analyst Peter J. Siris, who was clearly in a snit. "The stock price today would be higher if he hadn't joined it and the company had gone on its own way."

In reality, QVC's share price had more than doubled from the low-30s to more than $70 after Diller gained control of the company. Understandably, the stock collapsed after Diller's unsuccessful forays against Paramount and CBS, but the profits were there to be taken by all except those shareholders who chose to hang on for the very last dollar. As the Wall Street saying goes, "Bulls make money, bears make money, pigs get barbecued." Had shareholders sold half their shares when the price doubled, they would have turned a huge profit, even after the deals fell through.

Diller took his latest setback in stride, growing uncharacteristically reflective. "I came upon QVC one summer day two years ago. I had left Fox and was traveling around the country to think about what I would do next. I went to QVC's headquarters, and I watched in awe. A live television show on the air twenty-four hours, processing more than 130,000 telephone calls a day, tracking hundreds of millions of dollars in inventory.

"I stood there watching and thought, 'It's TV, it's not TV. It's computers, it's not computers. It's retailing, it's not retailing. It's advertising, it's not advertising. It's an odd art.' Today and for the next twenty years, those who are awake and able and willing will be playing a defining role in what is surely going to be a radical transformation of all we hear, see, and know. And what a piece of great good luck it will be to have been present at the creation."

Diller dreaming, Diller fantasizing about the future, Diller regretting what might have been, Diller disappointed about the way things turned out during the past two years, but Diller still undefeated, still planning his next move. Diller driven to succeed, to get up off the canvas and gather his strength for the next round, for the inevitable next battle that was just over the horizon.

While all the speculation about what he would do next swirled around him, Diller kept a surprisingly low profile. Forced into early retirement, with no office of his own in which to hang his hat, Diller spent most of his time analyzing his current situation. Clearly, he could not afford a third colossal defeat in the corporate takeover arena. Aside from the public humiliation, Diller's credibility with the money men on Wall Street would be damaged beyond repair.

In the spring of 1995, Diller surfaced at the annual Academy Awards extravaganza in Hollywood. Everyone who counted in the business felt an obligation to be seen and heard this time of year, and not at just any event. Any *putz* could wangle an invitation to one of the B-list parties, but making a prominent appearance at the right affair was crucial to one's career.

"The Academy Awards are an annual rite of passage, a social and economic boost in an industry in which the two are intertwined," said Women in Film president Joan Hyler. "Which parties you're invited to, and which ones you're not, say a lot about your standing in this town."

The mandatory first stop after the awards ceremony was the Governors Ball, which was held at the Shrine Auditorium with superstar chef Wolfgang Puck catering the $500-per-seat dinner. Appetizers featured "Jewish Pizza" topped with smoked salmon and caviar, spring rolls with lobster meat, and shrimp on skewers. The main course included filet mignon, lobster tails, and pheasant. However, in an effort to show how unconcerned they were about getting their money's worth, the truly elite usually passed up the gourmet offerings and ordered a tomato salad. Barry Diller went a step further and asked for half a cantaloupe stuffed with cottage cheese.

The two "in" parties afterward were *Vanity Fair*'s soiree at Morton's and Elton John's AIDS Foundation fund raiser at the Four Seasons Hotel. Diller made an appearance at both, exchanging fixed-smile pleasantries with President Clinton's former press secretary Dee Dee Myers, S. I. Newhouse, Jodie Foster, Quentin Tarantino, Tom Hanks, and Arnold Schwarzenegger, one of Hollywood's rare superstar Republicans. Others had included, at different times, such superstars as John Wayne, Charlton Heston, and Clint Eastwood.

Diller gave no hint of what he might be up to next during any of the festivities, so it came as a jolt to his confederates in Hollywood when he announced in August that he had bought a 20 percent equity position in a St. Petersburg, Florida, company called Silver King Communications. Most stunning of all was that everyone had been expecting a grand move on the scale of Paramount and CBS, and Silver King seemed so bush league. It was as though he had reverted to playing Double-A or Triple-A baseball after an unsuccessful season in the major leagues.

Silver King owned twelve UHF television stations in such top-tier cities as New York, Chicago, and Los Angeles, but they were all located in electronic Siberia, generating far weaker signals than those affiliated with the networks. What could Diller possibly want with such low-rent properties, the media world's version of the South Bronx or Duluth? He had to have a grand design in mind, a master strategy not immediately apparent to the naked eye.

"It's not always clear to the rest of us where he's going," said Jeffrey Katzenberg, a co-founder of DreamWorks SKG, the acronym for Spielberg/Katzenberg/Geffen, "but for his entire career, Barry Diller has been a pioneer and a visionary, able to see over the horizon. He's building another network that will be neither conventional nor predictable. When Barry steps up to the plate, he hits a grand slam."

Katzenberg's evaluation was more diplomatic than prescient. In reality, it was doubtful that hardly anyone else on earth had the foggiest notion of what Diller was up to, and Barry was not confiding in anyone. The idea that he could take twelve nowhere stations with channel numbers like 54 and 67 and turn them into a viable network, the way he had done with the Fox affiliates, was too farfetched to be believed.

According to Betsy Frank, executive vice president with Zenith Media in New York City, "Anybody who has any acquaintance with Barry knows that everything he does is a step up to the next level. But if it's a network he's after, it's going to be a lot harder to put it together than it was a few years ago. The environment has changed considerably. It's a lot tougher now. Who knows what he's really after? Barry doesn't show too much of himself. He's always been extremely guarded."

The stakes required to gain access to a major network were mounting every day. Most recently, the Walt Disney Company had paid about $19 billion for Capital Cities/ABC. If Diller had not been able to top the $10 billion Sumner Redstone spent to buy Paramount, he was hardly likely to raise double that amount to buy a network for himself in the current environment. That meant that he would have to build his media empire from scratch, which could be his only possible reason for investing in Silver King. But creating a truly competitive communications empire was going to require all the programming genius Diller had demonstrated throughout his career at ABC, Paramount, and Fox, plus a tremendous amount of luck and good timing.

As soon as Diller's move was announced to the public, his investment in the Florida-based company soared by 50 percent in a single day. Silver King's stock price jumped from $26 a share to almost $40 on Friday, August 25, 1995, fueled by speculators looking to hop aboard the latest takeover bandwagon. Barry Diller may have had trouble buying the companies he wanted, but he surely knew how to increase shareholder value by driving up the price of a stock. Mutual fund manager Mario Gabelli, who specialized in media stocks, coined a new word for the investment community to chew on.

"The stock had been Dillerized," Gabelli said, "by the mere fact of having Diller's name attached to it."

The rise in share value did more than increase Diller's net worth by a significant percentage; it provided him with greater leverage or borrowing power should he use his Silver King shares as collateral for future purchases. Diller would be better able to expand his reach in various markets by paying cable operators to put his stations on the low end of the dial.

"It doesn't matter if you are on UHF channel 86 if you appear on channel 11 on the cable dial," explained an executive close to Diller. This is where Diller's relationship with John Malone would come in handy, since Malone's TCI had almost twelve million subscribers.

"Malone's stations reach 30 percent of U.S. households," Diller said, tipping his hand more than was usual for him about his possible intentions at Silver King. "You establish local broadcast stations with entertainment, news, and sports, and as that is taking place, you begin network service."

That was the skeleton of his plan perhaps, but it was only a bare-bones sketch of what he hoped to build. The meat he needed to flesh it out with could only come from good, solid programming. This time around, Diller did not intend to compete against the networks with a better lineup of youth-oriented shows the way he did with Fox. Too many others had tried that formula since Diller's initial success, and the market had become overcrowded with "me-too" shows all trying to fill the same niche. In his latest incarnation as an empire builder, Diller intended to follow a different path by concentrating on local programming: local news, local sports, local entertainment, all eventually tied together in a national network of disparate stations satisfying regional needs. However, whether or not he could pull it off as planned was still open to conjecture.

Over the years, Diane Von Furstenberg had remained Barry Diller's closest friend and confidante. She had launched her own reputation as a fashion leader in the 1970s with the wrap dress, a sexy latter-day version of the toga. The genius of Von Furstenberg's creation was that the folds did, indeed, fall apart in all the right places, but just enough to show off a little thigh here and there, transforming the wrap dress into one of the sexiest inventions in modern history. It promised much, but most of what it delivered was in the eye of the beholder.

Von Furstenberg grew tired of the fashion game by the early 1980s and sold the rights to her designs for a royal sum, which allowed her to pursue her greatest love of all: handsomely designed coffee table books. For the next seven years, she built a new empire comprising oversized, high-priced, variegated, glossy books extolling the wonders of the modern bath and bedroom. This pursuit also showered her with great wealth, but in the late 1980s, Von Furstenberg grew increasingly embarrassed by the quality of the fashions that were being sold under her name by licensees. She reentered the fashion business in the early 1990s, creating new lines called Silk Assets apparel, Surroundings aromatherapy, and Color Authority sportswear, some of which she marketed successfully on Barry Diller's QVC channel. Diller and Von Furstenberg were more than good friends; they enjoyed a mutually rewarding business relationship as well.

One of the creations Diane Von Furstenberg was proudest of was the interior of Barry Diller's home in Beverly Hills. Von Furstenberg floated through the luxurious home she had decorated, stopping long enough to plump up a pillow, to light a scented candle, to adorn a table with a vase filled with yellow roses. Sunlight streamed through the windows in the sitting room off the veranda, illuminating the greens and golds with brilliant rays. Von Furstenberg was perennially sensuous even in advancing middle age, a more exotic Martha Stewart stripped of Stewart's New England crustiness. Diane was also an astute businesswoman who had recently teamed with Avon to market her line of sportswear.

"Your best salesperson is your customer, so Avon had a great idea when they started," she said. "Also, they gave an opportunity for women to make money on the side."

Her intention was to design one collection for Avon four times a year that would be worn by women selling her line to their friends and relatives. "The closer we can get the sewing machine and the cash register together, the better value we have."

Von Furstenberg's Silk Assets apparel line was a mind-boggling success on QVC, generating $1.3 million in sales in two hours and lending a veneer of style and class to Diller's electronic bargain basement. Their loyalty to each other was a refreshing departure from the rough-and-tumble, dog-eat-dog world in which they operated. In an age of skyrocketing divorce rates and allies turning against one another in multibillion-dollar wars for corporate spoils, Barry Diller and Diane Von Furstenberg proved that a good, solid friendship can sometimes be the most satisfying relationship of all.

At least for the moment.

CHAPTER 25

THE KING OF MARVIN GARDENS
REGROUPS HIS FORCES

THE DUST FROM mega-media takeover deals continued to swirl around Barry Diller as he moved to strengthen his hold on Silver King's ragtag TV stations. Michael Eisner, Diller's old protégé at Paramount who now headed Disney, had recently put the final touches on his acquisition of Cap Cities/ABC; Westinghouse was locked in talks with Larry Tisch to buy CBS following Diller's aborted bid for that network; and Ted Turner was engaged in foreplay with Time Warner's Gerry Levin as a prelude to the merger of their two companies. In the midst of this game of media-style musical chairs, Barry Diller was starting to look as if he could not find a seat.

Backbiting journalists referred to Eisner as the "new Sun King" and his former mentor, Barry Diller, as "no more than the King of Marvin Gardens." Wall Street insiders joined in on the Diller gang-up, with one investment banker stating, "Barry Diller has no credibility whatsoever. We've been burned too often." A media executive close to Diller said,

"Barry may be a great programmer, and he could probably do a pretty good job running a network. But the difference between a job like that and owning a media empire is like the difference between White Plains and New York City. The perception is that Barry's not up to it." Suddenly, Diller was being cast as a has-been, a nonentity in the media world.

However, Diller had been written off as an overrated child prodigy before, one who had grown up to be no more than a talented acolyte for the real media giants. And he had demonstrated time and time again that those charges were unjustified, that without his talent and vision the Rupert Murdochs and Martin Davises of the world would not have accomplished what they did. Diller's natural caution had held him back from achieving on his own what he had achieved for others. This time it was going to be different. This time he would assemble his own empire, piece by piece, station by station. Diller was going to do it his way, not by paying what he considered to be inflated prices for an existing media conglomerate that was already saddled with someone else's problems.

In November 1995, Diller joined Ted Turner, Robert Redford, and Brian Roberts in a panel discussion that opened the Western Cable Show in Los Angeles. The event got off to a fiery start as Turner and Diller attacked each other publicly.

"You can't be content. I'm worth a couple of billion dollars and I feel poor. You've been wandering around like the Children of Israel in the Sinai peninsula," Turner snapped at Diller, referring to Diller's job-hopping career.

"And you're going to take a job for the first time in your life," Diller shot back, belittling Turner's impending merger with Time Warner, where he was expected to play second fiddle to Gerry Levin.

Next Turner directed his barbs at Rupert Murdoch, who threatened to launch an all-news channel of his own to compete against Turner's CNN. "I'm looking forward to squishing Rupert like a bug," Turner said, grinning madly.

Then Turner tweaked Robert Redford, who regarded the proceedings with amusement from his own perch on the dais, about Redford's vagabond social life compared with Turner's state of wedded bliss with Jane Fonda.

"Well I don't have Jane," Redford quipped, "although in the past I did."

A hush fell over the conference hall as Turner glared at Redford, vibrating in his chair as though he might leap at Redford's throat and strangle him. After an awkward moment, Turner thought better of a physical response and smiled. "Maybe I should follow you around and pick up your discards," Turner said, defusing the tense situation.

Afterward, Rupert Murdoch took a jab of his own at Turner, saying that Turner's performance and his newly discovered liberal politics could be attributed either to Turner's "marrying Jane Fonda or giving up Valium."

Barry Diller tried to rise above the schoolyard posturing when he was cornered after the panel discussion by hungry newshounds eager to hear about his plans for Silver King. His new network would begin to coalesce sometime in 1997, he said. "You can't do networking backwards. You have to have a prepared localism," he said somewhat cryptically. "When we built Fox, our first successes came from our owned and operated stations." He appeared to be implying that programs such as *America's Most Wanted* had been successful in local markets before they were widely syndicated, and that was how he intended to build his new network—from the bottom up. In other words, take what is already popular in Duluth and introduce it to the national market instead of creating national programming first and imposing it on localities.

Notwithstanding their attempts to taunt him for his recent failures, Diller's competitors still regarded him as a threat and studied his every utterance for clues to where he was heading. "Barry Diller put it best when he said, 'Everybody's eyes are in everybody else's world right now,'" said Jim Willi, president of Audience Research and Development, a media consulting firm. "All the different media are converging, and everyone's trying to see how he can get into the business."

Whatever worked for someone else was likely to be mimicked by others. Ted Turner announced that he was launching CNNfn, a financial news channel that would directly compete with CNBC. Turner also set up CNN/CNNfn web sites on the Internet to snare youthful techies and web surfers into his orbit. Sports Illustrated Television established a partnership with the NFL to develop interactive sports programming for Time Warner's cable systems. Pacific Telesis, a regional telephone company, accelerated its plans to enter the cable market by acquiring companies with licenses to provide wireless video services. One by one, the boundaries separating one communications business from another were falling. The media industry was exploding, and no one knew precisely what it would look like by the turn of the century. Regardless of his recent setbacks in the merger-and-acquisition arena, Barry Diller was positioning himself at the forefront of the new technological revolution.

In November, Diller announced a plan for his Silver King Communications to acquire a controlling interest in the much larger Home Shopping Network. "These steps will quicken our ability to proceed with our ambitions for the development of Silver King," Diller maintained.

By "our ability," Diller was referring to his continuing partnership with TCI's John C. Malone, despite Malone's role in undermining Diller's attempted merger with CBS. Malone had grown tired of the endless tide of red ink emanating from HSN, which was 80 percent-owned by TCI's Liberty Media, and he presented Diller with a deal providing him with cash flow for Silver King in return for Diller's taking HSN off his hands. The deal, in effect, would bind TCI, Silver King, and HSN together as an interlocking media conglomerate with common goals and interests. Silver King's stock had tripled to $35 a share during the three months since Diller took over as chairman.

"Mr. Diller essentially got the price of Silver King up based on an upside potential that has not yet occurred," said media analyst Craig Bibb of Paine Webber. "Now he's using the inflated Silver King share price to buy into HSN." Diller's magic in this area was still intact. His name lent marquee value to any enterprise he joined, driving up the stock price, which provided him with higher-priced collateral to use for acquisitions. As a result, Diller did not have to use any cash to expand his fledgling network-in-progress—his purchase of a major interest in HSN would be accomplished largely by an exchange of shares between the two companies.

This complicated arrangement would turn HSN into a wholly owned subsidiary of Silver King while simultaneously providing Malone with a 45 percent stake in Silver King. In addition, part of the newly issued shares of Silver King that helped finance the deal would be used to buy Savoy Pictures Entertainment, a Santa Monica, California–based entertainment company with four television stations of its own. There was something of value in the deal for all parties concerned. Malone would free himself of his continuing headache at HSN and become a partial owner of Diller's new media empire; Diller would receive a cash infusion from Malone as well as HSN's cable delivery system to help him fulfill his dream; and the joint Diller/Malone enterprise would acquire four new TV stations to flesh out Silver King's twelve.

Observers who lost sight of the intricacies of the deal could hardly be blamed. It was an inordinately complex high-wire act even by Diller's and Malone's lofty standards. Some analysts who covered the industry had a tough time figuring out exactly what was transpiring and who would gain or lose the most when the dust finally settled.

"On the surface, the whole thing looks dumb," said Josephthal, Lyon & Ross analyst Dennis McAlpine. "But Barry Diller isn't dumb, so he's evidently got some grand scheme. I'll be damned if I know what it is. When you've got John Malone and Barry Diller working on the same side, they don't do something as dumb as this appears to be without some reason."

From McAlpine's perspective, it was true that the numbers did not add up. Silver King, HSN, and Savoy Pictures were all showing losses. A loss plus a loss plus a loss is still a loss. Analysts are number crunchers first and foremost. They are paid to forecast future stock prices based largely on earnings projections. McAlpine was faced with a situation where the stock prices of three companies were lifting skyward, with no visible earnings in sight to sustain them. Measured strictly by a financial yardstick, it was difficult if not impossible to justify such high valuations for these stocks.

But investors do not always commit their discretionary dollars for obvious reasons. Sometimes they buy stocks on hunches or for reasons not immediately obvious to people whose vision was limited under the umbrella of green eyeshades. In this case, investors were banking on the special synergism that Barry Diller and John Malone might bring to sixteen struggling television stations.

"These steps will add early fiber to the companies, quickening our ability to proceed with our ambitions for the development of Silver King," said Diller. In effect, Diller was merely saying that he would create something of value down the road, and he was asking risk-taking investors to take him on faith, in effect saying trust me!

"What's the status of HSN's back-order business?" Diller asked his top executives during a meeting at Silver King's headquarters in St. Petersburg, Florida, in December 1995. "What's behind the concept of celebrity marketing at HSN? Could management vacate the corporate headquarters and rent that space out?"

Diller's questions plus the tone of his voice sent tremors through the conference room. Heads were going to roll, there was no question about it. The D word, "downsizing," was written all over Diller's brow. Jobs would be lost, survivors relocated, careers derailed in midcourse; it was not going to be pleasant. Diller, their new boss, was not happy today. He had to clean house and get this business turned around. In the third quarter that ended September 30, HSN had posted a loss of almost $18 million compared with a profit of $6.5 million for the same period a year earlier. Gross sales had slid 13 percent to $239 million. This type of performance was clearly unacceptable.

HSN's biggest problem was its misguided attempt to upgrade the merchandise it offered by introducing more expensive products than its television customers were used to. As one industry executive put it, "HSN used to have a high proportion of jewelry in its mix, but it has been reducing the quantity of jewelry and moving the merchandise upscale. In a nutshell, the strategy failed. It went too far upscale."

However, QVC's continuing success convinced Diller that the overall concept of marketing goods on television was viable. "The business of HSN is sound. It just needs management and discipline." Diller also believed that HSN could develop a lucrative new market producing infomercials for advertisers. "Over the next five years, direct selling is going to replace standard fifteen- and thirty-second spots as we know them. Direct selling has never been used in a mainstream way to replace local advertising."

Diller seemed to be floating a couple of ideas simultaneously: building a network through local rather than national programming, and producing infomercials for direct marketers. The putative media empire he intended to create seemed a lot less grandiose than his recent attempts to buy Paramount and CBS. The spectacle of Barry Diller, the man who established his reputation as a programming genius, suddenly touting infomercials as the wave of the future was hard to swallow. Diller was clearly struggling in his effort to carve out his niche. Turning Silver King's and Savoy Pictures' television stations into profitable enterprises remained Diller's primary challenge. By his own admission, he was "years away from being a real network."

Diller was a wounded barracuda swimming in a sea of sharks named Turner, Murdoch, Roberts, Redstone, and Malone. But he was still dangerous, and he posed a threat to his competition. At least one of those sharks, John C. Malone, remained convinced that Diller would recover from his recent setbacks and swim ahead to lead the pack. Malone was backing Diller with real money of his own. No one wanted to bet against John Malone, and no one was willing to write off the lean and hungry Diller as a has-been. Not quite yet.

CHAPTER 26

A LITTLE ZEN GOES A LONG WAY

"YOU AIN'T GOT any size," Ted Turner said, continuing to taunt Barry Diller after their joint appearance at the cable show in Los Angeles. Turner was referring to their relative positions, with Turner soon to become the largest shareholder in a combined Turner Broadcasting System and Time Warner conglomerate, while Diller cobbled together a veritable anthill amid media mountains.

However, Diller's vision for his fledgling network focused beyond the horizon to the potential offered by sixteen under-utilized television stations and Savoy Pictures' $100 million cash reserve. "I'm not just gathering chips to go after glitzier properties," he explained. "People think you do things for the dumbest reasons. I'm doing this to make it work. I may screw up but I have an absolutely clear idea of what business I want to build."

Diller had already contacted several major newspapers about providing news and sports content for his stations, and he had enticed his billionaire buddy David Geffen into investing some of his money in Silver

King. As Diller turned fifty-four in February 1996, he was determined to build his own empire from scratch and, in the process, put his credibility on the line.

"This is either a worthwhile or a worthless proving ground," Diller said. If he succeeded in his goal, Silver King/HSN/Savoy would become the nation's seventh network in a much more crowded field than it had been a decade earlier, when he successfully turned Fox into the nation's fourth network. "Do I wonder why I have this need to keep proving myself? No. Well, yes. From enthusiasm to total failure is a crooked-straight line."

For a man who claimed to despise hype, Diller sounded a bit too Delphic and a trifle too coy. He sometimes used paradox with Zen-like equanimity, a curious role for a man accustomed to screaming at his underlings and hurling crockery against the walls to emphasize a point during meetings. Paradox and balance, yin and yang, were not attributes one associated with a man who enjoyed racing taxicab drivers down Second Avenue in Manhattan in either his BMW or behind the handlebars of his motorcycle.

Yet, Diller did seem strangely in balance as he paced the floor in his New York apartment with its stunning views of the city. He seemed restless and in repose at the same time, his middle-aged body still muscular and compact, his beatific grin becoming slightly menacing when he opened his mouth to reveal the sizable gap between his two front teeth. He suddenly stopped pacing and twisted himself into a Buddha-like position, folding his legs beneath him on the sofa.

"What is a network?" Diller asked rhetorically. "When is a network not a network? Am I interested in a national voice? Probably. Sure I am. But that's not what I'm trying to do. Local broadcasters all look exactly the same. Local newscasts are terrible. Except for weather and sports, they're uninformative. They should just have one master shot of police and ambulances and yellow police tape because that's all they run."

This was Diller's moment to do things his way for a change. He could have accepted any number of high-profile jobs; running MCA Universal for Edgar Bronfman of Seagrams was just one offer he declined. But why bother at this stage of his life? Diller already had more money than he needed for ten lifetimes. Working for someone else was out of the question. He had done that many times in the past. He had to take his shot now, or he would never have the chance. Diller was either going to be king of an empire he built himself or fail spectacularly trying. He was a man possessed, bedeviled with inner demons. Diller was wound up tighter than ever. He exuded psychic energy. Internal conflict drove him—paradox and turmoil. Diller was seething with frustrated ambition and yet strangely calm at the same time.

"A lot of it has to do with willfulness," he said, "whether you're capable of imposing your own will on the process. To the extent that you insist, you at least have a prayer. It's a process of bashing idea against idea to get stuff out of yourself and other people. Maybe it's harsh. Maybe it's not harsh enough. I have never functioned in an environment of support."

Diller was being a tad disingenuous, overlooking the financial support he was receiving from Malone, Geffen, and Herbert Allen, Jr. of the investment banking firm Allen & Company. "We have profitably bet on Barry Diller in the past," said Allen, "and look forward to betting on him in the future." Without support like that, Diller's dream for a network of his own would have evaporated overnight.

Ironically, in acquiring an astounding fifteen million options to buy a controlling interest in HSN, Diller would be competing directly against QVC, the home shopping company he ran a year or so earlier. Most analysts doubted that there was room for two major retailers on television. QVC was in better financial shape than HSN, whose programs were aired only on Silver King's twelve stations. Diller needed to turn HSN around before he could concentrate on launching his stations as a viable network. But that was the price Diller had to pay to gain Malone's support, and he bristled at the notion that Malone had pressured him into taking HSN off his hands.

"I was not pushed into anything," Diller said, fuming as he erupted

from his Buddha-like repose. "I wished to do it and was able to do it!"
Observing Diller was like watching the weather change in the mountains.
Sunny and calm one moment, turbulent skies the next.

In late February, Diller attended another A-list party, this one in
Washington, D.C., and hosted by none other than the President of the
United States, William Jefferson Clinton. Diller arrived on a cold sunny
day along with Ted Turner, Michael Ovitz, Rupert Murdoch, and twenty
other media executives. The president, blowing leftward one day and
rightward the next, depending on the latest polls, had assembled the dignitaries to discuss a ratings system to monitor sex and violence on television developed by the Motion Picture Association of America.

For years, the industry had resisted any attempt by the government to
influence programming as an infringement on free speech. Suddenly
and inexplicably, the most powerful media titans in the world filed,
sheep-like, into the White House to chat up President Clinton and Vice
President Al Gore about a plan to insert a "V-chip" in televisions so
parents could block shows they did not want their children to watch. Not
one of these latter-day Goliaths had the temerity to warn their hosts that
a system for rating shows and allowing the government to influence technology could be a prelude to further governmental demands for "correct"
programming. Everyone was opposed to gratuitous violence, but what
would stop Big Brother from seeking additional controls?

Following a feel-good lunch, as though the politicians and the communications gurus had actually accomplished something of value, everyone
traipsed into the East Room for a photo opportunity. To his credit, the
only dissenter to this alarming spectacle was Barry Diller. Speaking to
reporters afterward on Pennsylvania Avenue, Diller said, "This makes no
sense. It's a nice idea, but unfortunately you cannot rate 100,000 hours of
TV programs. It's unworkable. Those ratings can't distinguish between
one episode in which the main characters have sex one week, and a very
valuable discussion about teenage pregnancy the next week.

"This is an industry that is trying to forestall what it considers to be a worse alternative," Diller elaborated, "that is, a ratings system devised by the Federal Communications Commission that the industry would be under intense political pressure to adopt."

Diller put his finger right on the crux of the problem. This was a case of government muscle-flexing at its worst. Either embrace this watered-down, sugar-coated system or have a more draconian alternative rammed down your throat by an overly paternalistic government. Diller finally had a Democrat occupying the White House, but he was less than sure he liked the way this administration was tilting—at the moment. As far as Gore was concerned, the future apostle of Global Warming was allowing his wife Tipper and her concerns about "offensive" programming to temper his views about the First Amendment.

Like parties to an uncertain peace treaty ending a nasty war, the media representatives fixed frozen smiles on their faces that merely masked the uncertainty underneath. How was this going to work? Did anyone have a clue? No matter. Clinton's attention span extended no further than the election in November. His guests that day were little more than hostages in his bid for reelection. What they consented to was an agreement in principle to devise a system that would determine whether a show is suitable for children. Whatever happened to parents' responsibility for their own children? Did citizens of the United States, or any country, need Big Brother to discipline their kids for them? The brainless charade was an embarrassing exercise for everyone associated with it. But what else could you expect from a president who had trouble keeping his trousers zippered up in the Oval Office?

Notwithstanding all the smiling and handshaking in the nation's capital, an agreement to insert a V-chip in televisions was anything but a done deal. Other media representatives not present at the Washington powwow had a different perspective on the situation. In the words of one network executive, "We want to preserve our options, including the option to sue. If this system is voluntary as it's supposed to be, then we don't want to appear to be under the boot of government censorship by announcing it at the White House or any other governmental setting."

Diller's campaign to create a network of his own received a boost in March from the Federal Communications Commission, which approved his bid to take control of Silver King's stations. The FCC, in effect, abandoned its earlier restraints on cross-ownership rules, which would have restricted TCI's efforts to expand its own cable business.

With a green light flashing for him to move ahead, Diller raided his old company, Fox, for talented media executives. One of the first to join Diller at Silver King was Doug Binzak, a former scheduling and marketing whiz at Fox. Next to come aboard was Adam Ware, another Fox talent who got the job of executive vice president of broadcasting at Silver King. In raiding Fox for heavy hitters to flesh out his programming and distribution team, Diller sent a message to the industry that he would concentrate first on creating local identities for his stations before launching a national network. This formula of building a core of owned and operated stations worked spectacularly for Diller at Fox, and he hoped to duplicate it at Silver King. Once he succeeded with Phase One of his campaign, it would become the springboard for Phase Two: assembling a peripheral lineup of affiliated stations with the combined entity evolving into the nation's seventh network sometime in 1998.

Or so he hoped.

Diller's new hires were nothing if not enthusiastic. "Doug's experience is programming and promotion, and my experience is in distribution," said Ware, "but we are now going to be sharing the duties to some extent. Barry offered us this incredible challenge to make over the Silver King stations from Home Shopping Network into a whole new programming structure and business plan. Whatever branding we create for the Silver King Stations will dictate the direction we take in the future."

Developing the type of creative programming necessary to build a viable new network in such a competitive environment was going to take a heroic effort from both Diller and his lieutenants. They were in desperate need of solid new content from external series producers and syndicators. Although he refused to discuss his strategy publicly at the time, Diller's initial emphasis was going to be on non-primetime "fringe" periods during the day and late at night. Through this type of envelopment tactic, he hoped to build viewer loyalty during periods the other networks were not concentrating on, before closing in later on the coveted primetime slots.

"I know for a fact that Barry is not looking for primetime network programming off the bat," a syndication executive confided off the record. "When Barry first started at Fox, he was looking to exploit weaknesses the big three networks had in daytime, and that was most evident in his launch of the Fox Children's Network programming on weekday afternoons. Barry already knows that CBS's morning and afternoon programming is struggling. Fox is losing kid viewers to the cable networks like Nickelodeon, so that's where he will be looking for nontraditional fare such as game shows, relationship series, things like that."

Coming up with that type of programming was going to cost Diller plenty. His sixteen television stations reached approximately 35 percent of American households. The four he was acquiring from Savoy were actually affiliated Fox stations that Diller expected to lop off from Fox and cobble onto his own embryo network.

"Diller has a long way to go to fix those stations," said a Hollywood executive close to Diller. "My sense tells me that Diller is going to have to pay cash for any programming, since his stations have weaker signals. I just can't see any syndicator taking a barter split."

Diller was already in the process of building his cash hoard. Silver King had $22 million in reserves, while Savoy had $140 million in its coffers. In May 1996, as Diller prepared for what promised to be one of the most bruising battles of his life, he sat back and took inventory of his resources. The stations he was about to command included Silver King's WHSE in New York City; WHSI in Smithtown, New York; KHSE in Los Angeles; WEHS in Chicago; WHSP in Philadelphia; WHSH in Boston; KHSX in Dallas; KHSH in Houston; WQHS in Cleveland; WBHS in Tampa;

WYHS in Miami; and WHSW in Baltimore; and Savoy's WVUE in New Orleans; WALA in Mobile; KHON in Honolulu; and WLUK in Green Bay.

The only thing Silver King's stations had in common was their remote position on the band, ranging from channel 24 in Baltimore to channel 69 in Miami. Savoy was better-positioned with channel 2 in Honolulu through channel 11 in Green Bay. It was a ragtag lineup to be sure. Diller apparently wanted to duplicate the genius of Gaius Marius, the Roman general who commanded a motley army of far-flung provincials in 100 B.C. and succeeded in whipping them into an invincible fighting force. Could Diller accomplish what Marius did more than 2,000 years earlier?

Like Marius, Diller's odds were stacked heavily against him.

CHAPTER 27

THE BARRACUDAS BEGIN
TO BLEED

AT FIRST GLANCE, Barry Diller appeared to be fighting an army of Goliaths with his legion of provincial warriors, but the opposing forces were wounded Goliaths at best. In the major enemy camp Diller faced Ted Turner and Gerald Levin, the respective heads of the Turner Broadcasting System and Time Warner. Turner and Levin proposed to merge their two empires, but Time Warner was hamstrung by staggering debt and ill-conceived deals that encumbered its most valuable assets. Management was shaky, starting with Levin himself, who had run the company into a dead end. To survive, Levin either had to sell off assets or revamp his executive ranks, preferably both. Levin needed Turner more than Turner needed him, and most insiders were betting that Terrible Ted, the Mouth of the South, would emerge as top dog once the two companies were officially united.

Three years earlier, Levin had taken over as CEO of Time Warner following the death of his boss Steve Ross, who succumbed to a long bout with prostate cancer. Ross, Levin, and other senior executives had fattened their own bank accounts at the expense of shareholders while the company was reeling. Wall Street bankers had demanded that Time Warner retire most of the debt it had incurred over the years, and in attempting to do so, Levin blundered into one of the most incredibly stupid deals in modern corporate history. He formed a so-called strategic alliance with a group of investors, giving them effective control over Time Warner's most cherished assets: Warner Brothers Studios; the company's enormous film library; Home Box Office; Cinemax; and other media jewels.

"Jerry made the worst mistake in the book," said a former Time Warner executive close to Levin. "He handed veto power over his best assets to outsiders who had their own agenda."

In order to extricate himself from this costly blunder, Levin was faced with the prospect of ceding control over Time Warner's cable systems to a minority partner, U. S. West Communications, which imposed controls of its own over Levin's management style. In the end, Levin turned to Ted Turner to bail him out of his predicament, which was tantamount to a flounder forming an alliance with a shark to help him fight off encircling barracudas. The likeliest outcome was that eventually the shark and the barracudas would arrange a truce and eat the flounder for lunch.

From the beginning, Levin's dealings with Ted Turner provided comic relief for the investment community. First Levin attempted to trade Time Warner's 20 percent stake in Turner Broadcasting for some plum, like Turner's Cartoon Network. Turner just smiled smugly and told Levin no. That approach having failed, Levin next offered to buy the 80 percent of Turner Broadcasting it did not own for $10 billion, further increasing Time Warner's already monumental load of debt. In doing so, Levin was offering Turner approximately twice as much as his company was worth and, in effect, giving away 30 percent of his own company in return for a 15 percent boost in cash flow.

After they digested all the numbers, Wall Street analysts sat back in amazement and laughed themselves silly. With one stroke of his pen, Levin was getting set to turn Ted Turner into Time Warner's biggest shareholder, and none other than John Malone—a major Turner share-holder—into the second-largest shareholder. Through Malone, Barry Diller might also manage to get a foot inside Time Warner's door. While Levin was trying to explain to the media how and why he was buying Turner Broadcasting System, Malone was joking to intimates that "in his mind, Turner was acquiring Time Warner."

To win Malone's approval before he could consummate this preposter-ous union, Levin was cajoled into sweetening the pot further—as though it were not already sweet enough by half for everyone except Levin. Levin offered Malone, among other items, a twenty-year, 15 percent dis-count on key Turner Broadcasting services, including CNN, TNT, and the Cartoon Network, concessions worth $500 million, in addition to the $2 billion-plus that Malone's TCI would receive in Time Warner shares. All in all, it would not be a bad day's pay for Turner, Malone, and company.

Diller observed this financial legerdemain from his own battle sta-tion, a solitary general sizing up enemy forces with amused but hardly disinterested detachment. While Turner, Levin, and Malone, Diller's ostensible and highly volatile ally, positioned themselves for ultimate power, Diller could not help but take comfort in the skirmishing that would weaken them all at least temporarily, no matter what the outcome. Divide and conquer was a strategy that had served warriors well since time immemorial.

With all his loud-mouthed bravado, Turner was not without problems of his own. Turner Broadcasting was hardly a model of financial deco-rum as CNN, the all-news channel that accounted for half of Turner's annual cash flow, faced stiff competition from Disney's ABC, NBC, and Murdoch's Fox, all of whom were planning to launch all-news channels of their own. In addition, Turner was forced to take a $60 million write-off in the first quarter of 1996 because of dismal performance from its Castle Rock movie studio. Malone was struggling with persistent cash flow problems at TCI that threatened to get worse before they improved. So, while Diller may not have had "any size," as Turner had put it, compared with the assets his opponents commanded, he was slowly consolidating his own forces while the others were busy bloodying one another.

Diller's relationship with Malone was somewhat schizophrenic. While Diller wanted his biggest supporter to remain financially sound for obvious reasons, he did not want Malone to become so powerful that he could dictate all the terms of their relationship. Diller needed to retain some leverage over Malone so that their alliance was mutually beneficial, lest he be perceived as a mere junior player in Malone's sprawling media kingdom.

In the summer of 1996, John Malone reigned as the undisputed Cable King of the United States, but there were visible signs of turmoil in the realm. Malone had spun off stakes in Liberty Media to the public twice, and twice he yanked them back into the aegis of his flagship company TCI. Liberty Media was one of the largest players in cable programming, owning pieces of ninety-one separate enterprises, including Turner Broadcasting, Black Entertainment Television, Court TV Network, Discovery Communications, MacNeil/Lehrer, QVC, and others. Malone hoped that his interlocking network of interests would boost the price of TCI's stock and increase shareholder value, but his various gambits into the financial markets had so far produced mediocre results at best.

"The company is difficult to understand," said Dennis Leibowitz, a media analyst with Donaldson, Lufkin & Jenrette. Mr. Leibowitz's confusion was understandable, considering that Liberty's tentacles reached into so many diverse areas that its financial strength was almost impossible to quantify.

Malone was also concerned about the Federal Trade Commission, which was spending an inordinate amount of time scrutinizing the concentration of media power in the hands of a few titans. The attempt to join the nation's two largest cable operators (TCI and Time Warner) with several of the biggest cable programmers in the country (Liberty, Turner, and HBO) had Washington's full attention, and John Malone was not a man who liked the federal government looking over his shoulder.

To help him navigate his way through these increasingly complex waters,

Malone called on the expertise of Liberty Media's president Peter Barton, whom Malone regarded as "top banana in his squadron of second bananas," admittedly a mixed and shaky metaphor. Malone and Barton formed an even more unlikely business couple than Murdoch and Diller had been at Fox. Barton was a gregarious liberal Democratic whose wife Laura was a key fund-raiser for President Clinton. Malone was almost religiously reclusive and politically as far to the right as Barton tilted to the left. He once startled a roomful of analysts by announcing, "I exist," when they complained about his reticent nature. Yet, oddly enough, in business Malone and Barton complemented each other like opposite sides of the same coin.

"Peter has a patience for detail that John does not have," said Diller, who worked closely with both men. "Peter sat in an office for twelve hours, or some insane amount of time, negotiating one deal point."

Notwithstanding their differences of temperament, Malone and Barton saw eye-to-eye on the essential issues. Both understood that a Turner/Time Warner merger was in the best interests of TCI and Liberty only if the federal government did not force Malone to divest himself of major cable properties for antitrust purposes.

"If things get stalled, we'll bail out," Malone threatened, in order to sink the deal if he did not get his way. "It'll either be done by October 1 or it'll be dead. We're not prepared to be self-sacrificial."

As far as Diller was concerned, he was hoping that the deal would eventually go through, but only in a way that left all parties marginally weaker, even if only temporarily, while he gathered his own forces and attacked from the flanks. In May 1996, Diller painted an optimistic scenario about his ability to make HSN more upscale by offering shopping services on the Internet.

"This could be an absolutely huge business," he said during a meeting with shareholders in New York City. Diller planned to succeed where other providers such as America Online and Compuserve had failed, by offering viewers "exactly what they want." His formidable database, Diller said, could rapidly revamp its lineup of products to correspond to consumer buying patterns. But not all analysts were convinced he could pull it off.

"Home shopping is still basically a flea market and a vehicle for broken-down movie stars," said fashion consultant Alan Millstein after listening to Diller's pitch.

Flea market or upscale electronic mall for yuppies? Diller was gambling that he could take a sow's ear and transform it into a silk purse.

Each year in July, Diller's investment banker Herbie Allen invited a select group of media titans on a power retreat in Sun Valley, Idaho. "All sorts of deals can be hatched," said one industry executive, "because it's the perfect opportunity for titans to meet outside the scrutiny of the press." For example, in 1995, a chance meeting among Michael Eisner, Warren Buffett, and a few others in the parking lot outside the conference center resulted in Disney's $19 billion acquisition of Capital Cities/ABC. Allen's gathering, which took place from July 9 through 13 in 1996, was not expected to lead to a deal of that magnitude, but there were enough high-octane mergers already being discussed to start the rumor mill churning before the guests even arrived.

Allen had sworn all his guests to secrecy during the thirteen years he had been hosting the event. This latest gathering of 130 chieftains of the entertainment world was no exception, and anyone suspected of leaking information to the press was crossed off Allen's list for the following year's soiree. In 1996, Diller appeared on a panel moderated by Tom Brokaw with Microsoft's Bill Gates, Intel's Andrew Grove, and others.

"The press was filled with stories about Turner and Levin," said Tom Pollack, former chairman of the film group at MCA, "but everyone was curious about what Barry Diller was up to. He had yet to announce what his specific plans were. We were all waiting anxiously to find out if he was going to start another network or if he had something else in mind. Personally, I think he was looking to set his own agenda rather than conform to someone else's agenda. But only he knew exactly what he had in mind, and he wasn't saying what it was."

Diller refused to tip his hand from the opening barbecue on Tuesday night, July 9, until the final cocktail party four days later. The mornings were taken up with presentations by various corporate heads, but the guests were free to spend their afternoons swimming, fly fishing, river rafting, golfing, or in any number of athletic pursuits. A vigorous game of tennis was still one of Diller's favorite diversions, as was racing his motorcycle along mountain trails surrounding the compound.

The mega-mergers that had taken place in recent years had left many conglomerates reeling under an avalanche of debt, resulting in financial distress for many of the companies involved. Diller intended to avoid that mistake in his next venture and seize opportunity where his competitors had found only grief. Most of the competition had done little to rein in costs, cut overhead, or come up with more efficient ways to do business.

"There were so many years of success without anyone being called to account," Diller said after the conference, "that it masked growing fissures in the way the industry does business. Many of the old entertainment companies that are now conglomerates have lost sight of the basics."

Others caught up in the merger mania agreed with Diller's assessment. According to Robert Daly, co-chairman of Time Warner's Warner Brothers studio, "There are movies that we want to make, but until we get the budget down, we will not give them the green light. How do you say to a Tom Cruise or a Mel Gibson that they are not worth the money they want? It's hard to ask them to take a cut."

Many had faulted Diller for not having what it takes to compete against the industry giants after his failed bids for Paramount and CBS, although he believed his conservative business nature would serve him well in the long run. But he was determined not to take on more debt than he thought was prudent to acquire a property, no matter how badly he wanted it.

"Change only comes with real pain, and there hasn't been enough yet," Diller said. "Two or three companies will have to suffer through major losses before the industry turns itself around. There will have to be blood on the floor."

That was just fine with Barry Diller, as long as the blood on the floor belonged to someone else.

CHAPTER 28

WHEN 1 PLUS 1 = –2

WHILE BARRY DILLER'S competitors continued to pummel one another unmercifully, Diller worked quietly to build the foundation of his own empire. In August he addressed a gathering of media executives at InfoWorld's Spotlight conference in Laguna Niguel, California, and intimated that he hoped to establish a new television network through something called "niche TV" sometime in 1997.

"He's a canny operator, and it's possible he'll be able to come up with something entirely new to make his venture work," said Scott Wright, a media analyst at Argus Research. "His new programming will be 'narrowcasting,' appealing to specific groups who'll pay to see what they want. The new programs won't have to appeal to everyone in the country. We'll see Diller come up with some idiosyncratic programming."

Diller, as usual, played his cards close to his vest, refusing to give away whatever surprises he had in mind until they were fully unveiled. "We are on track," he said. "Do we know what sort of programming we are planning? Yes. Are we ready to talk about it? No. Today, movie and book publishing companies are spending millions of dollars to slap their properties on the Internet and CDROMs in the happy belief that their intellectual property is becoming interactive. That's lazy. We can't simply recycle our old products."

In saying as much as he did, Diller was risking more than was usual for him, ridiculing the efforts made by others and implying that he was going to invent a new way of doing business. He put the finishing touches on his acquisition of Home Shopping Network in a $1.3 billion stock swap that gave Silver King an 80 percent stake in HSN. The union of the two companies provided Diller with greater leverage to make additional acquisitions and develop his new lineup of programming.

"This opens up our options for acquisitions, for use of available cash flow, and for securing an additional line of credit," said Jason Stewart, a close associate of Diller.

Two weeks later, however, Diller confused everyone by reverting to his playful, happy-Buddha, paradoxical persona by denying that he planned anything resembling a conventional network. "Another generic programming service is hopeless," Diller told a reporter for the *Wall Street Journal*. What he had more specifically in mind, Diller said, were local video versions of "a city magazine or alternative newspaper," relying heavily on local sports, news, and political issues. "Each city has a distinct personality. Broadcast TV, unlike local radio, unlike newspapers, alternative weeklies, or city magazines, does not in any way capture it. We mean to fill that gap."

In other words, Diller seemed to be saying, "If you really want to know what I'm up to, stay tuned for the next episode." Some Wall Street analysts doubted that Diller himself had a clear idea of how he would structure his budding media kingdom. "I don't think Barry really knows what he wants to do," said one executive close to Diller. "I think he's just going to experiment until it hits."

Diller and his associates were more open about what their new enterprise was *not* going to be than about what it *would* become. "The way that

Warner Brothers Network and Universal Pictures Network each went about trying to get 100 stations to clear a two-hour block of primetime programming for one or two nights initially is not the direction we want to take," said Doug Binzak. "Right now, our sole focus is on developing programming for our stations' schedules from the beginning of the day to the end of it. Once we think we have some programs that have established a strong presence, then we may start looking at broader national platforms."

Diller was not too busy with his empire-building pursuits to pay attention to another of his favorite activities: helping Democrats get elected to office. In September he attended a fund-raising event for President Bill Clinton at Greenacres, the former home of silent screen star Harold Lloyd. Barbra Steisand, the Eagles, and the Neville brothers were on hand to serenade the president and his contributors, and Maya Angelou read excerpts from her poetry. Steven Spielberg, David Geffen, Tom Hanks, Steve Jobs, Edgar Bronfman, and many other heavy hitters whipped out their checkbooks to help ease the way for Clinton's reelection campaign.

Four years earlier, Streisand's appearance at a glitzy fund-raiser netted $1.2 million for Clinton in one afternoon in his race against a hapless, tongue-tied ("the vision thing") George H.W. Bush. Previously, she had warbled at fund-raising events for a bevy of Democratic losers like Michael Dukakis and Walter Mondale. Finally, Hollywood had a winner in the smooth-talking former governor of Arkansas, and their enthusiasm was boundless.

David Geffen liked to boast that he had raised "many millions" for the Democrats over the years. Geffen hosted two private dinners for Clinton early in 1996 that netted about $2 million for the party. It was no secret to anyone, least of all to Diller and his cohorts, that Hollywood was overwhelmingly liberal in its political orientation. Then again, one could hardly expect Diller and his friends to beat the drums for the Republicans, who had recently attacked the film industry as "a nightmare of depravity."

Even a Democrat like Clinton, a political weathervane who took his direction from the latest polls, was preferable to the fire-breathing dragons of the right.

As Diller concentrated on building the foundation of his media kingdom, the animosity between his main rivals grew nastier by the minute. In one corner was Rupert Murdoch, ranked by a leading trade weekly as the most powerful man in media, complaining in court that big, bad Time Warner was out to destroy Fox by refusing to air its all-news channel in New York City. Squaring off against him was Ted Turner, who compared the Australian-born Murdoch to "the late Fuehrer" Adolph Hitler.

New York Mayor Rudolph Giuliani and Turner's wife Jane Fonda entered the act, the former by offering to broadcast Murdoch's channel on municipal television and the latter by labeling the mayor a puppet of Murdoch. Jane had come a long way from her days as a feminist revolutionary, more recently reduced to Barbie Doll status by doing the Tomahawk chop in Atlanta, which offended Native Americans, as well as bolstering her modest bosom with silicon implants.

"Terrible Ted is either veering dangerously toward insanity" or else he is "off the medication he takes to fight his manic depression," suggested an editorial in Murdoch's *New York Post*.

Sensibly enough, Diller stood apart from all the squabbling, concentrating instead on shoring up HSN's sagging stock price and keeping an eye on ally John Malone's cash flow problems. For his own purposes, Diller wanted Malone slightly wounded, but he did not want his chief financial supporter turning into a complete financial basket case. In October 1996, TCI asked its vendors to "temporarily suspend all shipments" until further notice to "ensure the successful deployment of our current inventory and control unnecessary capital spending." Wall Street analysts had grown concerned about TCI's ability to roll out new equipment and services that it promised to its cable subscribers. It was a chink in Malone's armor that bore watching lest it degenerate into a full-fledged battle wound.

* * *

In the fall of 1996, Barry Diller armed himself for the most challenging campaign of his life, one that would determine his future as no other had before. This was make-or-break time for Diller. What he accomplished during the next year of his life would decide whether he would continue to be an annoying mongrel nipping at the heels of the front-runners or become a bona fide top dog occupying center stage with the media mastiffs—a couple of whom he had once worked for.

Diller contemplated his options calmly, shrugging his shoulders at the suggestion that time was running out and he might not be able to accomplish all the goals he had set his sights on. There was little question that he felt more than a small measure of disappointment at his failure to establish his own media empire thus far. But there was some comfort in the knowledge that Turner, Murdoch, Malone, and the other moguls were all experiencing growing pains of their own. Yes, Barry Diller hoped to surpass them all, but he wanted to fulfill his dreams without repeating their mistakes. When he finally reached the summit, he wanted to be sure his feet were firmly planted on solid ground.

The final months of 1996 found him crisscrossing the country in a feverish campaign to convince large institutional investors that his hybrid enterprise was financially sound. On December 19, the shareholders of Silver King, Savoy Pictures, and Home Shopping Network approved the merger of the three companies, which was renamed HSN, Inc., headquartered in St. Petersburg, Florida. Diller's months of hard work propelled him another step forward in his drive to create a major group of television stations anchored in the nation's largest TV shopping channel. One of Diller's major challenges as he approached the new year was to make sure that the cost of new programming for the Silver King and Savoy stations did not drain HSN's growing cash flow.

Independent stations such as Diller's were having a difficult time competing against powerful station groups for desirable programs. Diller had hoped to rely on mandatory "carry rules" to gain access to markets where his signals were weak. However, the federal government threatened to change these rules and allow cable operators to drop less popular independent stations in favor of cable channels requested by subscribers. If the cable operators were no longer forced to carry Diller's independent stations, he would have to create a demand for his own unique programming without bankrupting his operation.

Diller understood that there was opportunity in the bloodletting taking place among the giants in the entertainment industry. After a protracted period of frenetic deal making, Time Warner, Viacom, News Corporation, and Disney were staggering under an avalanche of debt. Most had stretched themselves to the breaking point, extending their tentacles into the diverse worlds of movies, TV, cable, magazine and book publishing, theme parks, and retail outlets. All this "vertical integration" had put an undue competitive strain on the industry.

Diller saw a fundamental flaw in the direction his competitors had taken. Previously lean operations had become diffuse, stretched to the snapping point. Without exception, they had neglected a key tenet of thriving growth enterprises: paring costs to the bone while focusing on maximizing growth. Diller's main competition had suddenly metamorphosed into flabby, stagnating, debt-crippled mastodons. The common stocks of these once-booming enterprises were being unmercifully punished by investors who no longer saw any potential for earnings growth in the near future. Profit growth had stalled in the once-glamorous businesses of music and films. The entire entertainment sector woefully lagged behind during the rollicking bull market of the mid-1990s, choking on the dust thrown up by other stocks.

The misfortunes of the industry were reflected in the temper tantrums thrown by media bigwigs like Turner and Murdoch, whose name-calling snits had generated headlines across the country. While his competitors were stalled, Diller took the opportunity to consolidate his own little empire and avoid everyone else's mistakes.

"These companies need to do what the rest of industrial America has done in the 1980s and '90s," said analyst Gordon Crawford. "They need to reduce debt, cut costs, sell off non-strategic assets, and get focused. It's critical if these stocks are going to start performing again."

John Malone continued to be mired in his own problems at TCI and was frantically slashing operating costs while spinning off various units. Disney announced in February 1997 that it wanted to shed publishing assets acquired in its $19 billion purchase of Capital Cities/ABC. Time Warner haggled with its own partner, U.S. West, about divesting itself of vast cable holdings and trimming $18 billion worth of debt. Viacom struggled to sell various radio stations and spin off Blockbuster Video, which it bought in 1994 for $18.4 billion. News Corporation owned a mountain of unprofitable magazines it needed to sell.

"Over the next twelve months," said David Geffen, "huge assets from these conglomerates will be sold."

Investment banker Herbie Allen, adviser to Geffen and Diller, agreed. "All these companies will trim down to focus on businesses that have strong cash flow and growth and get out of the businesses that don't have them."

Meanwhile, Diller's budding empire was lean and mean and flush with cash. In addition, he did not suffer from some of the other problems his competitors had: bloated movie production costs, outrageous salaries for stars, or astounding compensation for top executives. Ironically, Diller's innate fiscal conservatism had landed him in a position that his daredevil competitors aspired to.

Bear Stearns executive Alan Schwartz summed up the situation succinctly: "The entertainment deals merged two portfolios of assets where one plus one was supposed to equal more than two. Now, they have to analyze whether all the pieces of the portfolio are necessary to enhance the whole and ask if all the assets are going to be able to produce above-average returns and growth."

Sometimes, one plus one equals minus two.

When Diller launched Fox as a network in the 1980s, there were only three existing networks to compete against. In 1997, that number had grown to six while the viewing audience was increasingly shifting to cable. The Internet had also surfaced as an unlikely competitor, drawing viewers away from television. Consumers were being bombarded with too many movies to choose from, 417 in 1996 alone, with production costs ranging from $75 million to $100 million.

Adding to the pressure and the confusion was the difficulty of forecasting which aspect of the communications and entertainment business was going to prosper the most. Disney chairman Michael Eisner faced a dilemma in deciding whether to concentrate on his failing ABC network, on his theme park, or on his movie business. His original rationale for owning ABC was to use it as a venue for promoting his other businesses, but ABC was faltering badly with the unpopular Peter Jennings driving viewers to the other networks. Eisner had to find a way to make ABC healthy if it were to become an effective marketing tool for Disney's movies and resorts.

Barry Diller had come to feel a bit like the odd man out when Turner, Murdoch, Eisner, Redstone, Levin, and Malone captured the spotlight in their battle to rule the media world. But in the early months of 1997, Diller's lack of engagement in his competitors' bloody battles had left him unscathed and relatively healthy by comparison. He found himself in a better position to launch his own attack against their battered enterprises than the wounded giants were in to defend them.

"Owning content and distribution makes sense where it is affordable," he said in February 1997. "The market says these companies are all too complicated, too diffuse, and each for different reasons. Everybody is stuck like molasses in their own mess."

Everybody but Barry Diller, that is.

CHAPTER 29

PLAGUED AGAIN
BY THE DEVILS OF THE PAST

BARRY DILLER RARELY had much time or patience for self-analysis, but he was unusually reflective in the late winter of 1997 as he surveyed the field of battle. He was suddenly more aware than ever of the events that drove him relentlessly toward greater and greater success.

Only recently had his resentment of his parents and the circumstances of his early life turned to a small measure of understanding. First, there was the question of his Jewishness. Diller was raised a Jew, identified with fellow Jews, and traveled comfortably in the largely Jewish world of show business.

Diller never discussed his personal life with anyone but his closest friends, mostly because he himself did not care to dwell on the more painful aspects of his early life. But in 1997, just past his fifty-fifth birthday, he was suddenly more candid than ever. Was he, strictly speaking, really a Jew? According to strict Orthodox law, a child received his Jewish heritage from his mother's line, but Barry's mother was a Gentile. His own grandparents would not recognize him as one of their own. Feeling a bit downcast, if not despondent over his inability so far to outdistance Murdoch and his other rivals, Diller's mixed ethnic heritage appeared to be troubling him more than he had ever admitted to anyone.

Barry Diller had not thought about his brother Donald much in more than two decades. He had never discussed the circumstances of his brother's life with either of his parents. Indeed, he had pushed the memory forcefully away whenever it popped to the surface of his consciousness during the intervening years. It had been a painful, unpleasant occurrence that was better repressed, better consigned to the junkyard of history and not dwelled upon. Suddenly, in 1997 as he stood on the threshold of one of the most important campaigns of his life, Barry Diller could not get Donald—or Michael or Reva—out of his mind. The devils from his past, which he had driven into the shadows for decades, had arrived to haunt him.

The idea that he might eventually fail to realize his major goals was more terrifying to Diller than anything else. His father had tormented both of his sons with cruel taunts from the time they were children, telling them that failure is the worst thing that could happen, calling them failures whenever they failed to live up to his expectations.

"You're a failure!" he screamed at them over and over. "You'll never amount to anything!"

Barry had stood up to the old man, but Donald was crushed by him. And now Barry, at this relatively late stage of life, had to wonder if he would ever attain his dream of running his own media empire.

"I can't fail," appeared to be his mantra. "I won't fail. Failure is death!"

Failure would mean that his father had finally beaten him, and that the Diller curse, personified in his brother Donald who had been murdered after a failed marriage and a life given over to drugs, had afflicted Barry as well. Barry was not one to worry about failure, but as he contemplated his sixtieth birthday only five years in the future, the time remaining for him to truly make his mark was running out. Suppose he had not fulfilled his dream by then? What were the chances that he would ever make it all the way to the top?

Number one! He was obsessed by that goal. Top of the heap! King of the media moguls! Barry Diller was afraid of failing for the first time in decades. Failure is death!

On one level, it was absurd that a man worth $100 million or so and had achieved such incredible success in life could be considered a failure. However, Barry Diller did not find it absurd. He had not driven himself all these years to be number two or three or four. He was Barry Diller, the one everyone else expected to rule the roost. Now people were questioning whether he would ever fulfill that destiny.

"I function best in a skeptical environment," Diller said, defying his critics. "What I have done in the past that has worked best everyone said would fail."

What exactly was HSN? What was the logic behind the consortium he had assembled? Barry Diller himself was the only rationale that mattered. He was the power behind the enterprise, his own *raison d'être*. Barry Diller was Existential Man; he did, therefore, he would succeed. If he had to go back to basics and offer more items at lower prices on his shopping network, he would do it. Back to the bazaar. Diller hired James Held, a former Bloomingdale's executive who worked with him at QVC, to boost revenues at HSN. Held recommended upgrading the company's phone lines, credit check system, and distribution outlets, which would eventually enable Diller to rent his system to other companies that wanted to market products through HSN. Amway, perhaps the most successful multilevel marketing company of all time, quickly climbed on board.

Then Diller focused more directly on CityVision, the new regional programming he was developing. He would still not be specific about exactly what CityVision was, except to say that it was a unique concept of targeted programming for specific groups in a community, Hispanic soap operas for Miami residents, for example. Local news, local sports, local culture, local . . . whatever. If his programming proved successful and was picked up by other cable operators, HSN's stations would reach 40 percent of all American households by the turn of the century. If Diller needed more cash, he could spin off his four Fox stations in Honolulu, New Orleans, Green Bay, and Mobile for $300 million and still accomplish his goals.

"In twenty-five years, anybody who has been skeptical about Barry Diller has been a fool," said Jeffrey Katzenberg. David Geffen also lent Diller his vote of support by buying half a million shares of HSN with his own money. At $26 a share, the price of the stock in March 1997, Geffen's investment represented a $13 million stake in a company that might not show any profits for several years. Geffen was anything but a stupid man. He did not invest in HSN; he invested in Barry Diller.

Just as Diller was putting together his plan of attack, his old boss and some-times rival, Rupert Murdoch, upped the ante and changed the rules of the game. Diller, Turner, Malone, Geffen, Ovitz, Eisner, and others laid legiti-mate claim to the sobriquet Media Mogul. Murdoch threatened to outdo them all by assuming the title of *Multimedia* Mogul solely for himself.

In March 1997, Murdoch announced a plan to invest upwards of $1 billion in a satellite television service that had ominous implications for his competition. Murdoch proposed to combine his satellite operation with a company called Echostar Communications to create a joint ven-ture known as Sky. The new service was a direct threat to cable televi-sion since it had the capacity to beam local stations from major markets like Boston and New York to anyone anywhere with an eighteen-inch receiver dish. If Murdoch had his way, viewers in Podunk would be able to see local broadcasting from major metropolitan centers along with their own homespun shows.

Barry Diller was concerned enough about this new development to travel to Pebble Beach, California, on Tuesday, March 11, with 100 other media executives to discuss the matter with King Rupert. Murdoch put on a dog-and-pony show designed to allay the fears of his industry colleagues.

"We are local programmers ourselves," said Preston Padden, a News Corporation executive. "We will seamlessly integrate your own program-ming with our own."

Murdoch's attempt to mollify Diller and the others fell mostly on skep-tical ears. Murdoch was threatening to take over the world and was in effect asking them all to stand by peacefully and let him have his way. It was important to Murdoch that nobody interfered with his efforts since he had yet to clear his plans with the regulatory authorities. Murdoch was taking the line that his own grand venture would expand the program choices for television viewers without hurting local stations. He promised Diller and the other executives that he would not beam local stations from distant markets to customers who could receive their own local programming with either a cable hookup or an antenna. This was critical since the advertising revenue of local stations, necessary for their survival, depended on their reaching 100 percent of their own individual markets.

"Rupert's trying to soften up this group," Diller said, "so we don't stand in the way of his negotiations with broadcasters and the regulators. Anybody who thinks he's doing anything for charitable reasons is dangerously out to lunch."

In the words of Peter Martin, general manager of the CBS affiliate in Burlington, Vermont, "We are following this issue microscopically. My sense of Congress is that they are also keenly aware of the importance of the local television market."

Most observers had little doubt that Murdoch posed a direct threat to the cable industry. He had spoken in the past of "burying" cable, maintaining that satellite transmission provided more choices than cable did and was a far superior means of distribution.

"People in the industry are somewhat annoyed about Murdoch's belligerent remarks about burying cable," said Richard Aurelio, former president of Time Warner's New York City cable system.

Yet, Barry Diller was not totally opposed to Murdoch's grand design. Yes, it would provide fierce competition for cable operators like his sometime friend and ally John Malone. But for Diller, who was earnestly cobbling together his own patchwork empire of independent stations anchored in local programming, Murdoch offered a ray of opportunity. All Diller had to do was figure out a way of hitching his own star to King Rupert's Sky wagon.

CHAPTER 30

GLITZ, SCHMALTZ, AND CHICKEN WINGS

ON MONDAY NIGHT, March 24, 1997, Barry Diller hosted one of the in parties for Hollywood's A-list following the annual Academy Awards ceremony. Forever struggling to outdo itself with greater and greater extremes of poor taste, Hollywood's elite was determined to stage the most obscene display of self-indulgent extravagance in Academy Award history. The show put on in 1997 did not disappoint anyone; it surpassed the loftiest levels of vulgarity reached over its sixty-eight-year history, ever since the movie industry threw its first publicity party for itself at the Hollywood Roosevelt Hotel, in 1929.

The 1997 event employed more than 10,000 people at various levels of enterprise, from the lowliest stagehand through the Academy's executive director. It generated more than $100 million in revenue, which was about the same as the annual budget of Little Rock, Arkansas.

"I've done the Emmys, the Grammys, the Kennedy Center Honors, and the Presidential Inaugural," said Michael Seligman, the associate producer of the show, "but the Oscars are the only time creative people have a budget big enough to create their dream."

Whether it was a dream or a Bacchanalian phantasm was strictly in the eye of the beholder. It depended on whether one was impressed or horrified at the notion of paying $3,000 at a Beverly Hills hairdresser on the day of the nominations, or $5,000 for an eyebrow tweeze at Valerie of Beverly Hills, which was normally closed on Mondays but opened its doors for this occasion. Even the limousine drivers dined like royalty on Academy Awards night, having been dispatched to the Clipper Club down the street where 1,100 of them gobbled up $13,000 worth of chicken wings and sausages.

In 1996, Italian fashion firm Dolce & Gabbana flew an employee over to Milan to pick up a $10,000 custom-made gown and hand-deliver it personally to actress Susan Sarandon in Hollywood. In 1997, actor Jim Carrey upped the ante when he received fifty-six gowns from thirteen separate designers, worth from $2,000 to $20,000 each, in the designers' hopes that his wife might wear one of them on the night of the Awards. The lucky designer would be bestowed with millions of dollars in free publicity.

No one personified this larger-than-life glitz-fest better than Barry Diller. Barry was bred to the occasion, born and raised in Beverly Hills, the heart of the heart of Fantasy Land. Glamour, glitz, schmaltz, and conspicuous consumption flowed in his veins. He had been glad-handing and schmoozing all his life, flashing his mirthless grin while slipping the knife through the ribs of his opponents since he was barely out of high school. Barry loved the ritual, the pomp and ceremony of being seen in all the right places by all the right people.

Seventy-five million Americans were glued to their televisions during the main event of the evening, second in number only to the Superbowl. ABC paid the Academy almost $20 million to telecast the show, which generated about $36 million in advertising revenue plus additional millions in licensing fees to ninety-eight television markets throughout the world.

Before heading home to host his own party after the ceremony, Diller strolled over to the Governor's Ball, maneuvering his way through the throng with his hand outstretched and his broad smile set firmly in place for the rest of the evening. Eight hundred waiters worked their way among the crowd, carrying platters piled high with caviar, lobster, and smoked salmon displayed on Oscar-shaped matzo bread. Barry raised his hand in front of him, waving all of it off. Later in the night, in the early hours of the morning after his guests had finally left, he would treat himself to a bowl of cottage cheese and fruit salad on a lettuce leaf before retiring to bed. His business manager would inform him later, after all the bills had come in, that the cost of his *soiree* for a few hundred of his nearest and dearest friends was close to $200,000. It was just the cost of doing business. The only thing was, the cost was going up every year while business was getting harder and harder to perform.

In the spring of 1997, Diller was preoccupied with the growing battle between satellite and cable television systems. In which direction should he tilt? At this stage of his life, it was critical that he not cast his lot with one contender in the struggle, only to see the other side win. Somehow, Diller had to find a way to keep one foot firmly planted in both arenas.

John Malone was still the King of Cable despite his mounting problems at TCI, and Diller remained linked to him for better or worse through a complicated interlocking corporate structure. Leo Hindery, Jr., the man Malone had tapped to refocus TCI, sat on the Board of Directors of Silver King. TCI also maintained a small stake in Silver King through a fairly significant ownership position in Silver King's parent, the Home Shopping Network. Diller's budding empire, whether he liked it or not, was inextricably bound in one way or another to Malone. Now Diller's old boss Rupert Murdoch had clouded the heavens with his new Sky satellite venture, referred to as the Death Star by Malone and other cable operators. Diller still enjoyed a good working relationship with Murdoch, notwithstanding their past differences, and needed to figure out a way of tapping into Murdoch's project without alienating Malone.

By his own admission, Malone had lost 70,000 subscribers in 1996 to satellite program distributors. TCI was being ravaged by flesh-eating bacteria called capital expenditures, which were rising as the company's profits were falling.

"My vision for the company has not really changed that much," Malone said, "but the course we take to achieve that vision is constantly adjusted."

Diller shrewdly and diplomatically sided with Malone in public, even as he formulated his backup plan in the event Malone self-destructed. "John Malone is going to remain in the business," Barry said. "If you believe in cable, believe in him." Privately, however, Diller was keeping his options open.

"All this talk about Death Star is just silly," said Decker Anstrom, president of the National Cable Television Association. "The cable industry is not about to have its lunch eaten by Mr. Murdoch."

Diller smiled at that remark. All he really cared about was that Barry Diller did not have his lunch eaten by anyone. Diller was not accustomed to dining on the crumbs of someone else's meals. Even after his failed bids for Paramount and CBS, he had managed to land on his feet. Killer Diller the cat, fangs and claws sharpened for any eventuality. He intended to eat his fair share, if not the lion's share, of whatever course was being served.

Diller felt no guilt about keeping his options open. Business, like politics and war, sometimes made for strange bedfellows. Diller's current allies were not beyond forging strategic alliances with their own enemies. A week before the Academy Awards ceremony, John Malone met secretly with Diller's old boss and Malone's present nemesis Rupert Murdoch at the airport in Denver. Malone told Murdoch he was upset about Murdoch's plans for Sky, particularly in light of an agreement Malone had to sell his sports properties to Murdoch.

"One deal has nothing to do with the other," Murdoch snapped.

"I can't agree to give up Liberty's valuable sports enterprises to someone who's trying to gut my cable operation."

"Suit yourself," Murdoch said, knowing he had Malone temporarily over a barrel because of his cash flow problems.

By the end of March, Malone had little choice but to capitulate, without informing Diller of his plans. The $1 billion transaction would transfer major stakes in fifteen regional sports networks from Malone's Liberty Media Group to Murdoch's News Corporation. The deal was likely to have an impact on Diller, although he did not find out about it from Malone, but rather from third parties who enjoyed a closer relationship with Malone than he did. Loyalty played no part in the business world Diller traveled in, not when billions of dollars were up for grabs.

The U.S. Supreme Court gave Diller a helping hand at the end of March when it upheld federal rules requiring cable systems to carry local broadcasts of the type Diller transmitted from his independent stations. The decision was as close as it could get, five justices voting in favor and four against, closing the door on a thirteen-year effort by Malone and the rest of the cable industry to overturn the rules.

Malone and his colleagues had maintained that the "must carry" rules violated their First Amendment guarantees of free speech by forcing them to air programs they did not want to carry. However, while the justices had some misgivings about the First Amendment aspects of the case, they viewed it more as a question of keeping the airwaves free of domination by the networks and large cable systems. The Supreme Court ruling did not specifically apply to satellite systems, but there seemed to be little doubt that satellite operators like Rupert Murdoch would be affected as well. It was unlikely that the courts would allow Murdoch to escape the strictures imposed on his competitors in the cable industry.

For Barry Diller, the decision was doubly sweet. It meant that the local programming dynasty he was building would continue to enjoy access to the public through cable and, most likely, through satellite as well. The ruling would leave two industry titans—Malone and Murdoch—a little weaker, and independents such as himself a little stronger. The outcome could not have been better had Diller orchestrated it himself.

"While it's great to shout about how worthy your programming is and how deserving of carriage by the great cable industry," Diller could not help gloating, "it's far better to have it guaranteed by the Supreme Court's ruling."

The decision also benefited shareholders of Diller's HSN stock with a $2.50 jump in share price to more than $25 a share. Not bad for the common stock of a company that had yet to show a nickel in earnings.

Broadcasters of all types had been served well by their contributions to both political parties. The coffers of Democrats and Republicans alike had been fattened to the extent of about $10 million each during the past ten years by the networks, cable and satellite operators, and independents. Diller's Silver King had made so-called soft money contributions totaling well over $300,000, while Disney, GE, News Corporation, and others more than doubled that amount. Additional millions were funneled to politicians through the broadcasters' various PAC groups. Common Cause maintained that the money had bought the broadcasters favorable legislation from Washington, permitting wider ownership of television and radio stations amounting to a gift of about $70 billion, a significant return on their collective investment.

Peggy Binzel, a spokesman for Murdoch, denied the charge. "They have a view that money or power leads to votes, and that's not the way it is."

It was a lame defense, considering that everyone who was not comatose understood that money was the grease that kept the political machine operating smoothly on behalf of special interest groups. Diller was smart enough not to deny the obvious. When confronted with Common Cause's report, he simply smiled and shrugged his shoulders. "It's just the cost of doing business," he said.

Another issue that affected the industry was a decision made in April by the Federal Communications Commission to give each of the country's 1,600 television stations a second channel to broadcast digital programming. Digital TV would offer super-sharp, high-definition images and digital audio systems on a wide flat screen. In effect, the ruling would render obsolete all 240 million television sets in use in the United States by February 2009.

It was a bonanza for television manufacturers, who were already getting ready to market HDTV sets for the 1997 Christmas season, at prices ranging upwards of $2,000 at first, although prices would fall sharply as the fateful day drew nearer. It was a gift to the networks as well, since the cable and satellite industries were scrambling to realign their operations with the new technology. The FCC decision would also benefit the independent operators like Barry Diller, whose local programs would be beamed into more and more living rooms across the country via the latest available technology.

In the 1996 presidential campaign, Republican contender Bob Dole had attacked the FCC plan, which was in the proposal stage at the time, as "a big corporate welfare project." Even FCC chairman Reed Hunt admitted it was "the biggest single gift of public property to any industry in this century."

Now that the decision was official, the gargantuan "corporate welfare project" was a *fait accompli*. The Clinton administration may have passed a law downsizing welfare for ordinary citizens, but corporate and even industry-wide welfare had definitely been increased. The cost of doing business, as Diller put it, had paid out handsome dividends. The administration in Washington rewarded its fattest contributors with one of the biggest public garage sales in history—dwarfed only by the monumental bailouts of the financial services industry in 2008.

CHAPTER 31

HE'S NOT AN EMPLOYEE ANYMORE

ANOTHER MAJOR BENEFICIARY of the Supreme Court ruling in favor of must-carry rules was Lowell Paxson, CEO of Paxson Communications. Paxson owned forty-nine local television stations that reached 22 million homes with a steady diet of canned infomercials. Before the Supreme Court ruling in March 1997, Paxson lived in fear that his stations were going to be bounced off the air by the cable systems because of lack of viewer interest. Paxson's ultimate dream was to eventually beef up his stations with more creative programming, of which he was in scant supply.

Suddenly Paxson was a man in demand.

"I'm now a network in search of programming," he said. "When that ruling came in, I cried. Twenty-five minutes later, everybody in my office was drinking champagne, and by 11:30 I had a hangover. All of a sudden I'm the prettiest girl at the ball."

Barry Diller thought Lowell Paxson was pretty enough to invite him to

HSN headquarters for a powwow in April. Paxson had something Diller wanted very badly: distribution clout. In return, Diller offered Paxson the type of programming that could turn Paxson's network of stations from ghetto franchises into major league operations.

"I don't want to hold the programming cards," Paxson admitted. "I don't think there's anybody in our company smart enough to know what they mean."

"In broadcasting, new ideas are rare," Diller said, his eyes sparkling in anticipation of a new business marriage, this one made in heaven. "There is an opportunity for alternative programming here."

Diller and Paxson were a genuine odd couple in more ways than one. Paxson was a born-again Christian, a supporter of the Christian Network, a small cable channel that scrolled Bible verses down the screen with inspirational music playing in the background. He was a political conservative. Diller, of course, was a liberal Jew from Beverly Hills who couldn't have been more culturally removed from Paxson's world if he had come from a different solar system.

They were linked, however, by Paxson's role in launching the Home Shopping Network back in the 1970s, when he peddled can openers on radio. Paxson sold his stake in 1992 for $70 million, bought up a string of UHF stations that nobody else wanted, and then sold time on the air to producers of infomercials that featured everything from face cream to exercise bikes. Ironically enough, Diller found himself presiding over HSN several years later, just as he was developing the kind of programming Paxson needed to gain market share for his stations. Diller was planning a major launch of his local programming lineup in Miami for the spring of 1998. Paxson's network of cable stations would quadruple Diller's distribution capabilities if the two men could get together on terms. All they needed to do was hammer out the details.

Diller sought to further broaden his franchise in May 1997 when he proposed to acquire a 48 percent stake in Ticketmaster in a stock swap deal valued at about $210 million. According to the terms of the transaction, Paul G. Allen, one of the founders of Microsoft who sat on the boards of both Microsoft and Ticketmaster, would become an 11 percent owner in Diller's HSN by exchanging his shares in Ticketmaster for HSN stock. Ticketmaster's president Frederic D. Rosen and Allen's associate Bill Savoy would join HSN's board of directors along with Allen. Diller also planned to buy additional Ticketmaster stock in the open market to boost his stake in the company to more than 50 percent.

At first glance, the pending merger of the two companies seemed like a corporate oddity. However, in recent years, Ticketmaster had expanded its own operations far beyond the ticket-selling business into the marketing of a wide range of merchandise, including compact discs, videos, T-shirts, and other apparel. Rosen, in particular, had long dreamed of capitalizing on Ticketmaster's distribution clout by offering a broad assortment of products. By linking their operations, Diller and Ticketmaster would become a marketing powerhouse with total annual revenues of approximately $3 billion in sales through cable television, telephone, and the Internet.

Diller's move, following in the wake of Murdoch's struggling effort to expand his satellite capabilities, revealed a lot about the direction in which Diller intended to lead his empire in the years to come. The other media czars could tear one another to pieces as they fought for market share both in the heavens and underground via their cable delivery systems. Diller would pursue a more mundane path of selling popular items and local programming over the telephone, the Internet, and via a far-reaching network that included his own television stations and Paxson's, if the two could eventually agree on terms. The schemes being spun by Murdoch and the others might be more grandiose than Diller's, but Diller was creating a sound, more down-to-earth enterprise. After decades of helping to build media empires for other captains of industry, Diller was finally launching one of his own with a solid foundation beneath it.

"If you believe that the transaction process business will continue to grow, and you want others to use electronic shopping, then the companies can provide the infrastructure to do it," said Diller's associate Jason Stewart.

"As all forms of electronic commerce grow," Diller explained in his own breathless style, "the need for efficient transactional capability will exponentially grow, and we intend to be an aggressive player in offering these services to the thousands of companies that will need them as they develop their own versions of interactive direct commerce."

Though his growing operation was not yet as grand as he had envisioned several years earlier, Diller had the satisfaction of knowing that he was finally running a fledgling empire of his own making. Finally he could say he was his own man. Diller would not suffer the fate of Michael Ovitz, who had once been regarded as the most powerful man in Hollywood. Ovitz had started out in the William Morris Agency, where Diller, Geffen, and many other media titans had learned the business, then went on to create CAA in 1975, which evolved into the most influential talent agency in the country. After twenty years at the helm of CAA, Ovitz decided for some inexplicable reason to give it up and take a job at Disney as second in command to Michael Eisner. Ovitz's tenure at Disney was nothing short of disastrous, and he was forced to resign in disgrace (although with an obscenely large severance package) in January 1997.

"He's not Michael Ovitz anymore," said David Geffen before Ovitz resigned. "He's a guy who has a job working for Michael Eisner."

Diller was kinder on the subject of Ovitz, saying simply that Ovitz had made a career move that turned out to be a mistake. Diller had been there himself, working as second banana to higher powers such as Murdoch, Bluhdorn, and Davis. It was not a mistake Diller was going to make again. No one would ever be able to say again that he was just a guy who has a job working for somebody else.

In July 1997, Barry Diller sat alone in his lavishly furnished apartment in New York City's Waldorf Towers, adjacent to the larger Waldorf-Astoria Hotel. He took comfort in the knowledge that as a resident of the Towers, he was nestled among the elite of international society. His fellow tenants included Princess Elizabeth of Yugoslavia; Jean MacArthur, the ninety-eight-year-old widow of General Douglas MacArthur; Patricia Kluge; and entertainment world royalty including Frank Sinatra. The

Tower's twenty-four-hour concierge and business center, valet service, dry cleaning establishment, and other amenities were a constant reminder of just how high Diller and his neighbors stood in the ranks of rarified society. Diller had never been in the game for money alone, but as oil titan H. L. Hunt once said, "Money was just a way of keeping score." Money was important because of the privileges it could buy.

Diller's apartment, like most of the others in the Tower, measured some 6,000 square feet, trimmed down from the 9,000 square feet the apartments once occupied, but not exactly snug by anyone's standards. It rented for close to $80,000 a month, more than most people earned in a year. The table in his huge dining room could comfortably seat upwards of a dozen guests, his closets were larger than most studio apartments in Manhattan, Aubusson carpets graced his floors, and Baccarat chandeliers hung from the towering ceilings above his head.

As he took stock of his life at this critical juncture (he had turned fifty-five in February), Diller understood that he had yet to achieve his major goals and he had a fair distance yet to travel, but his star was still ascending. He was not a principal player in the mega-deals that roiled his industry, but when the dust finally settled around him, Diller would be left standing on his feet in one piece. At the moment, Bill Gates's Microsoft was planning to invest $1 billion in Comcast, the fourth-largest cable company at the time, to gain a foothold in the industry. Malone's TCI and Cablevision Systems announced that they would swap assets in an effort to lighten TCI's massive debt while strengthening Cablevision's grip on the lucrative New York City market. And Rupert Murdoch, who had put his finger to the wind and realized that he needed to join forces with various cable operators to compete effectively, had decided to put his grand satellite plans on hold for the moment.

Diller's planned merger with Ticketmaster was relatively puny by comparison, but he had never been one to erect a monument overnight; he believed in building his structure brick by brick, stone by stone. In the end, he knew he would play a major role in the media and telecommunications industry and be instrumental in influencing the direction it would take. He was as driven to succeed as always, never content to rest on his accomplishments, still combative, scarred by his battles but lean and mean as he anticipated the battles that loomed ahead.

In the spring of 1998, Barry Diller planned to launch a new television network and realize a profit on it within two years. Through HSN he owned stations in eighteen markets. He would start in Miami with a $150 million investment, then roll out his network city by city over time, eventually reaching 40 percent of U.S. homes within eighteen months. Diller planned to offer eighteen hours of programming a day (the number eighteen seemed to be popping up frequently for some reason), three or four of them devoted to news and the bulk of his broadcasting time to local talk shows and sports.

"With the economics, it seems like a pretty good bet," Diller said following a speech he delivered in New York City. "We could lose our shirts or make a fortune."

Diller's old pal David Geffen was betting on the latter with a multimillion dollar stake in Diller's enterprise. Not a fortune by their standards, but a significant vote of confidence in Diller's dream nonetheless.

Diller could not contemplate failure; it was unacceptable to him.

To ensure that he would succeed, Diller stunned the media world in October 1997 with the boldest move of his life. While everyone's attention was focused on Turner, Murdoch, and Malone, Diller struck a deal that would finally enable him to fulfill his lifetime goal of creating his own media colossus. He announced that he would pay more than $4 billion—$1.2 billion in cash and about $3 billion in HSN stock—for Seagram's Universal Studios properties, including the USA and Sci-fi cable networks. In return, Seagram would acquire a 45 percent stake in Diller's HSN.

The deal was nothing short of brilliant. It immediately launched Diller into the top ranks of the entertainment business alongside those he had either worked for or competed against all his life. The arrangement with Seagram was good for both Diller and Edgar Bronfman, Jr., the fortytwo-year-old bearded scion of the family that controlled Seagram. Diller had long been a friend and advisor to Bronfman, who had at one time offered Diller the job of running Seagram's media properties. Diller had turned it down on the grounds that he never wanted to work for anyone else again.

In Bronfman, Diller had an ally he could trust—insofar as anyone could be trusted in a world where power and money reigned supreme. Bronfman needed Diller's expertise to run the media end of Seagram's business, and Diller needed Universal Studios' assets to put him on equal footing with his rivals. Another benefit for Diller was the reduction of John Malone's equity stake in HSN from 30 percent to 15 percent. Diller would still have Malone looking over his shoulder, but with less control than before.

Among the programming that Diller acquired were rights to *Law & Order*, *Hercules: The Legendary Journeys*, and *Xena: Warrior Princess*. There was little question that Diller intended to overhaul USA and turn it into the linchpin of his media empire.

"Partnerships between cable programmers and broadcasters make sense," Diller said, further stating that he would fold the USA and Sci-Fi networks, as well as his Savoy Pictures channels and stake in Ticketmaster, into HSN and change the name of his new powerhouse company to USA Networks, Inc. Diller was suddenly in a position to go head-to-head with Turner, Murdoch, and the other giants, and he was determined to prevail.

After all, he was Barry Diller. Those who had underrated him in the past had paid a heavy price for doing so. He was Killer Diller. No one who truly knew him would ever count him out as long as the war was still on and he was dressed for combat. He was convinced that he was going to succeed. Not for one moment could Barry Diller admit even to himself that, at the end of the day, he was destined to be a failure.

CHAPTER 32

BARRY TAKES A BRIDE
AND BUILDS AN EMPIRE

THE PAST FEW years had been a blur for Diller, but he had not yet reached the pinnacle of success that he felt was his by birthright. As far as he had risen, towering figures still occupied higher niches than his in the media landscape—Murdoch, Malone, even Turner in his somewhat tarnished and weakened state—and he could not rest as long as their profiles continued to loom larger than his own.

No one could diminish what he had accomplished to date. In establishing USA Networks as an E-commerce powerhouse, Diller had positioned himself at the forefront of the next big wave to rock his industry. His track record for reading popular tastes before they fully emerged was unimpeachable, from pioneering made-for-TV movies for ABC in the 1970s to launching Fox as the fourth network in the 1980s.

"He is unparalleled in jumping on the hot button of the moment," said Porter Bibb, a media analyst with Ladenburg Thalmann & Company.

Others, however, were not overly impressed by Diller's assemblage of media properties. "It's a disparate collection," said analyst Dennis McAlpine. "I'm not sure how it all fits together."

Diller had nothing but contempt for criticism of that nature. "I'm getting sick of this," he fumed. "Television programming and direct selling *are* related, and our bet is that they will become *more* related." It wasn't Diller's fault if people didn't *get* what he was up to.

No one could deny that whatever Diller was up to was highly profitable. The corporate machine he had constructed was minting money and, according to Diller, that should be proof enough that it was working properly.

"What people fail to get," Diller said, "is that USA is essentially two different companies. One is based on TV entertainment and the other on electronic retailing, and a thread links both of them. They have a relation to each other because our broadcast and cable businesses are supported by advertising, and we think that direct selling is going to be a big component of advertising."

Diller was busy enhancing his electronic retailing capabilities by purchasing CitySearch, a website dedicated to helping Web browsers discover what was going on in different cities, and merging it with Ticketmaster, where they could buy tickets to whatever event they wanted to attend. At the same time, Diller was beefing up his entertainment-related enterprises such as USAnetwork.com and SciFi.com. Down the road a bit, the media mogul was still thinking of blending the emerging Internet entity with his more traditional media properties, including movies and television shows—although the entertainment side of his empire would eventually become less and less important to him. He viewed his Internet empire as a perfect marketplace for selling merchandise based on hit movies and TV programs.

"At the end of the day," said Alan Citron, CEO of USA's Internet operations, "if we do our jobs right, USA will have a whole host of sites churning out profits. I don't want to be crass about it, but we're basically about money."

The financial community understood Diller's genius for generating profits better than anyone else. According to Bear Stearns analyst Victor Miller, "If anyone can figure out a new television model, we're confident that Barry Diller can." Institutional investors had no problem putting their clients' money to work on any model Diller wanted to come up with, funneling assets into his bonds and common stock and creating new layers of wealth for Diller, his employees, and his company's shareholders.

His sprawling operation encompassed thirteen television stations owned by USA Networks, a cable service also under the banner of USA Networks, a television production entity called Studios USA, the Sci-Fi Channel, Home Shopping Network, Ticketmaster, and the newly created Ticketmaster Online-Citysearch. The empire generated revenues of well over $2 billion a year. Whenever he introduced new programming into any one of his market areas, he had a gift for making them succeed against overwhelming odds.

"Introducing new programming is always done in an unfriendly environment," Diller said. "It is like bouncing off the side walls of a squash court. It's like constant carom shots, and you find your way like a fool. Each year, as fragmentation continues, it gets more difficult."

Early in 1999, Diller announced that he was pursuing what would have been the biggest and gutsiest deal of his life, the $22 billion acquisition of Internet colossus Lycos. The purchase would be a quantum leap forward for the cautious and financially conservative media king and enable him to create an even larger E-commerce juggernaut, which he wanted to rename USA/Lycos Interactive Networks.

"It will be a powerhouse in the world of electronic commerce," predicted SG Cowen media analyst Ed Hatch. The new operation, according to Hatch, would have "unparalleled size, scale, and reach."

Lycos was the third-largest Internet portal, and under Diller's stewardship the new venture would have the capacity to reach half of the country's Web surfers as well as 70 million television sets, and to field more than one million phone calls a day. In his bid for Lycos, Diller enjoyed the backing of Seagram's Edgar Bronfman and Liberty Media's John Malone, his old ally, both of whom owned a substantial stake in Diller's enterprise.

Diller intended to finance the deal with a combination of assets and so-called *Diller Dollars*—the rising price of his stock, which he leveraged to the max. He personally controlled 61.5 percent of his expanding empire, with an assortment of investors owning the rest of it. In the end, the deal collapsed to Diller's benefit as Lycos fell victim to the dot-com implosion that shortly followed. However, Diller moved abruptly into a more profitable area, the online travel industry, when he purchased a stake in the Hotel Reservation Network and bought travel service Expedia from Microsoft.

Booz-Allen partner Geoff Sands did not think Diller was finished yet, now that he had the taste of real empire-building in his mouth. Not by a long shot. "Not only is Barry Diller not done," he said, "we'll see more of these deals in the future. There will be a rush for more of these alignments. This will be the name of the game—generating multiple revenue streams from E-commerce, advertising, and subscription over multiple platforms."

Over the decades, Diller had been troubled by the recurring stories in the media about his sexual orientation. According to media journalist Michael Wolff, who was with *New York* magazine at the time, Diller once said to him that "you can't say anything about my personal life."

"Of course," Wolff had replied, "only to the extent that your personal life is relevant to the story."

"No. I don't think you understand," Diller clarified in his most menacing whine, which was simultaneously amusing and terrifying. "I would kill you."

According to Wolff, he was truly intimidated by Diller's threatening way of joking and later referred to him as "not only a megagorilla but, every rumor agreed, a gay one in what was still, in the late seventies, a highly homophobic business."

In an effort to put the rumors behind him and end, once and for all, the discussions about his sexuality, Diller decided to take the plunge with his long-time friend, confidante, and companion, designer Diane von Furstenberg. On February 2, 2001, a cold, sunny, sparkling winter day in New York City, Diller and von Furstenberg hopped into his limo and sped down the East River Drive to City Hall in lower Manhattan, within the shadow of the Brooklyn Bridge. In front of a bevy of special guests, including actors Warren Beatty and Lauren Bacall, Disney head Michael Eisner, and author Dominick Dunne—David Geffen was conspicuous by his absence—they exchanged wedding vows and legalized their relationship.

"I didn't want to miss it. It's a real love story," Dunne told a reporter from the *New York Daily News*.

It was a quiet ceremony that ended quickly and was celebrated by a private dinner afterward for the couple and their closest friends. The gay community has had a lot to say about Diller's marriage ever since, and Diller has done little to dispel insinuations that his marriage was a platonic affair. His sexual inclinations have been considered fair game for at least two decades among journalists, fellow media magnates, and the gay community.

Several authors have gone beyond mere innuendo. *The Operator*, Tom King's biography of David Geffen, states emphatically that Diller is gay, and many in the gay community were incensed by Michael Ovitz's charge that his career was destroyed by a gay cabal in Hollywood. Writer Maer Roshan, who is openly gay, condemned the denials of gay celebrities in *New York* magazine and discussed Diller's long-term relationship with the former editor-in-chief of *The Advocate*, a gay magazine. In the homophobic Hollywood of the 1970s, it made good sense for Diller to avoid discussing his personal life. But, according to Roshan, with so many high-profile people coming out of the closet, or being outed by the media, there seemed less and less excuse for it. The dam has long been broken, and newspapers and magazines are no longer intimidated by privacy-obsessed moguls. Diller's marriage to Diane was even described in the stodgy *New York Times* as a "merger," not a marriage. Diller has no children of his own, and Diane von Furstenberg and her children Alex and

Tatiana are the closest people Diller has to family. People close to Diller say he is especially fond of her children. Diller has not only financed Diane von Furstenberg's fashion label, but many claim that he will eventually leave his fortune to her offspring.

In any event, the wedding barely slowed Diller down for a nanosecond from the torrid pace he had been setting during the past couple of years. Without breaking a sweat, Diller commenced negotiations on a new deal that would give French media conglomerate Vivendi control of most of USA's television operations and leave him with independent ownership of the rest of his empire, particularly the money-generating retail channels. In reality, the relationship was more complicated than it first appeared on paper, since Vivendi would pay Diller more than $10 billion for the properties but also let him run the entire show, encompassing not only the retail fiefdom, but the television operations and Universal's film business as well. No one knew how to run the empire better than the man who had assembled it, and Vivendi's top management was smart enough to figure that out. In effect, Diller was ceding official control over the television enterprise in exchange for the cash, but he would be gaining independent *de facto* control over all the properties he had accumulated over the years. For the first time in his life, the corporate independence he had always craved was now within his grasp. The structure of the deal was nothing short of brilliant from Diller's perspective.

Jean-Marie Messier, the chairman of Vivendi, made no secret of his desire to expand his company's presence into the United States. He openly favored American culture and society over his own, earning the enmity of his fellow Frenchmen, and moved his wife, family, and entire base of operations from Paris to New York in September 2001. Messier was enamored of American movies in particular and was somewhat starstruck by the recent success of Universal Pictures' *The Mummy Returns*, *The Fast and the Furious*, and *American Pie 2*. He was interested in putting the USA television and Universal film businesses under joint management and perhaps leveraging the success of the movies as spinoffs for television shows.

For his part, Diller's newfound autonomy would provide him with the freedom to pursue other acquisitions without the consent of Malone and other investors who had thwarted him a few years earlier in his bid to buy CBS and NBC. Diller wanted nothing less than to change the entire way Hollywood did business. He was a long-time critic of the star system, which placed film studios in financial straits by paying movie stars $20 million to $25 million per picture, gave directors a cut of every box-office dollar, whether a film was profitable or not, and also paid production companies hundreds of millions of dollars for filming that could have been done by the studios themselves.

"Over the years, Barry became more and more disenchanted with the movie business," said Leonard Goldberg, a former producer, studio head, and mentor to Diller. "The economic margins were shrinking and shrinking, and the egos were getting bigger and bigger. It became harder for him to justify the way the business was going."

"I want to stir things up," Diller admitted, and buying new companies and restructuring the way they did business was the most effective way for him to do that.

His model for the way he envisioned movies being made in the future was *Traffic*, a politically charged movie that slammed the government's futile War on Drugs. The film cost only $45 million to make and grossed more than $250 million, mainly because Michael Douglas and other stars agreed to work for relatively low fees in exchange for a percentage of the profits. The movie was a financial and critical success and won four Academy Awards for Diller's company. Earlier movies from the 1980s that fit this pattern were *Reds*, *Ordinary People*, *Terms of Endearment*, and *Broadcast News*. Diller had similar plans for the television business, which he also considered to be poorly managed.

"Barry's feeling about television is it's a terrible business," said a Diller aide who preferred to remain anonymous. "You spend all this money on development, you hire producers and writers, you take all the risks, and the odds are slim that you'll make back any money, especially if you give large pieces of the show to the talent."

In Diller's view, syndicated shows and repeats of past hits were far more profitable and less risky than new network series, and they were the main money-makers for his television operation. Now that he was sitting in the catbird seat as chief executive officer of Vivendi Universal Entertainment, the entity created by his deal with Vivendi, and with billions of dollars of cash in his treasury, the big question was just how well he would get along with his new French bosses. In other words, how much of a team player would he—*could* he—be given his history of compulsive and abrasive micromanagement?

Diller downplayed his reputation for being a tough, strong-willed executive who liked to get things done *his* way, on his own terms. "There is a lot of mythology in my life," he said through a steely smile. "Will I have opinions? I always have opinions. When I express them, it can get noisy, it often can get argumentative. But my purpose is to draw out others, what they really think."

The only problem with that, according to people close to Diller, was that the media king had a way of slicing people into confetti when they expressed opinions that differed markedly from his own.

CHAPTER 33

DILLERAMA

THE MARRIAGE BETWEEN Vivendi and USA—essentially between Jean-Marie Messier and Barry Diller—was an odd one from the start. The two executives appeared on stage together at a news conference in New York City to announce their merger in December 2001, putting their best smiles forward. Diller always looked as though he were girded for combat, while Messier, at age forty-four, still retained the look of a freshly scrubbed Boy Scout. Ostensibly, Diller would be reporting to Messier and his colleagues in Paris and would be held accountable by them, but Diller looked strangely enough the more energetic and formidable of the two even though he was sixteen years older. Already, before the ink was dry on their corporate nuptial agreement, many analysts were wondering out loud just how long it would take the older man to eat the young Frenchman's *foi gras* and send him packing back to Paris.

"Where is his money?" said one skeptical media analyst. "You have to follow the money," meaning that Diller's priorities would remain on the interactive side of the business.

"I have grown to like Mr. Messier," Diller replied somewhat cryptically, defending himself against charges of divided loyalty. "I like our process together, and I think we can do stimulating work."

For his part, Messier stated that he was struck by Diller's "industry vision" and his "track record for growth in asset value and cash flows."

USA's cash flow was growing at a rate of 10 percent a year, ahead of the industry average, and USA was the third-most popular primetime cable channel after HBO and Turner Broadcasting. But Diller's link to Vivendi was tenuous at best. He agreed to work for the French concern without either a salary or a contract. He could walk away from his handshake arrangement with Vivendi anytime he found Messier and his colleagues too intrusive, too overbearing, or at odds with his own agenda. Meanwhile, he had already pocketed more than $10 billion of their cash. Before too long, Messier could wind up asking himself just what he had gotten out of the deal.

Their corporate marriage, such as it was, ended before the next year was out in a way that Diller could not have foreseen. By July 2002, Messier's expansion into the brave new world of American entertainment had put such a strain on Vivendi's finances that the company was close to defaulting on its debt obligations. Vivendi fired Messier, leaving him high and dry on American soil, and replaced him with Jean-Rene Fourtou, who proceeded to skirt the rocky shores of bankruptcy by selling off $5 billion worth of assets, including American publisher Houghton Mifflin. Vivendi's stock plunged 90 percent on the news that Messier had spend $77 billion on acquisitions designed to transform his company, a former water utility, into a rival of AOL Time Warner. Worst than Messier's profligate spending spree was the mounting suspicion that he had engaged in an accounting fraud to hide Vivendi's perilous finances as far back as 2000.

By December, the Finance Brigade of the Paris Public Prosecutor's Office had gathered enough evidence to take action. The investigators sent police storming into Vivendi's Paris headquarters to seize the company's accounting books, and they also raided Messier's mansion in Rambouillet, a village outside of Paris, to take possession of his personal papers. French prosecutors charged Messier with fraud and other criminal activities but eventually dropped charges against him on the grounds that their case was not strong enough to lead to a conviction. Diller, who had a reputation for being as honest as he was tough, lost no time in distancing himself from Messier's fiasco. He promptly resigned his position as co-chief executive officer of Vivendi Universal Entertainment while maintaining his financial interest in the company.

"We will remain a minority shareholder in VUE," Diller said. "But we are not part of that group, we are not part of any plot, and we will see what happens here." Diller personally owned 1.5 percent of the French entertainment concern, and his company owned another 5.4 percent.

There was delicious irony in the speculation that Diller might be able to buy back at bargain basement prices the entertainment properties he had just sold to Vivendi. With Vivendi on the ropes and Messier threatened with the prospect of spending a good chunk of his middle age in a Parisian prison, Diller was faced with the opportunity to buy back his old assets for fifty cents on the dollar. Indeed, he let it be known that he would play a key role in the sale of the assets, since Vivendi had to pay Diller as much as $2 billion to satisfy tax obligations in the event their partnership was dissolved within fifteen years, according to Diller.

In the end, Diller was more interested in separating Vivendi from another billion or so in cash than he was in reacquiring his old entertainment properties. The man who had launched his career on the entertainment side of the business, and had created a brand new network for Rupert Murdoch in the process, was less interested than ever in providing entertainment for anyone.

"Say goodnight, Gracie," he said, sarcastically dismissing the head of VUE's entertainment network, after she had pitched him on the value of his former movie and television properties. Diller later summed up his sentiments colorfully and succinctly: "Hollywood today is mostly a pain in the ass." And as far as television was concerned, "a handful of companies are in charge of everything both vertically and horizontally that you get to see through a screen, a television screen, not a computer screen. There's no *air* in it anymore."

From now on—until further notice at least—the name of the game for Diller was the Internet, and he spelled it *Interactive*. He believed in his new operation so passionately that he renamed his company InterActiveCorp (IAC). His interests had shifted dramatically during the past few years. He had evolved into the most successful *shopkeeper* on the planet, a nonpareil purveyor of goods and services sold across the global electronic marketplace.

Diller helped orchestrate the sale of VUE's entertainment assets to the NBC unit of General Electric and reflected on what his next step would be. At the end of 2003, IAC was positioned as the largest E-commerce retailer in the world, generating annual revenues of more than $6 billion—larger than Yahoo!, Amazon.com, and eBay. Diller's company owned Expedia and Hotels.com, the two most profitable online travel services in the marketplace; Ticketmaster, which controlled 90 percent of ticket sales for concerts, shows, and sporting events; LendingTree, a mortgage broker with revenues growing 50 percent a year; Hotwire.com, the discount travel site; CitySearch, with its symbiotic relationship with Ticketmaster; Interval International, a timeshare owner; and HSN, a cable channel cash cow.

The various entities fit together like pieces in a puzzle. Expedia sold tickets for Ticketmaster and offered time shares for Interval International. HSN was slated to promote travel services on the air. Hotels.com inserted hotel discount coupons in Diller's Entertainment Publications discount books. Ticketmaster planned to offer online auctions on HSN for tickets to various events. Hotwire was linked directly to Expedia and Hotels.com. CitySearch restaurant listings fit perfectly with Entertainment Publications discount books. And LendingTree referred its mortgage customers to the Expedia and Ticketmaster sites.

After his spending spree of the past few years, Diller was still sitting on a cash hoard of $5 billion, which would enable him to finance new acquisitions that he expected to mesh with his sprawling interactive empire.

Travel, finance, real estate, classified ads all made sense to him, and he hadn't even begun to tap into overseas markets with his concept. Diller had quietly, but purposefully, assembled his interactive Internet powerhouse by fusing previously fragmented businesses into a dynamic whole.

"In every one of our businesses, we're playing a role in defining new economic laws," he explained. Economics for Diller meant advertising the products of companies that offered him the biggest discounts, much like an online Wal-Mart putting pressure on suppliers to squeeze out fatter profit margins for itself.

"Diller has the ability to punish," said Jim Young, an executive vice president with InterContinental Hotels Group.

The hotels had to play ball with Diller since "Expedia has 18 million unique users a month; that's humongous," elaborated Kurian Jacob of the Radisson Lexington chain, which filled about 100 hotel rooms a day with Expedia customers.

While the analysts had been trying to figure out exactly what Diller was up to, the former media czar had cagily positioned himself as the king of E-commerce during the past six years. He sat atop an Internet empire dedicated to consumer demand *precisely* because he was the first man on the planet who realized that shopping was the true *entertainment* medium of the twenty-first century. Movies and television shows were now passé. *Shopping* was entertainment, and not just any kind of shopping. *Shopping for bargains* was America's favorite pastime as the new century was beginning to build up a head of steam. Finding the *best deals* on hotels, airline tickets, theater tickets, travel packages, restaurants, real estate, and other luxuries was what interested Americans the most. Nobody paid retail anymore, and Diller had become the king of discounting. And if discounting was what America was all about, it was just a question of time before the rest of the world followed America's lead. Much as the rest of the world professed to hate American culture, the rest of the world couldn't get in line fast enough to mimic America's lifestyle. The whole world was destined to go on a shopping spree of unprecedented proportions, and Barry Diller owned the biggest discount store in the marketplace.

CHAPTER 34

INSANITY CAN RUIN THE BEST OF MARRIAGES—AND PUT THEM BACK TOGETHER AGAIN

LIKE ALL BAD marriages, it was inevitable that two partners with monumental egos like Barry Diller and John Malone would develop some relationship issues. Barry Diller built his $18 billion media empire with a lot of financial help from Malone. It was Malone who referred to his relationship with Diller as a "marriage." Like most marriages, when the journey was going smoothly, the partners left each other alone. But when the road got bumpy, the marriage threatened to come unglued.

At the beginning of 2008, with the U.S. economy teetering precariously on the edge of a recession, the stock market gave way to a barrage of selling. The stock price of Diller's IAC/InterActiveCorp was not spared from the bloodletting, and Malone, whose Liberty Media Corporation owned a majority voting stake in IAC, began to fret. "There was a time when there was, I think, a 20 percent 'Barry premium' in the stock," said Malone, gazing out of his office window overlooking the Rocky Mountains in

Englewood, Colorado, according to one report. "Today you could argue there is a 'Barry discount.'"

Malone entertained the notion, for the first time in years, of unraveling his internecine business ties to Diller. For his part, Diller admitted that "we've been frustrated with each other at times," but he believed that given their longstanding history together, they would be able to patch things up. Malone had granted Diller the power to vote Liberty Media's shares in IAC, but now Malone was having second thoughts about that arrangement. "The hook is set," said Malone. "It is our company, and Barry ain't going to be able to spit the hook"—a reference to a fish spitting out the hook before the fisherman can pull him in.

Diller was incensed. "John is insane," he said.

It wasn't just IAC and Liberty that were reeling from the bear market that had taken hold of Wall Street. The entire media and telecommunications sector had been in turmoil since 2003, when competition in the online travel industry intensified and growth began to slow. Key industries within the sector were in disarray, including television and movies, both of which were being buffeted by rapidly emerging technologies and the influence of the Internet. Top executives in the entertainment field were scrambling to develop new business models in an effort to stay ahead of the curve. They all tried to get a handle on the *next big* thing, if only they could figure out exactly what it would be.

Barry Diller had recently turned sixty-five, and Malone was a year older. Both had regarded themselves as unparalleled influences in their businesses, but now they were afraid of becoming irrelevant, of being overtaken by younger players with brand-new ideas. Aside from their uneasy business marriage, however, they had little else in common. Malone started out as an engineer and built his company into the largest cable-TV operator in the country. He sold a piece of it to AT&T in 1999 but maintained control of its programming arm. Unlike Diller, Malone was a political conservative, something of a gunslinger who feuded regularly with government regulators. He was a family man, married for forty-four years to his wife Leslie. He preferred to spend a good deal of time on his Colorado ranch, and he often bragged that he had thrown out most of his tuxedos. Diller, of course, remained entranced by the over-the-top glitter of Hollywood celebrityhood and all the parties that went with it. One of the few things the men had in common outside of business was sailing. The two men sailed as frequently as their busy schedules allowed, and Diller once sailed up the Intracoastal Waterway from Florida at Malone's suggestion.

A few years earlier, Liberty Media acquired full ownership of QVC, giving Malone direct control of HSN's biggest rival. It wasn't long before Diller and Malone began to quarrel about IAC's weakening balance sheet, as well as Diller's astronomical compensation package. Diller was the most highly compensated executive on earth in 2007, with a combined annual income of more than $250 million. Other differences surfaced: Malone had always used debt to boost his stock returns, while Diller had a life-long aversion to borrowing money. The price of IAC's stock had begun to languish in 2005 when the company was sitting on a $2 billion cash hoard. Malone advised Diller to assume some debt and buy back IAC shares in the marketplace in an effort to support its price—a common practice of many companies when their stocks are being battered.

"What are you sitting on all that cash for?" Malone asked Diller.

Both men disagreed on how to structure their takeover deals. When Diller bought the search engine Ask.com (originally Ask Jeeves) in 2005, Malone urged him to use his cash instead of exchanging stock for the other company, since Diller would get better tax treatment if he ever decided to sell the shares. But Diller ignored the advice, insisting that a stock transaction was the only option the sellers would agree to.

"If it had been me," Malone said, "I would have been willing to pay a higher price and pay cash. Barry doesn't use his balance sheet effectively. He is not a financial guy."

Malone originally declared that he thought Diller would be able to turn his company around over the long term. "I would still bet on Barry," he said. But in the next breath, he took the onus off himself for criticizing his erstwhile buddy and transferred it to Liberty Media's CEO Greg Maffei, who left Microsoft to join Liberty Media in 2005. "There is not quite as much love for Barry on average" at Liberty, said Malone. "Greg has made it clear that he isn't as enchanted with Barry as I am." In effect, he had appointed Maffei as his pit bull.

Maffei and Diller had clashed when Maffei was chairman of Expedia and Diller bought the firm. Now it was payback time, and Maffei encouraged his new boss, Malone, to tighten the screws on his old nemesis, Diller. Diller tried to be diplomatic about the situation, maintaining that he had a lot of respect for Maffei but wasn't about to be intimidated by him. The tension mounted, and at the end of 2007, Malone and Diller met to discuss ways of putting an end to their long-term marriage. One possible solution, put forth by Diller, was for Liberty Media to assume full ownership of HSN in exchange for Diller receiving Liberty Media's shares of IAC.

It appeared at first as though this arrangement might be mutually acceptable when IAC's stock price climbed from $24 to $40 a share at the beginning of 2008. At that price, Malone believed the stock swap that Diller proposed looked attractive. The stock price, however, could not hold up for long and began to sink back to earth once again. Malone quickly lost interest in the deal and asked Diller to sweeten the pot.

"I am not about to abandon Mr. Diller unless he offers me something a hell of a lot better than a swap for HSN," said Malone.

Well, Diller was not about to offer Malone any more than he already had. Malone pressed him to toss in Expedia, which Malone had expressed an interest in owning for quite some time, but Diller would not budge. Once again, Malone tried to use more pressure to bend Diller to his will. "It is a little uncomfortable for Barry," he said. "Right now we are the shadow that walks around behind him." Malone's comment only stiffened Diller's resistance. Next, Malone tried a tactic that made him sound more like a Mafia hit man than a high-level executive. "If a bus gets Mr. Diller," Malone mused, "Liberty Media gets control of IAC."

Diller had to laugh at that one. He joked that he drove a motorcycle instead of a car around Manhattan because "It makes it easier for Liberty to run me over."

Diller knew that the best defense is a good offense, and he lost no time in striking the next blow. He sent out a press release in January 2008, stating that he wanted to spin off various segments of his company in an effort to create greater value for shareholders. Malone interpreted Diller's plan as an effort to dilute his own equity interest in IAC. If Diller couldn't get rid of Malone one way, he would try another. Malone responded with a lawsuit that would restrain Diller from breaking up his company into five separate, publicly traded entities. In March, a Delaware judge dismissed Malone's lawsuit, and the two titans ended up settling out of court with a deal that gave Malone additional representation on the board of each new company. In return, Malone agreed to a so-called standstill arrangement that limited his ability to increase his stake in the new companies.

The spinoff gave Diller the right to retain most of IAC's Internet assets, including Ask.com and HSN. Ticketmaster would be allowed to function as a separate entity, and a new subsidiary would bundle IAC's online travel businesses and be called Interval Leisure Group. IAC's housing-related businesses, which included LendingTree.com, would also operate separately under the name Tree.com.

It was a complicated transaction, but the net effect was to generate piles of cash for Diller at a time when the market value of his company was sinking—indeed, just months before the *entire* stock market dove off a cliff. The timing could hardly have been better. Had Diller waited a few months longer to implement his plan, he would have received considerably less for his assets considering that stocks fell 18 percent during a single week in October alone, the worst week in stock market history. Diller and Malone did their best to put a positive spin on the settlement. "Now it's really over, and that's great for both of us," Diller and Malone said in a joint statement crafted to appease Wall Street.

"I am pleased that we were able to amicably resolve our dispute with IAC," Malone added. "Liberty supports the proposed restructuring of IAC and looks forward to the ongoing success of each of the new entities."

Financial analysts agreed almost unanimously that the spinoff would eventually prove to be lucrative for both parties. "The spin is just in the nick of time, given that the company in its previous form was really not responding to therapy. Keeping it all cobbled together was a bad idea. The restructuring, to management's credit, will bring shareholders a lot of value," said Sanford C. Bernstein analyst Jeffrey Lindsay. IAC would hold on to Ask.com, Match.com, and some smaller Internet properties, while the other four publicly traded businesses would trade under the names Tree.com, Ticketmaster, HSN, and Interval Leisure Group.

"Focusing on consolidated results is only about the past," said Diller, who had become a spinmeister *par excellence*, "and I would think it far more productive for the future to analyze and judge the entities on their own merits. As a large shareholder in each, that is certainly what I intend to do."

The spinoffs put Diller in an ideal position to look around for a major asset to acquire now that he had added considerably to IAC's cash reserve. The question that analysts immediately began to ask was just what type of company would interest Diller the most. Stock prices were depressed across virtually all sectors of the market, thanks to the bear market that took hold in the early summer of 2008. That meant Diller could buy a company for a fraction of what it would have cost him a year earlier.

There was little doubt that Barry Diller would use the situation to reinvent himself once again. "The work is done, and our focus now is moving forward," said Diller in the office of his futuristic headquarters looming over West 18th Street in Manhattan. The building had been designed by architect Frank Gehry to look as though it were constantly in motion, just like the company's chairman. Diller was sixty-six years old now, and his reputation as one of America's preeminent media moguls was firmly in place. He owned more than thirty separate brands under the IAC umbrella, constituting the components of a perfectly focused Internet company. Diller's chief financial officer, Tom McInerney, maintained that the new IAC's capital structure would prove to be crucial, as it boasted net cash reserves of about $1.3 billion—roughly one-third of the company's total market capitalization—which would be used for acquisitions in the foreseeable future. Diller's newly spun-off companies, apart from IAC, had an estimated aggregate fair market value of almost $4 billion: $1.4 billion for HSN; $1.3 billion for Ticketmaster; $1 billion for Interval; and about $200 million for Tree.com.

One of Diller's recent purchases was Lexico, owner of Dictionary.com, which he bought with a view to improving Ask.com's search results. After the spinoff, Diller announced he would be launching Rushmore Drive, a search engine for the black community, and The Daily Beast, an online journalism project led by Tina Brown, the former *Talk* magazine editor.

Diller was definitely hungry for more deals. Some of his likely targets included a buyout of, or alliance with, Time Warner's AOL, in which Yahoo, Microsoft, and News Corp. had also expressed an interest. It was not out of the question that Diller would team up again with John Malone, notwithstanding their contentious courtroom battle. Businessmen, generals, and mafia dons thought alike. "Don't take it personally, it's only business." Joining forces with old enemies to do battle against another marauder is standard operating procedure. If Diller and Malone could find a way to make money and dominate the media landscape together, there was little question that they would reunite their forces—if only to fight each other again another day. Neither Diller nor Malone had lost sight of the 235 million visitors to their various web sites, and the challenge for both men was to find the best way of maximizing profits from those hits.

"I don't know how long I'll be at this," Diller said after the spinoff. "Maybe as long as Rupert . . . certainly not as long as Sumner, however old he is, wherever he is, alive or dead." But no one truly believed he was done doing deals, not as long as his health held out, which he apparently had no problem with at this stage of his life.

"These guys don't like to sit still," said Peter Kreisky, a Boston-based media consultant. "Growth is important, and the assumptions that existed when they put together these companies in the first place no longer are valid." The ability to deliver content via high-speed Internet connections, for example, has set off a new scramble for assets that Kreisky called "the broadband shuffle."

Diller maintained that he wanted to focus on acquisitions that fit in with his other assets. "Agglomeration is not what the market wants now or in the future," he said. "We'll either invest in our businesses or in acquisitions. But if we buy, the mandate will not be to be serial acquirers, but rather to invest in businesses we know. . . . The truth is, if you have a decent idea and there's a business model to it, you need to stay with it."

He gave the public some insight into which direction he might turn when he announced in October 2008 that Ticketmaster would take a $123 million minority stake in talent agency Front Line Management Group and appoint its founder Irving Azoff as its new chief executive. Ticketmaster changed its name to Ticketmaster Entertainment after the deal closed.

"Today we took a significant step in solidifying our position in the music business," said Diller.

Front Line represented about two hundred artists, including the Eagles, Jimmy Buffett, Neil Diamond, Van Halen, Fleetwood Mac, Christina Aguilera, Aerosmith, and Guns 'N' Roses. The acquisition represented a first baby step back into the entertainment business, where Diller got his start more than forty years earlier.

Diller was looking for a way to extend the reach of his existing businesses, and for the moment at least, only he was privy to what his strategy might be. As always, good poker player that he was, he was not going to tip his hand to anyone until he was ready.

ACKNOWLEDGMENTS

YOU MIGHT SAY that I began researching this book more than twenty years ago when I was writing my biography of Australian-born media czar Rupert Murdoch—although I did not realize at the time that I would one day write a biography of Barry Diller. I had recently published a book about real estate tycoon Donald Trump, the first biography written about him. *Trump* turned out to be highly successful and sold more copies than any book I had written before. When my publisher asked me if I was interested in following it up with a biography of Murdoch, I agreed without hesitation. Murdoch was the most influential and powerful figure in the media world, an area I was acquainted with through my work on Wall Street. I started out as a stockbroker in 1975 and went on to become a supervisory analyst and financial writer, authoring several books on personal finance. It didn't take me long to become intrigued by the idea of writing biographies about the rich and powerful figures who have dominated the financial landscape during the past few decades—the

Hunts of Texas, Trump, Murdoch, Alan Greenspan, the Gallo wine family, and now Barry Diller.

In the course of researching my biography of Murdoch, I interviewed hundreds of individuals including Murdoch himself, Barry Diller who worked for him at Fox in the 1980s, dozens of people who knew both of them, financial analysts who covered the media and telecommunications sector, and many others who believed Diller would one day rise to the head of the pack and surpass his former boss as king of media. In retrospect, it was probably inevitable that down the line at some point I would take on Barry Diller as a biographical subject. This book, then, is the natural outgrowth of all the legwork and interviewing I did over the past couple of decades. Biographers are snoops first and foremost. We enjoy poking around in the shadows of other people's lives, looking for details that have never before seen the light of day. I have often felt that had I not been compelled to become a writer, the profession that would have attracted me most is that of private detective.

I would like to especially thank Barry Diller, Jason Stewart, Tom Pollack, Mel Harris, Rupert Murdoch, John Malone, Ted Turner, Porter Bibb, Dennis McAlpine, Alan Citron, Victor Miller, Edward Hatch, Geoff Sands, Jim Young, Kurian Jacob, Jeffrey Lindsay, Tom McInerney, Peter Kreisky, Lucy Salhany, Betsy Frank, Herb Schlosser, Alan Cole-Ford, Richard MacDonald, Steve Dunleavy, Dennis H. Leibowitz, and countless others in the financial and entertainment fields who were courteous and cooperative while I was researching this book. I would also like to acknowledge the contribution made by my old friend Andy Thibault, an investigative journalist with the nose of a bloodhound and the instincts of a pit bull when it comes to getting to the bottom of a story. In addition, this book would not be as complete were it not for the talent and efforts of other writers who covered this beat before me. A complete bibliography of source material is included in the following pages.

BIBLIOGRAPHY

Adamson, Joe. *Groucho, Harpo, Chico, and Sometimes Zeppo: A Celebration of the Marx Brothers and a Satire on the Rest of the World*. New York: Simon & Schuster, 1973.

Anderson, Christopher. *Hollywood TV: The Studio System in the Fifties*. Austin: University of Texas Press, 1994.

Anger, Kenneth. *Hollywood Babylon*. New York: Dell, 1975.

Auletta, Ken. *Three Blind Mice: How the TV Networks Lost Their Way*. New York: Random House, 1991.

Balio, Tino, ed. *Hollywood in the Age of Television*. Boston: Unwin Hyman, 1990.

Barnouw, Erik. *Tube of Plenty: The Evolution of American Television*. New York: Oxford University Press, 1990.

Basten, Fred E. *Beverly Hills: Portrait of a Fabled City*. Los Angeles: Douglas-West, 1975.

Bedell, Sally. *Up the Tube: Prime-Time TV in the Silverman Years*. New York: Viking, 1981.

Birmingham, Stephen. *The Rest of Us: The Rise of America's Eastern European Jews*. Boston: Little, Brown, 1984.

Boyer, Peter J. *Who Killed CBS? The Undoing of America's Number One News Network*. New York: Random House, 1988.

Brook, Stephen. *L.A. Days, L.A. Nights*. New York: St. Martin's Press, 1992.

Brown, Les. *Televi$ion: The Business Behind the Box*. New York: Harcourt Brace Jovanovich, 1971.

Brownstein, Ronald. *The Power and the Glitter: The Hollywood-Washington Connection*. New York: Pantheon, 1990.

Bruck, Connie. *The Predators' Ball: The Junk Bond Raiders and the Man Who Staked Them*. New York: Simon & Schuster, 1994.

Csida, Joseph, and Jane Bundy Csida. *American Entertainment: A Unique History of Popular Show Business*. New York: Billboard, 1978.

Dannen, Frederic. *Hit Men: Power Brokers and Fast Money Inside the Music Business*. New York: Vintage, 1991.

Davis, Genevieve. *Beverly Hills: An Illustrated History*. Northridge: Windsor, 1988.

Eames, John Douglas. *The Paramount Story*. New York: Crown, 1985.

Evans, Robert. *The Kid Stays in the Picture*. New York: Hyperion, 1994.

Friedrich, Otto. *City of Nets: A Portrait of Hollywood in the 1940s*. New York: Harper & Row, 1986.

Gabler, Neal. *An Empire of Their Own: How the Jews Invented Hollywood*. New York: Crown, 1988.

Gaines, Steven, and Sharon Churcher. *Obsession: The Lives and Times of Calvin Klein*. New York: Avon, 1994.

Goldenson, Leonard H., with Marvin J. Wolf. *Beating the Odds*. New York: Scribners, 1991.

Halberstam, David. *The Fifties*. New York: Villard, 1993.

Howe, Irving. *World of Our Fathers*. New York: Simon & Schuster, 1976.

Kent, Nicholas. *Naked Hollywood: Money and Power in the Movies Today*. New York: St. Martin's Press, 1991.

King, Thomas R. *The Operator: David Geffen Builds, Buys, and Sells the New Hollywood*. New York: Broadway, 2001.

Klein, Patsy. *Growing Up Spoiled in Beverly Hills*. Secaucus: Lyle Stuart, 1986.

Levy, Emmanuel. *And the Winner Is: The History and Politics of the Oscar Awards*. New York: Ungar, 1987.

Litwak, Mark. *Reel Power: The Struggle for Influence and Success in the New Hollywood*. New York: William Morrow & Co., 1986.

MacGraw, Ali. *Moving Pictures: An Autobiography*. New York: Bantam, 1991.

Mair, George. *The Barry Diller Story*. New York: John Wiley & Sons, 1997.

Maney, Kevin. *Megamedia Shakeout: The Inside Story of the Leaders and the Losers in the Exploding Communications Industry*. New York: John Wiley & Sons, 1995.

Marx, Groucho. *Groucho and Me*. New York: Bernard Geis, 1959.

McClintick, David. *Indecent Exposure: A True Story of Hollywood and Wall Street*. New York: William Morrow & Co., 1982.

Metz, Robert. *CBS: Reflections in a Bloodshot Eye*. New York: NAL, 1976.

Nelson, Howard J. *The Los Angeles Metropolis*. Los Angeles: University of California, 1983.

O'Donnell, Pierce, and Dennis McDougal. *Fatal Subtraction: How Hollywood Really Does Business*. New York: Doubleday, 1992.

Parker, John. *Warren Beatty: The Last Great Lover in Hollywood*. London: Headline, 1993.

Phillips, Julia. *You'll Never Eat Lunch in This Town Again*. New York: Random House, 1991.

Pye, Michael. *Moguls: Inside the Business of Show Business*. New York: Holt, Rinehart & Winston, 1980.

Rivers, Joan. *Still Talking*. New York: Random House, 1991.

Rose, Frank. *The Agency: The William Morris Agency and the Hidden History of Show Business*. New York: HarperCollins, 1995.

Rosenfield, Paul. *The Club Rules: Power, Money, Sex, and Fear in Hollywood*. New York: Warner Books, 1992.

Sarlot, Raymond, and Fred E. Basten. *Life at the Marmont*. Santa Monica: Roundtable, 1987.

Shawcross, William. *Murdoch*. New York: Simon & Schuster, 1992.

Skolsky, Sidney. *Don't Get Me Wrong—I Love Hollywood*. New York: G. P. Putnam's Sons, 1975.

Thomas, Danny, with Bill Davidson. *Make Room for Danny*. New York: G. P. Putnam's Sons, 1991.

Vellenga, Dirk, with Mick Farren. *Elvis and the Colonel*. New York: Delacorte, 1988.

Wagner, Walter. *Beverly Hills: Inside the Golden Ghetto*. New York: Grosset & Dunlap, 1976.

Weaver, Pat, with Thomas M. Coffey. *The Best Seat in the House: The Golden Years of Radio and Television*. New York: Knopf, 1994.

Williams, Huntington. *Beyond Control: ABC and the Fate of the Networks*. New York: Atheneum, 1989.

ABOUT THE AUTHOR

JEROME TUCCILLE IS the author of more than twenty-five books covering a wide range of topics. His biographies include *Gallo Be Thy Name: The Inside Story of How a Secretive but Well-Connected Family Rose to Dominate the U.S. Wine Market*; *Alan Shrugged: Alan Greenspan, the World's Most Powerful Banker*; *Rupert Murdoch*; *Kingdom: The Story of the Hunts of Texas*; and *Trump*. He has also written many financial books, among them *The Optimist's Guide to Making Money in the 1980s*; *Mind Over Money*; and *The New Tax Law and You*. Tuccille has written or co-authored four novels, including *Wall Street Blues*, a thriller set in the financial world, and *The Mission*, a World War II espionage tale.

Tuccille is a vice president of T. Rowe Price Investment Services, and he has worked in the investment area as a broker, financial writer, and supervisory analyst since 1975. From 1971 to 1973, the author taught at the New School for Social Research in New York City, and in 1974 he was a third-party candidate for governor of New York.